Rock Climbing

The Art of Safe Ascent

John Long and Bob Gaines

FALCON GUIDES

GUILFORD, CONNECTICUT

FALCONGUIDES®

An imprint of The Rowman & Littlefield Publishing Group, Inc.
4501 Forbes Blvd., Ste. 200
Lanham, MD 20706
www.rowman.com

Falcon and FalconGuides are registered trademarks and Make Adventure Your Story is a trademark of The Rowman & Littlefield Publishing Group, Inc.

Distributed by NATIONAL BOOK NETWORK

British Library Cataloguing in Publication Information available

Library of Congress Cataloging-in-Publication Data

Names: Long, John, 1953– author. | Gaines, Bob, 1959– author.
Title: Rock climbing : the art of safe ascent / John Long and Bob Gaines.
Description: Guilford, Connecticut : FalconGuides : Distributed by National Book
    Network, [2021] | Series: How to climb series | Includes index. | Summary: "Written
    by world-renowned rock climbers and veteran Falcon authors John Long and Bob
    Gaines, this go-to resource for the necessities of rock climbing safety stresses both
    fundamentals and state-of-the-art techniques for beginner and advanced climbers."
    Provided by publisher.
Identifiers: LCCN 2020049022 (print) | LCCN 2020049023 (ebook) | ISBN
    9781493052844 (paperback) | ISBN 9781493052851 (epub)
Subjects: LCSH: Rock climbing.
Classification: LCC GV200.2 .L66 2021 (print) | LCC GV200.2 (ebook) | DDC
    796.522/3—dc23
LC record available at https://lccn.loc.gov/2020049022
LC ebook record available at https://lccn.loc.gov/2020049023

♾️™ The paper used in this publication meets the minimum requirements of American National Standard for Information Sciences—Permanence of Paper for Printed Library Materials, ANSI/NISO Z39.48-1992.

Warning: Climbing is a dangerous sport. You can be seriously injured or die. Read the following before you use this book.

This is an instruction book about rock climbing, a sport that is inherently dangerous. Do not depend solely on information from this book for your personal safety. Your climbing safety depends on your own judgment based on competent instruction, experience, and a realistic assessment of your climbing ability.

The training advice given in this book represents the authors' opinions. Consult your physician before engaging in any part of the training program described by the authors.

There are no warranties, either expressed or implied, that this instruction book contains accurate and reliable information. There are no warranties as to fitness for a particular purpose or that this book is merchantable. Your use of this book indicates your assumption of the risk of death or serious injury as a result of climbing's risks and is an acknowledgment of your own sole responsibility for your safety in climbing or in training for climbing.

The Rowman & Littlefield Publishing Group, Inc., and the authors assume no liability for accidents happening to, or injuries sustained by, readers who engage in the activities described in this book.

Heather Weidner on Caustic (5.11b),
Red Rocks, Nevada
PHOTO BY JOHN EVANS

Contents

Aim and Scope

Many of us come to the adventure of ascent through a climbing gym. Back in the 1990s, when climbing gyms first appeared in major North American cities, even hard-core outdoor climbers were quick converts to what felt like a dream realized—to conveniently meet friends and make new ones, to grab a workout and polish technique when time was short or the weather turned. Fun? Absolutely, but still a proxy for the "real thing." Over the decades, gym climbing—like bouldering—grew into a sport unto itself, now part of the Olympic Games. But as long as there are crags nearby, even many World Cup–level gym climbers long for their place in the sun and look to start climbing outdoors. In states such as Florida, Michigan, and Missouri, the gym-to-crag migration is less frequent because outdoor venues are so far away. But rare is the climber who never climbs on real rock, and doing so requires additional gear and mastering new skills.

This book presents the most current techniques and equipment concerning the roped safety system as it applies to outdoor climbing. Basic methods have changed little in forty years, but the gear has so steadily evolved that belay and protection devices, harnesses, and shoes from as recent as 2000 look downright archaic today. Climbing's surging popularity is matched by a tsunami of lab testing data and field-based testimony about gear and rigging systems, and how to best use them. This information has shaped our methods and attitudes, sometimes incorrectly.

The art of climbing faces and jamming cracks is not covered in this manual. Countless articles and video tutorials are available to anyone interested in climbing technique. The burning questions most people have about outdoor climbing concern how to keep things secure while climbing outdoors and on a rope. With so many opinions about every aspect of the roped safety system, what are the soundest methods? How would we know? This manual seeks to answer those questions.

The following chapters derive from the ocean of physical data and technical analyses available, combined with our decades of teaching and writing about climbing, and shape it all into one coherent system. Most methods described here are known, exhaustively tested and widely used, but a collective review of proven techniques, clearly and simply presented in one sourcebook, is long overdue.

Orientation

How can I keep things as secure as possible?

That's the first and last question concerning all modes of ascent—on rock, ice, and snow. Absolute safety is never achieved in outdoor climbing, so we strive to maximize our *security*. But how do we achieve this in a heat wave or a snowstorm, with a strained elbow and a core-shot rope, all as the sun goes down? Changing conditions, many unforeseen, make a one-size-fits-all approach rather challenging.

John Cardwell on Misty Wall, Yosemite Valley, California
PHOTO BY JOHN EVANS

Nevertheless, "simplicity and security" remains a basic strategy that has stood the test of time in a majority of situations. Put differently, the highest level of security is generally achieved through using the simplest option. This harks back to Occam's razor, or the law of parsimony, a problem-solving principle that says the simplest solution is most likely the best one. There are many reasons, soon explored, why this is so in climbing. Achieving "simplicity and security" in outdoor climbing boils down to observing a handful of *fundamental principles* worth a brief review.

Simplicity and security is not a life hack applied to climbing and is not an accelerated means of increasing productivity and efficiency. Most climbing accidents occur because people seek a shortcut, intentionally or otherwise.

Fundamentals

This book or any instructional book can only complement, never replace, initial professional instruction. However, not all professionals provide good instruction. Guides are often vetted by four points of criteria: (1) Are they trained and certified for their advertised scope of practice? (2) Are they a legitimate business (permits, insurance, and customer service)? (3) Are they experienced locals? (4) Are they well reviewed? These points are easily confirmed; doing so is well worth your time.

If you are entirely new to the game, take a basic skills class from an established professional. It's the *simplest* way to learn, the *safest* too, because it removes the guesswork. Climbing technique is applied knowledge, slippery to grasp and nearly impossible to visualize as theory. At least for those first few outings, focused professional instruction roots the key methods and concepts in direct experience—vitally important because *our foundation is built through doing, not through words.* Building on that foundation is a lifetime vocation of performance (tasking) and review (including study)—then repeat. The words and explanations, the sidebars, the photos and illustrations found here all pertain to proven methods to keep the adventure as secure as we possibly can. Trying to "hack" this process through tricks and shortcuts leads not to increased productivity and efficiency but to accidents.

Learning Basics

Most climbing gyms hold affordable introductory courses every weekend. Here you learn how to belay, set a ground anchor, lower a leader, and pull and stand on holds (basic climbing movement). For over twenty years, a majority of climbers have learned the ropes this way. However, in this era of the coronavirus, gyms are often in lockdown or open only for partial use, so many first-time climbers are getting their initial instruction outdoors, avoiding the inherent hazards in throngs of people jammed into a confined gym.

Learn the Signals, and Consciously Use Them

Security in climbing requires clear communication, critically so regarding when a climber is on belay—or not. Miscommunication can and does kill people, so specific verbal signals were established to clarify a climber's status regarding being *on belay* (among other vital concerns). These signals were devised to avoid catastrophe, and must be used at all times by all climbers actively involved in the roped safety system. Most professional guides and schools teach standardized signals (see sidebar on page 168), though the wording might vary from team to team or whenever you climb with foreigners. Regardless, *experienced teams always make certain to know, announce, and mutually confirm the exact status of the belay.* Our lives depend on that.

Eternal Vigilance

The skill that brings us home is not in giving lip service to the signals but the vigilance we maintain while using them. Vigilance assumes three basic forms: (1) appraising difficulties, (2) regular reminders, and (3) scrutiny.

Appraising basic difficulties comes quickly with experience. Regular reminders involve the conscious and regular use of the signals. Scrutiny is achieved by partners routinely double-checking the overall status of the system and our personal links in the chain. We always keep a close eye on both the vertical world and each other.

Before every climb we check each other's knots, tie-ins to the anchor, belay devices, locking carabiners, and so forth. The key here is *how we check*. A cursory glance is not enough. Gravity never sleeps, so we need to be mindful and focused both when using the signals and when running our system checks. With practice, this takes only seconds, but these are the most crucial seconds of all.

Eternal vigilance. Every other skill and technique plays off our vigilance, without which nothing else matters. This subject is explored in greater detail in chapter 15, "Risk Management."

Basic Procedures

Refining basic skills is always a personal adventure. Nobody else can do it for you. But there are important reasons to start with a pro. When we are coached on basic procedures, we develop good habits from the start. If we are even slightly off with any of these techniques, it takes ten times as long to unlearn bad habits as it does to properly learn them from the start.

For those new to climbing on real rock, the challenge is not so much scaling the route—you start on *easy* terrain—but managing the roped safety system with some little confidence and security. After a few days' instruction, experienced gym climbers can usually learn enough basic skills to manage easy routes on their own. But questions

remain: Will that cam hold if I fall on it? Is this anchor stout enough? Answer these questions, and get accustomed to the process, *on routes that are simple to climb.* Enjoy the process of being a novice, because it rarely lasts long. Bump up the difficulty as your judgment and confidence grow. Whenever you plateau—and you will—consider taking another seminar from a qualified guide who will meet you on the plateau, wherever that is, and take you to the next level. This is the fastest way to improve. Even pro climbers have coaches.

As a cautionary note, give yourself time to feel comfortable on real rock before attempting to chase high numbers—a common rookie mistake. Countless are the stories of the 5.12 gym climber who straightaway hops onto a 5.9 crack, clueless about how to jam or hand-place gear. That's a certain path to terror, injuries, and disenchantment. In the gym, given adequate leading and belaying skills, basic security is a given, as the protection is fixed in place. Outdoors, it is not. That's the principal rub.

Placing gear and arranging anchors is a special study we will examine in detail later on. No one totally masters either skill, *but you must master belaying, lowering, and rappelling.* Because these techniques are relatively simple, attention can stray, *resulting in a disproportionate number of injuries and deaths that are entirely avoidable.*

Experience and Judgment

Seek mentors (guides, skilled friends, experts in groups, et al.) and continuously watch more experienced climbers to learn how they operate and stay secure at the crags. Equally important is to ask "Why?" when you see experienced climbers doing something you don't understand. As long as you're not interrupting, the climber has rarely been born who will ignore a chance to explain, if not demonstrate, their expertise.

Peer reviewing a tricky situation, seeking another qualified opinion, is a common trait among experts. No one knows it all. Over time you will develop the judgment to make your own decisions, but discussing the particulars is always a team exercise. While experience is not a principal per se, seeking experiences that can sharpen your understanding and judgment is a fundamental skill.

Learn to Do Your Part

Even a relative beginner can be an asset at the crags by schlepping loads, coiling ropes, belaying others, picking up trash, keeping things organized, and encouraging when appropriate. By offering what you *can* do, you develop leadership skills that immediately pay off. A leader is rarely the best physical climber; she's typically the person who galvanizes the group and keeps them sane, prepared, efficient, and secure. Such people always lead by example. Their MO (modus operandi) is to never leave others to do the tedious jobs. They are an asset *to the whole group.*

Knots

A few pages on knot fundamentals is a prerequisite for going forward, because most all the equipment described in chapter 1 works in concert with knots. Annual accident reports are full of accounts of serious injuries and even deaths from people either tying a knot incorrectly or getting distracted and never completing it. This has happened to everyone from rookies to world champion sport climbers, so it cannot be overstated: *Stay focused while tying all knots until they are correctly completed.*

Knot tying skill comes through repeatedly tying them correctly. Uncoil a climbing rope; grab a couple of slings and loops of cordage and practice. Sidebars illustrate the step-by-step instructions. If an active visual guide is needed, many excellent video tutorials on climbing knots can be found online.

Expect to fumble things at first. You'll quickly develop a feel for each knot, and your hands will simply tie it tidy as a Christmas bow. Adjustable

knots (soon described) are trickier to learn, but once you develop that feel, it's like riding a bike. You just do it. Then you check it to make sure it's tied correctly. *Visually inspecting every knot you ever tie is crucial for staying alive.* Then your partner looks it over as well. Focus, vigilance, and oversight—that's the drill. Every time for every procedure. Period.

A professional guide might find use for two dozen knots, while recreational climbers can usually get by with ten essential knots and hitches: the figure eight follow-through (the retraced eight), water knot (ring bend), prusik, figure eight on a bight, Munter hitch, double fisherman's, girth hitch, clove hitch, autoblock, and stopper knot.

These knots, and the others presented in the following chapters, (1) tie us into the end of the rope; (2) tie us into the "middle" (other than an end) of the rope; (3) tie or attach two ropes together; and (4) enable system backups and rope ascension.

The old saying about climbing knots is that no matter how long you climb, you'll only have one chance to tie them wrong. Our lives depend on the security of these knots, *so they must be perfectly tied every time*—"in rain or shine and in the dark."

Knot Terminology

Bend: Two ropes tied together by their ends

Bight: Two strands of rope doubled back on itself

Load strand: The strand of the rope that bears all the weight

Hitch: A knot tied around another object (such as a carabiner or a rope)

Standing end: The part of the rope the end of the rope crosses to form a knot.

Tag end: The very end of a rope that protrudes from a knot; commonly called the "tail"

Working end: The side, or the part of the rope that is being used during knot tying

Hitches

A *hitch* is a knot that is tied around something. The *clove hitch* is used to fasten a rope to a carabiner. A *friction hitch* is a knot tied with a cord or sling around another rope, utilizing friction to make the knot hold when weighted, but releasable/movable without untying when it is unweighted. Hitches are versatile, practical, and easy to learn and to tie. The moment you unhitch them from a carabiner or knob of rock, they unravel. There's no true knot to begin with, so there's no knot left to untie.

Clove Hitch

The clove hitch is tied around the wide base of a carabiner. The beauty of the clove hitch is easy rope-length adjustment without unclipping from the carabiner, making it a versatile knot for anchoring purposes—for anchoring a belayer, tying off an anchoring extension rope, or tying off the arms of a cordelette.

Especially for smaller, offset D carabiners, get in the habit of *tying off to the load-bearing strand on the spine side of the carabiner;* you'll ensure that you're loading the carabiner in the strongest configuration. Make sure you tighten the clove hitch properly by cranking down on both strands, and you're good to go.

The "clove" is initially tricky to tie, and easy to tie incorrectly. Experiment when it doesn't matter (on your couch, with a length of rope and a carabiner), so you'll get it right when it does.

Tying the clove hitch

Knot Strength

You might read or hear that knot Y is *stronger* than knot Z, though few sources make clear what "knot strength" actually means, or that it's the wrong metric to determine the best knot for a given task.

Knot strength does not mean, for example, that an overhand knot can sustain X amount of force before it pulls out or blows apart, much as our grip will fail at a certain threshold. Knot strength means that when weighted, the tight bends and crooked cinching that happens to knots compromises the maximum holding power of a rope—but at different ratios, knot to knot.

In both slow-pull and drop tests, the strands of the knot rarely pull through and the body of the knot rarely disintegrates. Most often the rope fails/breaks directly below or above the knot. Whatever measured force the rope can sustain when knotted this way or that is contrasted with the rope's full, unknotted strength (usually determined by wrapping both ends of a single strand of rope around smooth, round bars; when pull-tested, the rope breaks somewhere on the strand *between* the bars). The lower measurement (of the knotted rope) represents the "knot strength," which is given as a percentage based on the

Knot check, Joshua Tree National Park, California

unknotted rating (e.g., an "80 percent knot" tests 20 percent weaker than the tested, full strength of the unknotted rope).

Quantifying knot strength is a slippery slope because after testing, rope manufacturers average out huge amounts of data and then round the averages up and down when they publish the numbers. Actual figures are derived from *a range of results*, averaged out for easier understanding. The core problem with all testing done on ropes and slings is that these materials are textiles. Unlike testing done with metals, which do not flex or stretch, ropes and slings do stretch, if only slightly (as with high strength fibers), making it impossible to precisely calculate forces with much uniformity, therefore complicating attempts to make predictions. Many factors in real-world climbing can alter the test results, including (but not limited to) damage to the sheath or the core, twisting, relative humidity, rope fatigue, water saturation, air temperature, or any combination of the above. Furthermore, a knot's strength depends on rope and sling construction, and the wrapping radius of whatever you are pulling with. The bottom line: Averages give us a general sense of the performance properties of the rope; and relative to average human body mass, we can focus on knots and hitches that are "strong," "not as strong but uniquely useful," and "destructive."

A dynamic lead rope knotted with a figure eight follow-through breaks at (an average) 75–80 percent of its full strength. A lead rope with a double fisherman's knot blows at 65–70 percent. A clove-hitched lead rope goes at 60–65 percent of its full strength, making the clove hitch the "weakest" knot commonly used in climbing.

Modern dynamic climbing ropes simply don't "break" in climbing situations unless they are cut over an edge or in a worn-out, degraded condition.

Barring a fall on a static tether straight onto the anchor, as long as the dynamic lead rope transmits the loading (absorbing much force in the process), weaker components (slings, cordelettes, etc.) won't simply break if the gear is in good condition and the rigging is sound.

The takeaway is that if properly tied and utilized, all the knots commonly used in climbing and described in this manual are suitable for rigging the roped safety system. None of these knots will weaken a rigging system sufficient for it to fail *because of the knot*. The critical concern here is *properly tied*. There are many credible accounts of slow-pull knot tests where poorly dressed knots not only resulted in low breaking strength but also pullout, especially joining knots. Joining knots, as we will see, always require good dressing and adequate tails. And cinch them down tight before loading.

Buddy-Check Your Knots

1. Always check your knots.

2. Visually inspect your partner's knot before every pitch. If he or she leaves the ground before you can check, stop the show and ask, "How's your knot?" Ask that he or she check it and show you.

3. If someone asks you a question or tries to hand you something when you are tying your knot, finish before answering or taking the item. Do nothing else until the knot is complete (*completion before distraction*). Likewise, hold off on conversation if your friend is tying his or her knot.

4. Remember, a knot's not finished until you tighten it. A stiff new rope is more likely to loosen. Reef on it. Weight it.

We cannot say these things enough. Because doing it every single time is the hardest part.

—Alison Osius, *Rock and Ice* magazine

CHAPTER 1

Basic Equipment

Ropes, slings, carabiners, and protection devices are someone's personal property, but during a climb they are mutually shared by the climbing team. A climber's personal gear, used only by them, consists of six basic items: shoes, chalk bag, helmet, harness, belay device, and personal tether (as needed).

Since climbing gear has evolved into specialized equipment, it's very important to read the manufacturer's manual and instructions that come with any harness or belay device. Manufacturers have put a lot of work into explaining the best and proper usage of their products, and all of this information is in the manual or written material found with every piece of gear you buy. All manufacturers agree on the need to regularly check your equipment, preferably before and after each use.

Shoes

Climbing shoes are not a safety issue, but since they are the single most important item of your personal gear, they deserve a few words. There are three basic models, secured to your feet via standard lacing systems or Velcro straps ("hook-and-loop"). The models include *neutral, moderate,* and *aggressive* profile shoes.

Everyone new to outdoor climbing should consider starting with neutral profile shoes. This includes expert gym climbers used to wearing high-performance, reverse-camber (aggressive) shoes. Granted, many gym climbers venture outdoors to

Selection of climbing shoes from Nomad Ventures Climbing shop in Idyllwild, California

only tic short, clip-and-go sport routes, in which case aggressive shoes will do. But anyone interested in multipitch climbing will immediately encounter some crack climbing. Aggressive profile shoes are designed to toe-in on small pockets and footholds on overhanging rock, not for twisting your feet into cracks—the native turf of neutral profile shoes.

Neutral profile models feature flat-bottomed outer soles (like sneakers), allowing your feet to lie flat inside the shoes. They are less constricting (boxier), promoting all-day comfort, and remain the go-to shoe for long multipitch routes where some scrambling and hiking are expected. That said, Tommy Caldwell and Kevin Jorgeson made the

Rita Young Shin on The Sadness (5.12a), Lime Kiln Canyon, Arizona
PHOTO BY JOHN EVANS

first free ascent of the Dawn Wall on El Capitan—questionably the hardest long free climb in the world—in neutral profile shoes.

Chalk Bags

Legendary boulderer John Gill was first (c. 1950s) to use gymnastic chalk for rock climbing. Dry hands, Gill quickly discovered, meant superior grip. By the early 1970s, chalk became an accepted, necessary evil for climbers worldwide.

Chalk is carried in a small bag attached to a thin waist belt with plastic buckle (common) or a short bit of thin tech cord tied with a square knot (rare) and cinched at the waist. Both allow you to freely move the bag around your waist—crucial for battling up chimneys and body cracks.

There are two basic models of chalk bags. Sport bags are smaller and typically flat on one side, allowing the back of the bag to lie flush against the small of your back, where it usually rides. Reaching behind to chalk up quickly becomes an instinctual move.

Block chalk can be broken down into powder form once inside the chalk bag.

Wear your chalk bag on a belt so it can be moved around your waist as needed.

Cylinder-shaped bags are usually larger, better for multipitch routes where a generous reservoir is preferred. The lip of quality bags is stiffened with an insert wire or a halo of rigid sling that keeps the mouth wide open for ready dipping. A thin skirt (inside the mouth) and stout drawstring closure are required to avoid spillage. Many climbers clip their chalk bag onto gear loops outside their packs to thwart whiteouts. The totally leak-proof chalk bag is a fantasy item.

Some bags are lined with thin fleece, which holds enough powder for a quick swipe during cruxes. Many feature a zipper pocket for cell phones, keys, and lip balm, and a brush holder, in the form of a small sleeve stitched into the bag, normally housing a soft-bristle toothbrush used for cleaning holds.

Manufacturers enjoy adding exotic textures and graphic designs to select bags, from Monet prints to faux fox pelts. French designer Louis Vuitton offers their Chalk Nano Bag, an "elegant high quality refined adult brand," for $1,575. Plebian bags run $25 to $35.

Chalk comes in various block and powder forms. A recent innovation is alcohol-based liquid chalk, which is applied wet to the hands and dries white, which may have the added benefit of acting as a hand sanitizer. There is also discussion about the anti-viral properties of regular chalk, which purportedly kills the coronavirus by leaching out the moisture. Makes sense, though it likely will take some years before anything is known for sure.

Helmets

Back in climbing's formative years (late 1950s through mid-1970s), very few climbers wore helmets, then considered "not cool," to say nothing of being unwieldly to wear, fashioned as they were from fiberglass and other stiff composites. Nowadays perhaps 80 percent of active climbers wear helmets, particularly in trad climbing areas where some rockfall is likely. Borrowing from the foam cores used in bike helmets, the modern climbing helmet—like the modern harness—is so lightweight and form fitting that one move off the deck and you'll forget you're wearing one.

Even in seemingly benign single-pitch toprope milieus, hazards do exist, especially if there's loose rock atop the cliff and climbers are rigging anchors and setting ropes. Rocks and debris are easily dislodged by careless feet and ropes being pulled around. When teaching groups, most guides establish a mandatory helmet zone at the base of the cliff, then watch for clients who are lounging at the base without a helmet. Likewise, at a single-pitch sport cliff, particularly a newly developed crag with

Helmet selection from Nomad Ventures climbing shop, Joshua Tree, California

chossy rock, it's standard practice for the belayer to wear a helmet.

Wearing a helmet is a personal decision. Many climbers feel that removing their helmet is justifiable when they are confident they won't invert through rehearsed movements and falls; when they're burrowed in a squeeze chimney; or when they have to keep rotating while trying to on-sight a wide crack. It's hard to argue with such informed decisions. The problem is when the decision is not well informed, or is informed by poor information or misunderstanding. That said, only a maniac tackles a big, multipitch climb without a "brain bucket." In the past, hard shell helmets offered good protection from falling objects but were less effective protecting against side impact from leader falls. Today's modern helmets are good at safeguarding against both falling objects and head impact during leader falls. More sport climbers are choosing to wear helmets as well. Whatever you decide, know that many fatalities (particularly from leader falls) could have been prevented if the climber had been wearing a helmet. Rockfall, whether caused by other climbers, the rope, or natural causes, is always a danger. Top brands of climbing helmets include Petzl, Black Diamond, Mammut, and Camp USA.

Harnesses

In terms of *safety and simplicity*, the "right" harness hinges on two factors: a comfortable fit, and choosing the harness best suited (has the right features) for the bulk of your climbing.

An ill-fitting harness is a nuisance and a killjoy. In a few isolated cases, poorly fitting harnesses have caused serious accidents. Lucky for us, well-crafted harnesses come in a variety of models and sizes. Small buckles and straps, found on many models, allow adjustments to virtually all body types. But a comfortable, perfectly fitting harness might still be the *wrong* rig for the job. A lingerie sport harness

won't do for climbing big walls, as it lacks the features required to hang for days on steep rock while using and managing a mountain of gear. You need the right tool for the job, and in real-world rock climbing, not all jobs are remotely equal.

Harness Features

All modern harnesses feature a waist belt and leg loops connected with a reinforced belay loop. The waist belt consists of a waist strap, buckle(s), tie-in loop, gear loops, and haul loop.

The **waist strap** is a thin strip of flat, bartacked (industrial-strength stitching) webbing, featuring a tail that feeds through a small speed buckle (aka autolock buckle) on the side of the belt. Some designs feature two buckles (one on each side of the front of the harness) for easy adjustment.

Older harnesses featured double-back buckles, requiring you to double-pass the waist strap through the buckle to ensure it couldn't unthread itself. While double-back buckles are still (rarely) found on a few basic models, most all modern harnesses feature speed buckles, which crimp the waist strap between two small buckle plates, keeping the strap locked tight. The end of the waist strap tail is doubled and stitched, so it's too thick to unthread itself from the buckle.

Remember: Here and elsewhere, it's important to read the manufacturer's guidelines that come with your harness, especially in regard to proper buckling instructions.

Per fit, the rule of thumb is that while standing upright and relaxed, you should be able to slip two fingers between the waist strap and your skin. Once you get pumped (a certainty), your stomach and diaphragm need to expand, often a lot, to freely draw breaths. So cinching the waist strap down tight as a corset is not "safer." It's suffocating. Note: While nylon and polyester are not, strictly speaking, the same things, to keep things simple we use them here and elsewhere as interchangeable terms.

Modern lightweight harness

Harness with adjustable leg loops

Traditional doubled-back buckle

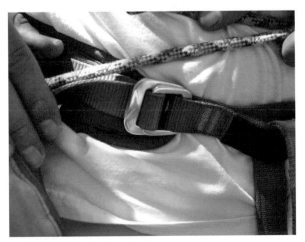

Modern "speed buckle"

The **waist tie-in loop,** also reinforced, is a small loop through which you pass the rope before tying your tie-in knot. It is situated so that when the waist strap is cinched, the tie-in loop rests dead center at the front of the waist belt. After adjustments, if the tie-in loop sits slightly off-center, the harness doesn't fit; you need a larger or smaller model. A proper fit is critical, so sizes run from XS to XL. Adjustable harnesses are also available (e.g., XS–M); they are great for growing kids.

Gear loops (two or four) are thin, stiff, nylon loops that are stitched onto the waist belt just above your hips.

The **haul loop** (if featured) is stitched dead center onto the back of the harness and is used for a variety of purposes, discussed shortly.

Leg loops consist of two leg loops connected by a thin piece of reinforced webbing that forms the bottom tie-in loop. All-around harnesses feature leg loop buckles, making them adjustable, and let you change or drop your pants while remaining tied in.

Many sport harnesses ditch the buckles and are fixed, or nonadjustable. Some models have adjustable leg loops; some have two buckles at the waist strap as well. Pro models commonly have a triangle of elastic mesh where the leg loops connect to the tie-in loop, which allows for (roughly) an inch of expansion. The leg loops stay snug while flexing a bit, as your leg muscles do.

Because the leg loops are only attached in front, the back of the leg loop can droop down the legs and inhibit movement, especially when straightening out a leg after a high step. To counter this, the leg loops are tensioned up on the back of the thighs and over your rump with **elastic risers**—two thin, durable elastic lines attached to the back of each leg loop, "rising" and connecting to the back of the harness (at the waist) with a small hook or buckle, through which the straps can be cinched to the desired tension. If the rise is too high, a climber can pitch backward when weighting or falling on the rope. Too low, and the impact force is mostly absorbed by the waist strap. Not dangerous, but painful. A well-fitting harness keeps you upright and balanced when hanging *and* during a fall. The bottom line is that fit and performance are in part determined by the rise. If the rise is poorly adjusted, a hanging climber must fight and juke about just to stay upright.

When the risers are unhooked or unbuckled, you have a "drop seat" harness, a feature common to alpine and trad harnesses, allowing us to step out of the leg loops (not always easy) when nature calls. So the riser hook or buckle is an important feature in some cases. Fiddling with a thorny riser hook is hateful with a full bladder or with anxious logs on board.

The **belay loop,** by far the burliest feature of the harness, is a reinforced (often tripled) nylon loop—roughly 3–4 inches in diameter—connecting the tie-in loop on the waist strap with the tie-in loop on the leg loops. The belay loop sits dead center (crotch level) between your legs to facilitate a belay device and to equally distribute loading in the weight-bearing triad formed by the waist strap and the two leg loops.

The **haul loop** is a small loop of webbing stitched onto the back of the waist belt, generally used for the leader to clip off and trail a haul line or second rope, to attach approach shoes (and other gear) during a climb, and in squeeze chimneys and body cracks to attach a sling of hardware or a short runner tethered to your crag pack. The haul loop is not meant for heavy load bearing or as a secure tie-in for any purpose.

Harness Models

Harness options for most rock climbers are basically just two: a lightweight sport or gym harness and a trad (traditional) harness.

"Trad" refers to the "traditional" method of ascent, where the leader hand-places all the protection in the rock. On sport climbs, both indoors and out, the leader's "rack" (collection of hardware) rarely involves more than twelve to fifteen quick-draws. Most trad leads lack *any* fixed protection, so you have to carry it with you, racked (organized) on your gear loops. In body-size cracks, gear racked on your harness might inhibit upward movement, so you rack the gear on a sling draped over one shoulder and running across your body, like a single bandolier. Otherwise, all equipment is racked on the gear loops. It's not unusual on long, involved trad leads for the leader to carry upwards of twenty-five items of gear on their harness—ranging from tiny wired tapers to 5-inch cams—making gear loops (especially their design and position) a critical issue.

A *sport/gym harness* offers minimal padding, features, and weight. The best ones are artistically spare in style and design. Most have four gear loops; some only have two, one on each side, for ten or twelve quickdraws. You'll need more for mega sport routes.

Few sport harnesses are actually padded; rather, a thin, spongy mesh is sandwiched over thin strings of nylon sling that dovetail into the waist and leg straps. It took years of small tweaks in fabric, design, and construction to realize this basic design, now shared by many brands, though the details of each harness vary slightly.

Because only the waist belt/strap has a buckle, the leg loops are not adjustable. What's more, the dimensions differ slightly for each model, making fit and comfort the primary concern. Fit a sport harness snug, but not tight or constricting. Most brands offer a female version with a shaped waistbelt, increased rise, and a smaller leg-to-waist ratio. Because many female sport climbers are thin-hipped, the male version is sometimes a better fit. Try on both to be sure.

The difference in weight between the lightest and heaviest sport harnesses amounts to a few ounces, making weight a nonfactor. The right harness is the one that fits you best (most comfortable) and has the features you need for your climbing. While sport harnesses will work in a pinch for trad climbing, the absence of a haul loop and the smaller gear loops add needless challenges.

Trad harnesses have bigger, burlier gear loops (four or more) to handle a full rack of gear; adjustable legs loops, cinched for summer climbing in

Trad Climbing

When sport climbing swept through the climbing world in the late 1980s, it represented a sea change in the traditional ("trad") mode of ascent where, by and large, a leader hand-placed all the anchors and protection used during a climb, and a follower cleaned the gear as they "seconded" the lead. Permanent bolt anchors, previously used only as last resorts on blank rock, became the standard anchors for all sport climbs, often installed on rappel with rotary power drills. It was a confusing transition for many climbers, who had played by a set of rules that held no sway in the sport climbing world.

Many modern-day climbers are unfamiliar with the history, so "trad climbing" is often misconstrued. As sport climbing became the new normal, many came to consider traditional climbing a niche genre known for derring-do—a characterization that is not only false but overlooks the fact that, worldwide, most of the big classic routes are usually trad routes. Colorado climber Willis Kuelthau put it like this:

"Trad climbing" is what some editors call a "retronym"—a term coined to replace a word whose meaning has become clouded. Just the way an analog watch was once simply a watch, trad climbing was once the only type of climbing there was. It was simply climbing.

shorts or tights, loosened for cooler temps and thicker pants; padded waist belt for lumbar support (read: comfort); thicker leg loops for those long days hanging/belaying off your harness and for cozy rappelling; and a haul loop, mainly for trailing a second rope.

Most experienced climbers consider fit and comfort the critical features when selecting a harness. But for ambitious trad climbing, gear loops and the haul line loop are also concerns.

Gear Loops

The best gear loops inhibit, if only slightly, gear bunching. Semirigid plastic loops, with a flat rather than round profile, are usually most effective for housing big trad racks. They can also be a nuisance when burrowing into a body crack or while humping a pack with your harness on. As with most gear and features, there are trade-offs.

Location is key. Too far forward, and gear on the front loops will swing across your thighs. Too far back, and retrieval off the rear loops is difficult. Gear loop position is in part determined by our physique, as gear loops on the same harness will be positioned a bit differently depending on trunk, hip, and leg size. Much is determined by fit.

A **reinforced haul loop** is required for trad climbing. No haul loop is made as an anchor point or to directly hang off. Rather, it's meant to hang gear off, sometimes even a crag pack or big trad rack (per the squeeze chimney example just mentioned), so if the haul loop is not reinforced (well stitched to the harness), it will rip off. Again, though not "weight bearing" insofar as bearing your full hanging body, a working haul loop *must be capable of bearing some weight*. Some haul loops are strength-rated and duly marked. Most are not. Read the specs to find out.

Lastly, while every haul loop is positioned dead center on the back of the waist belt, some haul loops are so small that reaching back blindly to clip or unclip a carabiner is nearly impossible. We can't

be wasting time on such routine procedures, made tough by poor designs. Get a harness with an easy-access haul loop.

What Harness to Buy?

If the money is there, consider having two harnesses: one for the gym/sport climbing and a second for multipitch trad routes. If not, and you practice both disciplines, buy a well-fitting trad harness. Sport climbs rated 5.15 have been climbed in trad harnesses, which are only a few ounces heavier than the skimpiest sport unit. If you're an all-around climber (or aspire to be) on a limited budget, go trad; you've got all bases covered. Most any reputable, well-fitting modern harness is so well-crafted and user-friendly that 5 feet off the ground, you'll forget you have one on.

Knowing the differences between models and sizes (test-driving for fit and comfort) is only possible by climbing in one; hanging from one; racking gear on one; belaying, rappelling, falling, and lowering in one. Many retail stores have practice walls where you swing and hang about. The other option is to test-drive a harness belonging to a climber of similar build and weight. Whatever means you can manage to demo a harness at the crags, do so *before* buying.

Safety Issues

Harnesses, like most climbing gear, are engineered for safety, comfort, and utility. Every harness just described consists of a waist belt and leg loops and has met the stringent strength criteria of independent testing groups. As with the climbing rope, the forces required to break a modern harness far exceed those ever encountered in real-world climbing. But that's when the harness is brand new and properly used. There are several considerations.

The belay loop connects the tie-in points on both the waist strap and the leg loops. Only these three components are strength-rated, and are designed for full weight bearing and absorbing the

Figure Eight Follow-Through (aka Retraced Eight or Trace 8)

The figure eight follow-through is the most common and trusted knot for tying the "business end" of the rope into your harness. It's also used to tie a rope around an object like a tree or through a tunnel. It is an easy knot to learn and to tie, and because it cinches on itself when weighted, it is impossible to untie itself. It cinches up tight after a hard fall, making it tough to untie, but the trouble pays dividends in security. Perhaps the biggest reason world rock climbing has gravitated toward the eight follow-through is that it presents a natural symmetry that makes it easy to recognize—and verify as being properly tied—when we're double-checking and watching out for each other. Tie the figure eight with a 5-inch minimum tail. Tighten all four strands to "dress" (snug up) the knot.

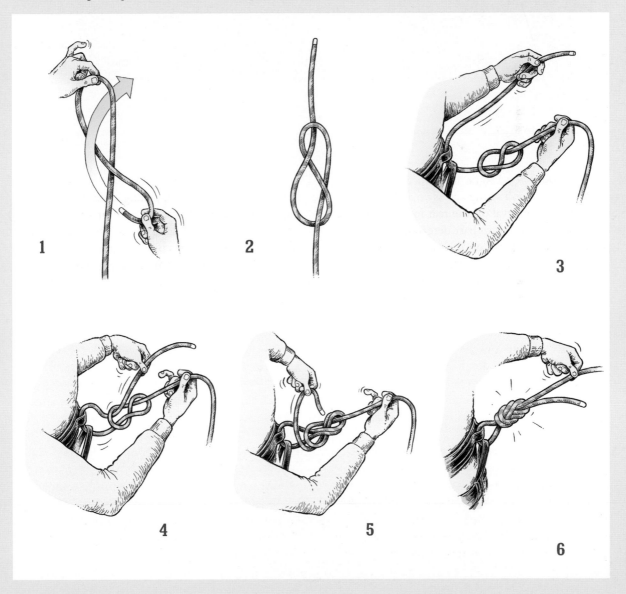

Tying In with a Figure Eight Follow-Through

The rope end generally "traces" the same path as the belay loop, which goes through the tie-in points on both your leg loops and waist strap. Tie the figure eight so that its loop is the same diameter as your belay loop, keeping the knot close to your harness. Since the figure eight is a "cinch knot," which tightens on itself under loading, a backup knot is not required. Every harness comes with manufacturer's guidelines. Read these carefully.

*All cinch knots take some wiggling to untie (and a lot if you fall on them). Because the **tucked figure eight** is much easier to untie after hanging/falling, it is favored by sport climbers.*

impact of a fall. All other points and loops on the harness are NOT strength-rated and should never serve as either tie-in or anchor points. Ever.

While a belay loop in good condition will never break during climbing, standard practice is to tie in by running the tail of the lead rope through both the waist belt and the leg loop tie-in straps, thus eliminating one link in the tie-in chain. Since these are high-friction areas, as the weighted rope grinds at the tie-in points, these are typically the first to wear out. Regularly inspect both tie-in points.

Check your harness for fraying straps; fuzzy, denuded stitching; tears or cuts in the webbing; bent or damaged buckles; stains (and possible chemical exposure); and so forth. If there's any doubt, retire the harness.

If seldom used, retire your harness based on the manufacturer's guidelines (typically 5 to 7 years) or

after it begins to show signs of wear, usually at the belay loop. Very active climbers, climbing about 10 days a month, might wear out their harness in a year's time. In one of the very few cases of harness failure, legendary American climber Todd Skinner had his belay loop fail during a rappel and perished. Examination disclosed that his belay loop had been badly compromised through wear and tear. Harnesses *do* wear out.

UV rays (sunlight) are hell on nylon. Imagine the hours, days, and weeks we all spend in a harness while in sunlight. Of course there is a huge difference between consecutive hours of sustained radiation versus intermittent exposure over the course of many short intervals. But it's clear that sunlight appreciably weakens nylon over time and exposure. Keep this in mind, and periodically inspect your gear for sun damage—the effects are real and can be dangerous, even fatal.

Conclusion

The ideal harness is the one that fits well and best addresses the demands of your style of climbing. For all-around climbers, go with a trad harness, which works well on any terrain. Cost is a consideration, but a harness is a personal item. You wear it. You hang in it. You live in it for hours, sometimes days, at a go. So consider saving up for the harness you want rather than settling for a cheaper model. Deals for even top-shelf harnesses are readily found online. Once you've narrowed your options, harness selection is largely a matter of fit and comfort.

Belay Devices

Belay devices are small, mechanical tools fashioned from metal (steel and aluminum). They function as a friction brake on a climbing rope, as needed, for holding a climber's weight (on the rope), arresting a fall, lowering a climber off the wall, and rappelling. Describing, selecting, and using belay devices is a critical safety issue for all climbing; the subject is given its own chapter (3) later in this book.

Personal Anchor Systems (aka tethers)

Daisy chains (a direct aid tool dating back to the early 1970s) start with a sewn, 5-foot sling onto which a dozen or so 2- to 3-inch "pockets" are bartacked (stitched), creating a "chain" of sewn loops. Several decades ago, daisies were sometimes used to secure a climber to an anchor, particularly when the climber wasn't tied into the climbing rope and on belay—while rappelling from the top of the cliff, say, or transitioning from climbing to rappelling. By girth-hitching the daisy through your harness, you could clip into the anchor with whatever pocket put you at the desired distance below, or to the side of, the anchor array. However, testing showed that even short falls onto the daisy

could rip out the stitching. So in the late 1990s, manufacturers updated the design to a series of individual belay-type loops, bartacked together to form a continuous chain, and the modern personal tether (aka PAS, or personal anchor system) was born.

A tether is a convenient, adjustable leash. *It is not a primary attachment to the anchor. Only the rope is.* A tether should *never* bear more than two or three times our body weight. Most of all, *we should never fall onto our tether.*

The tether is far too short to provide meaningful stretch (little with nylon; approaching zero with Dyneema), so the tether can do little to absorb the falling force/energy, resulting in a violent shock load directly onto the anchor *and* the tether, an impact created by a relatively high fall factor (total distance of the fall divided by the length of your attachment)—plenty to wrench backs, bruise ribs, and worse. Drop tests by manufacturer DMM, dropping an 80 kg dead weight onto a double-length (120 cm) 11 mm-width Dyneema sling, actually *broke* the sling (since it's essentially static) in fall factor 2 drops, even though their Dyneema sling is rated at 22 kN/4,950 lbs. breaking strength. The human body is more forgiving than a dead weight, but you get the picture.

A risky trend in recent years, mainly by novices, is using tethers and PASs as their principal connection to anchors on multipitch climbs. This is mainly an error of application. To be clear: *For multipitch rock climbing, the stretchy lead rope should always remain the belay's principal connection to the anchor, not a static tether.* People see videos of world-class climbers using tethers while speed climbing El Capitan, not understanding the context of their use or the safety compromises involved.

A PAS is a specific tool that has little use in most free climbing and multipitch situations. It snags on things and gets in the way when left permanently girth-hitched to a harness. Tethers come into their own where you're forced to untie from the rope, usually during big, complex, multistage rappelling featuring a variety of rappel anchor scenarios. For the climb, stash the PAS in the pack, *and only remove it for the descent.* Here, the PAS is the best tool to extend your rappel device and provide adjustable clip-in points to the anchors. "Safety and simplicity," our guiding principles.

Using a Tether

As far as you can, keep the tether weighted, which automatically keeps you *below the anchor.* Never climb up to—or especially past—the anchor where a short, wrenching fall is even possible, thus eliminating the chance of violently loading the anchor and the tether.

Popular PASs include the Metolius PAS and Sterling Chain Reactor. Many prefer the Sterling Chain Reactor, since it's made of nylon rather than Dyneema and so stretches a tiny bit. Likewise, if you're tethering with a sling, consider a $^{11}/_{16}$-inch double-length (48-inch) nylon sling over a Dyneema sling.

Metolius manufactures several PAS designs made from a Dyneema-nylon blend, including their PAS 22 (rated at 22 kN/4,950 lbs.) and their Ultimate Daisy Chain: "The only daisy chain to pass the CE/UIAA sling standard, the Ultimate Daisy has a strength of 22 kN/4,950 lbs. in any configuration, thereby eliminating the potential dangers of traditional daisy construction."

Recent designs are trending away from Dyneema/Dynex/Spectra, which is basically all the same stuff: UHMWPE (ultra-high-molecular-weight polyethylene), low stretch and "stronger then steel." The shift is toward stretchy dynamic rope, sewn in a loop-to-loop PAS-style unit, somewhat solving the issue of static shock loading while allowing adjustability at the anchor. These personal tethers comply with the UIAA 109 Dynamic Lanyard Standard, which requires a "flexible connecting element able to withstand the energy of a factor-2 fall." But that doesn't mean you want to take that

fall, so the cardinal rule remains: ***Never fall directly onto the tether.***

After spending weeks testing a variety of tethers, Kolin Powick, climbing category director at Black Diamond Equipment, wrote up his findings and closed with this: "If you like the security and convenience of a Personal Anchor System, always avoid putting yourself in situations where you can shock load the system—because you're gonna feel it."

1. Manufacturers recommend girth-hitching your tether to both tie-in points (waist strap and leg loops) of your harness rather than just your belay loop. The belay loop should be allowed to freely rotate on the harness, which limits constant friction and wear on a particular section of the loop.

2. For harness connection of any kind, including tethers, the rule of thumb is belay loops for metal (i.e., carabiners); tie-in points for fabrics (i.e., ropes and slings). This keeps your belay loop clean and free for its intended use: belaying and rappelling.

3. With any PAS or sling (including a dynamic lanyard), *always stay positioned below the clip-in point*, where the potential fall factor is less than 1.

4. *Never take a fall factor 2 onto your personal anchor system.* Some will break—many tests show as much. Some even break with a fall factor 1.

5. Only attach a tether to the front of your harness when you're going to use it. As a permanent fixture, it adds needless clutter to your personal safety system (*keep it simple*). Observe how many top-end sport climbers even use a tether. Few if any do.

6. Consider a dynamic lanyard–style PAS as your first choice. Static, polyethylene (Dyneema) tethers are asking for trouble. Edelrid suggests to untie your PAS when done climbing.

No! A traditional daisy chain with bartacked pockets like the one shown here is not recommended for rappel extensions or as a personal tether. If you clip a carabiner into two loops, you create an extremely weak and dangerous connection (3 kN/674 lbs.).

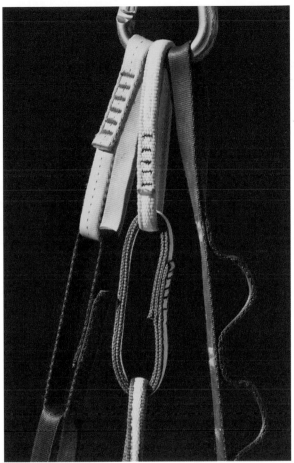

Tether comparison, left to right: Sterling Chain Reactor with loop-to-loop construction, Metolius PAS with loop-to-loop construction, Black Diamond Daisy Chain with traditional bartacked pocket construction

The Metolius Dynamic PAS. Metolius recommends connecting your PAS by girth-hitching it to both harness tie-in points.

CHAPTER 2

Ropes

The roped safety system is made possible by the stretch and suppleness of our lead ropes, the very qualities that make our lifelines vulnerable. Lead ropes can be cut (rare), but they never simply pull apart, no matter the impact force generated by a leader fall. However, the smallest abuse can retire a $200-plus rope in a second. Knowing our ropes, and the tactics to use and preserve them, is basic curriculum for all rock climbers.

Three basic rope types are used in climbing: dynamic, low-stretch, and static.

A *dynamic rope* is commonly used for toproping, and *always used* for lead climbing. Dynamic ropes stretch up to 25 to 35 percent during a leader fall, around 10 percent in a toprope fall. This is the case for new ropes (the ones they test), and actual numbers are relative to a climber's weight, how much rope is out in the system, the length of the fall, and so forth. Nevertheless, the percentages just given provide reliable parameters, while the exact numbers remain basically unknowable.

A *low-stretch rope* stretches (elongation) 6 to 10 percent at 10 percent of its minimum breaking strength. Low-stretch ropes are used mostly for rigging and toproping and should never be used for lead climbing, as rope stretch (explained further below) is key in absorbing the energy generated by a leader fall.

A *static rope* is not absolutely static, though it stretches very little (less than 6 percent at 10 percent of its minimum breaking strength). Think of

static rope as wire cable. Static ropes have a stiff "hand" (poor handling) due to their firmness, and are typically used for fixed lines, hauling, and rappelling, where rope stretch can complicate the task. More later on static and low-stretch ropes.

Dynamic ropes come in single, half, and twin configurations. A **single rope** (marked on the label with a "1" inside a circle), standard for rock climbing and rappelling, can be used as a single strand.

A **half rope** (marked on the label with a "½" inside a circle), used primarily for alpine rock climbing and mountaineering, consists of a pair of ropes; both are tied into the leader, who alternates clipping one strand at a time into protection. This arrangement reduces rope drag through protection and allows the leader to belay two followers at the same time, each of whom is tied to one strand. It also provides two full-length ropes to facilitate a rappel descent.

A **twin rope** (marked with two overlapping circles), mostly used in alpine climbing, should only be used with the two strands together; each climber ties into both strands, and both strands are clipped into each protection point. The big advantage of a twin rope (like the half rope) is that it allows for retrievable rappels down the entire length of the doubled rope. It also is lighter than a half rope. Additional pluses for half and twin ropes include divvying the load for carrying and redundancy in general.

With advancements in rope manufacturing technology, some ropes now have **dual certification**

Katherine Butler at Wild Iris, Wyoming
PHOTO BY JOHN EVANS

Selection of dynamic ropes from Nomad Ventures climbing shop, Idyllwild, California

(half and twin) and even all three certifications (single, half, and twin), offering great versatility. For example, a dual certified rope allows you to mix up the way the rope is clipped on a single pitch: If the

Deconstructed kernmantle rope showing the white twisted core strands under the more tightly braided sheath

route goes straight up, both strands can be clipped; if the route wanders, alternate clips can be used.

Half, twin, and dual certification ropes are specialty items having little to do with basic climbing security and almost nothing to do with normal rock climbing. The tool used in 99 percent of all rock climbing remains our focus: **single dynamic ropes.**

Every certified single dynamic rope has fantastic lifesaving qualities that are quickly, even profoundly, compromised through neglect. Experienced climbers consider the rope an extension of themselves and treat the line accordingly. Yes, we can withstand some sudden shocks, and on occasion we—and our rope—simply have to. But the key to longevity is conscious self-care.

Dynamic climbing ropes are typically fashioned from nylon (polyamide) and feature a tightly braided outer sheath containing thin strings of twisted fibers. The sheath is the rope's "skin," a thin, hollow tube that surrounds and shields the core against abrasion. Because the sheath is only a protective covering, its tensile strength is modest. The rope's strength and structural integrity come mainly from the twisted yarns at its core. Massive overkill is built into every certified climbing rope. They never simply break, but they *can* sever when weighted and are running over a sharp edge or rock feature. Rope failure, while extremely rare, *is* possible.

Strong and durable, light and supple, modern dynamic climbing ropes can stretch upwards of 35 percent of their length (hence the term "dynamic rope"), providing a comparatively slow deceleration for a falling climber, and a "soft catch" for the belayer arresting the fall.

The entire roped safety system hinges on this stretch in the rope. If the rope were a cable (or static rope), a checked fall would result in almost instant deceleration, generating forces great enough to shatter carabiners, blow out anchors set in the rock, and break a climber's back. While a saving grace, rope stretch can add significant length to a fall—while both leading and toproping—a fact every climber must carefully manage. More on this later.

Weight and Diameter

Over the past few decades, ropes have gotten thinner and thinner. Since a leader must trail the rope, dragging it over the rock and through whatever protection devices placed as they ascend, as long as thinner ropes were suitably strong and durable, lightening the line was a welcomed trend. But a 9.7 mm rope, say, is not *automatically* lighter than a 10.5. You might think that the total weight of a climbing rope is determined by the diameter times the length. However, in order to reduce the diameter, rope makers started tightening the weave on the sheath while using the same proportion of core materials to preserve strength and durability. Also, core construction varies rope to rope, sometimes making a 9.4 mm cord heavier than a

10.2. What's more, "diameter" is at times more of a marketing term than a true measurement. All rope diameters are measured while the line is slightly weighted.

All this suggests that the best indicator of performance and construction is probably weight. Nevertheless, diameter is a crucial factor in how a rope handles (its "hand") and performs, so climbing ropes are classified using this metric. It's crucially important that your rope's diameter is compatible with the belay device you'll be using. Once you determine what diameter rope best suits your needs, factoring in weight can help narrow your choices. It's a little confusing, but read on.

Fat Ropes (10–11 mm)

The core strands of a rope do not wear out. The protective sheath is always first to go. Just a gossamer jacket of nylon (polyamide) fibers, the sheath, at most, contributes 20–30 percent of a rope's strength. Once the sheath wears through—exposing the critical core strands to abrasion—that rope is done.

Because thick ropes have more surface area to absorb abrasion, the sheath on fat ropes usually outlasts those on thinner lines. Sheath percentage (information is available from the rope manufacturer) helps determine durability. The rope with the burlier sheath is more durable. For running laps in the gym, frequent toproping at the crags, "working" the moves on a sport climb, and certainly for big wall climbing (or any mode of ascent where repeated falling, hanging, and lowering can quickly trash a rope), fat ropes are the first choice. Many active climbers have workhorse "fatties" for everyday use and a thinner line, used sparingly, for performance ("sending") climbing. For group and recreational (not pushing your limits) climbing, the practical qualities of fat ropes almost always trump the benefits (mainly weight) of skinnier cords.

Fat ropes are the best value and provide high friction in belay devices (more secure for beginners). Fatties are also bulkier, heavier, and sometimes add troublesome friction to both the system and tube-style belay devices. There are always trade-offs when selecting a rope, but for overall recreational use, go fat.

Medium Diameter Ropes (9.5–9.9 mm)

Sport routes, trad climbing, multipitch, alpine climbing—anything goes with medium diameter ropes, which strike a functional balance between weight, durability, and performance. They are also easier to handle, manage, and pack/coil than fat ropes. They perform well on hard sport routes and are light enough for long climbs and to schlep into the mountains. Retail figures show that medium diameter ropes outsell fat and skinny ropes about 2 to 1.

Skinny Ropes (9.0–9.4 mm)

Though we define skinny ropes as ranging between 9.0 and 9.4 mm, even skinnier lines are available, including the 8.5 mm Beal Opera, rated single, and several others. But the normal usage of "skinny rope" refers to lines in the 9.0 to 9.4 mm range. We all have the right to buy skinny ropes, but few of us actually need one. Skinnier ropes are pricey, wear out comparatively quickly, and are only truly needed when every ounce matters: for max redpoint/on-sight attempts, freeing big walls, or extreme alpine routes. They offer the lowest weight and friction, are the easiest to handle, but may be too thin for some belay devices. A world-class climber maxing on a sport climb might benefit from a skinny cord, but the advantages are negligible. Even pros rarely break out the "skinny" till they're ready for the send (to climb the route, bottom to top, in one go without falling).

Skinnies are relatively fragile personal property, reserved for whoever owns them. Make friends climb on their own skinnies, not yours. Nothing will trash a skinny rope faster than working a sport climb or running herds up a scruffy toprope setup. Skinny ropes, though marvels of technology and craftsmanship, are specialty items few of us will ever need.

Length

Up until the 1980s, a 50-meter rope (165 feet) was the standard. Modern, lightweight gear allows for longer leads, and 60-meter ropes (200 feet) are now common. Most manufacturers sell 50-, 60-, 70-, and some 80-meter dynamic ropes in precut lengths. While 60 meters is still the standard and recommended length for someone's first rope, 70-meter ropes are the first choice for many experts, especially for multipitch. An increasing number of modern routes feature mega leads between bolt anchors, requiring 60-meter and occasionally 70-meter lines. Even longer ropes (up to 100 meters and more) are infrequently used—for uber sport climbs; for shorter, one-pitch routes, allowing the leader to climb to the anchor and lower off on a single cord; and on long multipitch climbs where rappelling, if needed, can often be done on a doubled long line. But by and large, ropes exceeding 70 meters are special-order items used by pros and specialists for specific projects. Because the ends of the rope are usually the first to wear out, starting with a 70 meter line allows you to cut off any frayed ends and still have a rope that is long enough for the majority of climbs the world over.

The go-to rope length is still (if arguably) 60 meters. This will cover you for everything from The Nose on El Capitan to toproping at the local quarry. You'll rarely need all 60 meters. You can lead and lower off most sport climbs, worldwide, on a 50-meter line. Even full 50-meter leads are the exception outside destination areas like Yosemite, Zion, or Red Rock. But a 60-meter (better yet, a 70-meter) rope allows multipitch climbers to link two shorter pitches into one lead, a boon when time is a factor—and it often is. A 70-meter rope also lets you toprope climbs approaching 110 feet long, opening up a nearly infinite number of crag routes, which infrequently run more than 100 feet. And for those times when a full 70 meters are required, the little additional cost will keep you in the game.

Middle Marks

Middle marks indicate the middle of the rope, critical information when setting up a rappel on a doubled rope, or when lowering a climber to the ground following a single-pitch lead (explained in detail later). Ropes are commonly middle-marked with 6-inch black bands painted onto or dyed into the sheath. Problem is, light-colored ropes quickly get filthy from regular use and repeated lower-offs, so darker earth tones are favored for many ropes. Unfortunately, middle marks (usually black) quickly fade or get rubbed off, becoming nearly invisible on darker, dirty ropes (most working lines are semi-dirty). Brightly colored middle marks are recent innovations and long overdue. But these too fade and wear off.

The ideal solution is bi-patterned or bicolored lines, where half the (bicolored) rope is red, for example, and the other half blue. This is usually accomplished by splicing different colored threads together on the sheath, which causes small irregularities (which in some cases become wear points). (Modern automized machines have done away with the splicing, but not all manufacturers use these.) A questionably better solution is bi-patterning, which avoids the splicing. This is accomplished by moving the bobbins around the braiding machine to change from spiraling stripes, for instance, to a scattered speckle pattern. The middle is exactly where the color or pattern clearly changes on the sheath, making the midpoint impossible to miss. Just expect to pay a little more for this convenience.

Middle marks can be reapplied with pens designed specifically for nylon ropes—if you can find one—but these too will eventually fade. Marking the middle with a few wraps of bright electrical tape is a cardinal error. The tape can gum up the line and jam in belay devices, or slip up and down the rope (especially while rappelling), resulting in a false reading/mark that might be 5 meters off center. Not good. That said, paying a little more for a bicolored or bi-patterned rope is a sound investment if multipitch routes (rock or alpine) are your focus and you commonly need to rappel.

Dry Ropes

There is no way to always avoid getting the rope wet (rain, belaying on river banks, etc.), but there is every reason to want to. Wet ropes lose up to 40–50 percent of their strength and can take on such weight as to become almost unmanageable. In cold temps they can freeze stiff as cables and cannot be used. To help keep ropes dry, manufacturers apply various water repellents to the sheath, core, or both (best option). The coatings slightly stiffen both the sheath and the core, which decreases rope drag (ergo, friction in the system) and increases durability. The coating adds some little cost to the rope, but except for the gym, where dirt and water are not issues, the increased performance justifies the price. The coating also inhibits UV damage, though normal wear and tear will (a) generally cook a rope before the sun does, and (b) rub off most of the sheath coating in short order. Currently there is no widely available product to reapply a dry coat to a rope, but several reasons to want one.

Additional Specs

Other common specs referring to rope performance include fall rating (how many laboratory drop tests a rope can sustain before failing); impact force (the force measured during the first drop fall test); stretch (how far a rope elongates during a drop test); and sheath slippage (which is self-explanatory).

While engineers go back and forth on these specs—as they should—in practical terms, as long as a rope is approved by the International Climbing and Mountaineering Federation (Union Internationale des Associations d'Alpinisme, UIAA), and certified to EN 892, these specs are largely academic.

For example, the number of drop tests a given rope can withstand means little when there's no confirmed case of a UIAA-approved climbing rope failing from the force of a real-world fall. Some ad copy promotes fall ratings as metrics for a line's durability, but 99 percent of all ropes are retired not because of diminished core strength but because the sheath wears out. The big stretch found in super skinny ropes is a good thing for overhanging sport routes, where there's nothing for a falling climber to hit but mountain air. But for everything vertical or less, where there's plenty to hit, we go with a less stretchy, medium diameter cord. Or a fatty.

Fact is, underperforming ropes quickly vanish from the highly competitive marketplace. And with the majority of climbers going with medium diameter ropes, almost all of which are UIAA approved, price is the determining factor for many when buying a rope. Deals are readily found on the internet. To help narrow your choices, ask friends and acquaintances what brand and rope model they prefer. And when you discover a rope (or ropes) you like and can afford, consider sticking with it. Most well-used lines of similar size and weight feel and behave relatively the same, but new ropes have vastly different "hands." Keep it familiar, and add to your peace of mind.

For your first rope purchase for outdoor use, go with a fat rope. They are the best value and most durable—an important factor for novices, who often can't avoid conditions that tax a line. No matter how fast you progress, it's likely your fat rope will wear out before you need the performance benefits of a thinner line. In the meantime, the fatty will do you proud on all terrain.

Low-Stretch Ropes

In my (BG) climbing school, we've used low-stretch ropes (also called low-elongation or semi-static ropes) for our toproping classes for more than thirty-five years. For dedicated toprope routes in the climbing gym, low-stretch ropes are the norm. These ropes stretch about 4 percent under body weight, slightly more in a toprope fall with a bit of slack in the line.

Low-stretch ropes are especially welcome when setting up relatively long toprope routes (up to 100 feet high), where it's desirable to limit the amount of stretch due to so much rope in the system. Likewise, go low-stretch when fixing lines, hauling, rigging extensions, and fixed-line rope soloing. A supple hand tells you the rope will hold knots firmly and handle well for belaying. Sterling makes an excellent low-stretch rope called the Safety Pro. A 10 mm-diameter rope is ideal for handling and durability.

Climbing shops typically sell static and low-stretch ropes from spools, cut to your desired length.

Static Ropes

Static ropes have a maximum elongation of less than 6 percent at 10 percent of the rope's minimum breaking strength (MBS). New technology allows manufacturers to create ropes with almost no stretch (think wire cable) under a person's body weight while rappelling down the rope. The Sterling Rope company's ½-inch-diameter HTP Static rope stretches only 0.8 percent with a 300-pound load and has a safe working load (SWL) of 908 pounds, which is one-tenth of its MBS of 9,081 pounds.

Because of their stiffness, static ropes handle poorly and are typically used—if used at all—for fixed lines and haul lines, where rope stretch can be an issue. *A static rope should never be used for lead climbing or toproping*, or where it may be subject to any impact force. It should be used only when stretch is not required, such as fixing lines/projecting on big projects, and for specific rescue operations, such as long hauls. Otherwise, a low-stretch rope is always the better option.

In Summary

In the wonky calculus of adventure sports, those who can afford single, dynamic ropes with all the features are least likely to need them, busy as they are making money. Active climbers typically have less disposable income and make do with the best dynamic rope they can afford, scam, or purchase on sale. Any UIAA-approved, EN 892 certified rope is plenty secure. Because most climbers toggle between moderate to hard routes, leading and toproping, short (majority) to occasional multipitch efforts; venture to urban, desert, and mountain milieus; and climb everything from slabs to overhangs, the best option is to own two lines: a fatty workhorse for day-to-day use and a thinner line for performance climbing. The cheaper route is to go with one medium diameter rope, but active climbers are certain to wear it out in a season, perhaps less. Ropes are a necessary expense, which is why most climbers seek deals on whatever rope they buy.

Rope Bags

Always use a rope bag to store your rope and for that first pitch off the deck. Rope bags keep your line organized and mostly tangle free, while keeping the rope out of the dirt.

Rope bags are rectangular tarps onto which you "flake" out (uncoil and stack) the line in arm-length loops. All viable bags have short loops of sling, or tabs, sewn onto opposing sides of the tarp. To pack a rope bag, roll out the tarp, tie one end of the rope into the dark tab, then layer the tarp with loops of rope, finally tying the "business end" (now on top of the pile) into the brightly colored (usually red or yellow) tab. Then you neatly fold and roll up the tarp, cinching the bag tight with compression straps sewn onto the bottom of the bag. Some bags roll into a small, lightweight pack—basically a day pack stitched onto one end of the tarp, replete with shoulder straps for carrying or a single strap to sling over your shoulder. The simpler models form a tight canister of rope you can strap to the top of a crag pack or stuff inside.

Once at the crag, you unfurl the bag/tarp onto someplace close to the bottom of the chosen climbing route and untie the business end of the rope from the tab. The leader ties in and the belayer feeds out slack directly off the tarp so that the rope never touches the dirt. For one-pitch sport routes, free rope on the tarp continuously feeds out and piles back up as climbers ascend and lower off the anchor, a process always managed by the belayer so that the rope remains organized and snarl free on the tarp, off the dirt, and away from where anyone can tromp on it. Rope bags are also the most efficient way (*safety and simplicity*) to pack up your rope between routes.

Rope bags come in countless designs, but all involve a thin nylon tarp onto which the rope is stacked in loops and is folded and secured with compression straps. Rope bags are for cragging, usually around small cliffsides. On multipitch routes you coil the line and pack it with you and avoid lugging the bag. Popular bags favor a simple, compact design. Fancy bags add price and convenience features but don't protect the line any better than the cheapest models.

A great source for current options for rope bags, and all climbing gear, is Outdoor Gear Lab, the most trusted gear reviewers in the United States.

Rope Care

So long as your rope is not wet (or even moist), store it in a rope bag—but not in your trunk, garage, or basement, where chemicals and rodents are found. And don't leave your rope in your car except on road trips. Heat is hard on nylon ropes. In between outings, store your line in a cool, dry place. Sans rope bag, loosely coil your rope and hang it or lay it up and safely out of harm's way, such as on a wooden peg or the top shelf or your closet. Never leave a stored rope exposed to sunlight.

Be especially careful to never let your rope anywhere near acids, bleaching or oxidizing agents, and alkalis. Acid is the archenemy of climbing ropes and can severely weaken, even melt, nylon and polyester fibers. Never expose your rope to battery acid or any type of acid commonly found in garages or the trunk of your car. Again, if possible, always store your rope in a rope bag.

Wash That Line

Through repeated use, even when using rope bags, sand, grit, and grime will quickly work into your rope, much as how our clothes get dirty, even when we work inside. The solution is age-old: We wash our clothes—*and* our rope—as needed, or after six months of regular use. Many sources say grit and dirt that has worked into the inner core fibers can compromise the rope's holding power, which makes sense. A more immediate issue is that a filthy rope

handles poorly and leaves heinous smear marks on whatever it touches—principally hands and clothes. A dirty rope is a nuisance, so wash it.

Do not use detergent, which can weaken nylon. Use a mild liquid soap made especially for climbing ropes, easily found online. Pour the soap into a half-filled bathtub or a big container, and swish the soap around. Flake out your rope into the tub and let it soak for an hour. Then agitate the whole rope in the soapy water, which will quickly get cloudy. Drain and refill the tub or container, swish the rope around again, and repeat the process (this might take three or four cycles) till the water runs clear. You can also use a washing machine—preferably a front-loading, industrial-size rig, because a top-loading machine's agitator can abrade the rope. If using a washing machine, do not spin-dry the rope.

Dark ropes mask dirt, more than you imagine— till you start washing that cord and the water turns to mud and a regular sandbar settles in the bottom of the tub or machine. Most climbers are amazed at how much better that old line looks and feels after a washing. To dry, flake the rope out on a clean floor and let it air-dry for at least forty-eight hours. Heaters (heating the room, *not* the rope) and fans can hasten the drying process.

Inspecting a Climbing Rope

Inspect your climbing rope frequently to spot any damage. Make it a ritual that before any big route or outing, you flake the cord out onto a clean floor and pass every inch of it through your hands; you are feeling around for sheath damage, bumps, and flat/soft spots in the core. A more casual inspection happens when we consciously feel the line while feeding it through our belay device. Mild fuzziness in the sheath is usually of no great concern and comes from normal use. But anything remotely alarming, like stretches of mushy core or a badly denuded sheath, and it's time to retire the line.

When to Retire a Rope

All ropes wear out. How fast depends on the wear and tear of usage. Obvious damage, as just mentioned, is a sure sign that it's time to hang up that rope. And we always retire a rope after a huge fall. If you are careful with your line and use a rope bag, most ropes can survive a year of weekly use, less if you typically climb on rough rock or are working sport climbs and fall and hang galore, which is part of the sport but hard on the cord. A rope used a few times a month might last three years, but don't count on it. Once-a-month usage might extend the life span to four or five years, barring obvious damage. A never-used rope, still in its plastic wrapping, should not be used if it's ten or more years old. A retired rope can be woven into artful rugs or used to make dog leashes.

As a matter of decorum, never step on the rope—a disastrous move when wearing crampons. Walking on the rope with soft rock shoes is unlikely to cause much harm, but it breaks the cardinal rule of always respecting the rope as the lifesaver it is.

Coiling and Uncoiling Your Rope

The concern whenever coiling a climbing rope—no matter the method—is to avoid kinking the line in the process, making it pesky and time-consuming to *uncoil*. This is especially true with new ropes, when the sheath is snug on the core strands. After buying a new rope, the Sterling Rope company recommends the following protocol: Start with one end and uncoil a few strands. Then go to the other end and uncoil a few strands. Go back and forth until the entire rope is uncoiled, then inspect the rope by running it through your hands (flaking it in a loose pile) from one end to the other. Another method is to simply unroll the rope from the coil, as if pulling it off a spool. Hold the rope and rotate the coil until the entire rope is stacked on the ground, keeping the rope free from any twists, then butterfly coil (explained below) it after inspection.

The Backpacker, or Butterfly, Coil

For toproping, the best way to coil your rope is to use the butterfly, or backpacker, coil, which puts fewer kinks in your rope. It is also the fastest coil to perform, since you start with both ends and coil a doubled line. Start by measuring two and a half arm lengths (both arms extended), then begin the butterfly. Finish it off by tying the rope ends with a square knot around your waist. To set up your toprope climb, start by flaking out the rope from the ends—you'll come to the middle of the rope when you're done flaking it out. Now you can clip the middle of the rope into your anchor, toss the ends down, and your toprope climb is rigged.

In situations where you'll need to scramble, the backpacker coil is an excellent way to carry your rope.

Backpacker, or Butterfly, Coil

The Mountaineer's Coil

Another standard coiling method is the mountaineer's coil. This traditional method makes for a classic, round coil, easy to carry over the shoulder or strapped onto the top of a pack. The big disadvantage of the mountaineer's coil is that it must be uncoiled as it was coiled; otherwise it's easy to form a mess of slipknots that are time-consuming and frustrating to resolve. A neat mountaineer's coil is also difficult to achieve on a kinked rope. The key when flaking out a mountaineer's coil is to take your time and uncoil it one loop at a time.

Mountaineer's Coil

New England Coil

This method butterflies the rope but as a single strand, making it easier to flake out and much less likely to tangle than the mountaineer's coil.

New England Coil

Summary

The rope is your lifeline. Learn how to care for it and inspect it properly.

- Choose a fat rope for everyday use; a medium diameter rope for performance climbing.
- Frequently inspect your rope for damage. It's almost impossible to damage the core without also damaging the sheath, which might indicate problems underneath. Fuzziness and wear is unavoidable, but whenever the sheath is worn through (*core-shot*), the rope is also shot. If the line is otherwise fine, you might cut it up and use shorter sections for gym climbing.
- Wash your rope a few times a year, or whenever it's clearly dirty.
- Observe the rope care precepts.
- Look for deals when purchasing any rope.

CHAPTER 3

Belay Devices

Statistics show there are four times as many climbers today as there were a decade ago. Under secure conditions, falling—once to be avoided—has become normalized, even expected, for any climber pushing their limits. This has birthed what one reviewer calls "a bewildering array of belay gizmos that each promise maximum safety and convenience." Such copy is misleading. There are trade-offs for every belay device on the market. No design is best for all conditions.

Modern belay devices come in both *passive* and *active* models. All passive braking devices (aka tube devices) involve folding the rope into a bight and pushing it through a narrow slot in the "tube." In turn, the bight runs through a locking carabiner connected to the belay loop on your harness— vague to describe, obvious in the illustrations. When the two strands of rope (one going to the climber, one to the belayer's brake hand) are held parallel in front of the belay device, there is little friction. When the brake strand is pulled down and held at a 180-degree angle (relative to the strand going to the climber), the device provides maximum friction, making it relatively easy to hold the force of a falling climber.

In exceptionally rare cases, a belayer might get struck by rockfall, rendering them unconscious and making a tube-style belay device immediately useless. In all other cases, tube-style belay devices are so effective and simple to use that belay failure using these tools is almost always user error.

Beginners, indoors and out, should first master belaying using a tube-style device, which covers all the basic tasks: belaying, catching falls, lowering a climber, and rappelling. While an ABD (assisted braking device, discussed shortly) is overwhelmingly our first choice for sport climbing (involving a leader repeatedly falling and sometimes hanging for hours while "working" a route) and big wall aid climbing, some prefer not to lug the often-heavier ABD onto multipitch climbs. While MBDs (manual braking devices) correlate to accidents at slightly higher rates than ABDs, a tube-style device remains a viable tool for everything from short crag routes to multiday wall climbs. With no moving parts and a simple design (*safety and simplicity*), there is little difference between models.

The best performing devices are asymmetrically shaped and don't much resemble a tube. Many popular designs have a flared lip on one side of the slot describing a toothed groove, better to bite the rope when arresting falls, while adding some welcome tension for lowering and rappelling. Standard tube devices feature twin slots for belaying on twin ropes and rappelling on two strands.

Many tube devices are cast aluminum, a relatively soft alloy. Given that a rope, often under high pressure, is continuously grating through the device, the outside edge of the brake-hand side of the slot can eventually wear thin and damage your rope. A few companies, like Edelrid, offer practically wear-resistant, stainless steel tube devices. Check the

Alex Honnold on the Changing Corners pitch (5.14a), The Nose route, El Capitan
PHOTO BY JOHN EVANS

Black Diamond ATC XP belay device in lowering/braking position

aluminum models, and retire the device as the edges wear and sharpen up. Tube devices are among the cheapest items on your rack, so retire them sooner than later.

Autoblock and Assisted Braking Devices

Active braking devices are ingenious space-age tools that achieve their braking power by running the rope through mechanisms (usually camming devices) inside the device. Autoblock tube devices are a favorite with guides, for various reasons.

Neither active braking nor autoblock devices are basic concerns per the roped safety system. But because both devices are popular with novices and predominate among advanced climbers, a short breakdown on their use is called for.

Autoblock Devices

Several manufacturers make hybrid tube devices that have both a manual braking mode and an auto-blocking mode, making them versatile choices for both belaying and rappelling in the regular manual mode, or for belaying directly off the anchor in the autoblocking mode. For multipitch climbing, they allow you to belay two followers at the same time. Their main disadvantage is the difficulty in lowering a climber when the rope is under tension.

Petzl Reverso in autoblocking mode

Assisted Braking Devices

ABDs with self-locking cams are widely used for sport climbing. The most popular model is the Petzl Grigri, the gold standard. It's the original upon which all other ABDs are modeled, in both basic mechanics and performance. All ABDs are designed to lock when suddenly weighted, as during a fall, but might not lock under certain circumstances: if there is a slow and accelerating pull; when the handle is pressed against the rock or a carabiner; when the belayer grabs the rope on the non-brake-hand side; or when the belayer grabs the device incorrectly and holds the cam down, preventing it from locking.

The Petzl Grigri Plus offers two modes: for toproping or leading, with a lockable switch.

For these reasons it is critical to remember that even though ABDs are self-locking, a brake hand should always remain at the ready on the braking side of the rope. ABDs are far from foolproof, and many accidents have occurred with ABDs, typically when someone is being lowered, when the handle is pulled all the way open, and the belayer loses control of the brake hand. The Petzl Grigri Plus addresses this problem with a built-in anti-panic function that essentially locks the device when the handle is opened too far during lowering.

As with any belay device, the cardinal rule is: Always maintain a brake hand! If for some reason you need to take your brake hand off the rope, tie a backup knot (e.g., overhand loop) on the brake strand side of the rope.

Petzl Grigri in lowering mode

Overhand Loop

Loop knots are used to clip the rope into a carabiner or to tie the rope around an object. The simplest loop knot is the *overhand*. It requires less rope than the *figure eight* and is useful for tying cordelettes (covered shortly).

Overhand loop

Finished overhand loop

ABDs are useful for direct belays. Their main advantage over multipurpose devices is that they allow an easy lower when the rope is under tension. When lowering with a direct belay using an ABD, the brake strand should be redirected. Consider using gloves when belaying with ABDs; they'll allow you to put more weight on your brake hand for smooth lowers.

Conclusion

Tethering a hanging climber on a taut line, holding multiple falls, and the constant lowering common to sport climbing can wear a belayer out using a simple tube device, tasks an ABD can accomplish with ease. That's why we love them. That said, a tube device has never kept a team from completing

Kevin Jorgeson on the West Face route, Sentinel Rock, Yosemite
PHOTO BY JOHN EVANS

a climb, nor has their use—in capable hands—compromised the security of anyone involved. For *safety, simplicity,* and versatility, tube-style devices are nonpareil. The more-complicated devices can foster dangerous belay habits; for example, when the device is expected to cover for a careless belayer. Not all active devices work well, or at all, on every diameter rope. And they often are liabilities on wet or frozen ropes. But in well-schooled hands, ABDs remain the favored tool.

These shorthand descriptions *will not* allow you to safely operate either an autoblocking device or an ABD. Each involves a specific setup and critical hand moves that are best learned through direct instruction. Once you've been coached through the basics, it takes little time to get handy with either autoblock devices or ABDs. But for that initial session, seek expert instruction. It's the simplest and safest way to go. The science of belaying is taken up in detail in chapter 11.

CHAPTER 4

Carabiners

All climbing that uses a rope also uses carabiners, a fundamental device for technical ascent.

There are two basic carabiner types (locking and non-locking) and several different shapes: oval, D-shaped, asymmetrical D-shaped, and pear-shaped. There are three different gate configurations: solid straight-gate, solid bent-gate, and wire-gate.

Locking carabiners come in two basic locking mechanisms: screw-gate or twist-lock.

Through various means, we all end up with a hodgepodge of carabiners in twenty shapes, colors, and sizes—but not entirely. Most climbers develop a personal system, where different types of carabiners are used for racking gear, for the business end of

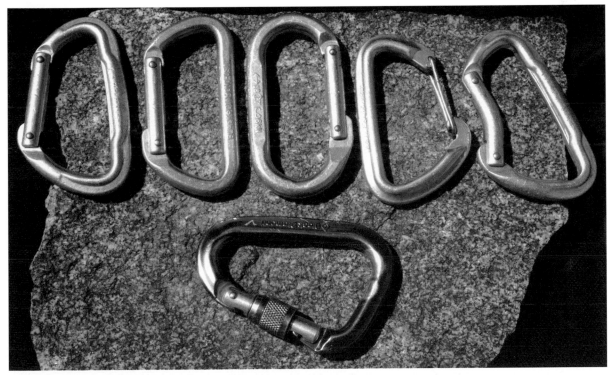

Top row (left to right): asymmetrical D, regular D, oval, wire-gate D, bent-gate D; bottom: locking D

Jenny Fisher leads Jupiter Crack (5.11), Indian Creek, Utah.
PHOTO BY JOHN EVANS

their tether, for the rope side of their quickdraws, and so forth. Though most carabiners will work in a variety of ways, ovals notwithstanding, every size and model was designed for a given task.

Compared to ropes, harnesses, and shoes, most carabiners are relatively inexpensive, averaging $6 to $15 apiece (though lockers can run up to $30 and more). Since any full-size rack requires upwards of fifty or sixty carabiners, total carabiner investment outstrips most everything else save camming devices. Well-maintained carabiners can last a decade, so buy the ones you want to live with, because you're going to, probably for years. Naturally, you'll want the best carabiner for the job, as funds allow, which starts with knowing some basics about carabiner design.

Heavy steel carabiners are useful for toproping, and a few other places where durability is critical, but steel carabiners are never carried on your rack. Carabiners we actually climb with are fashioned from aluminum alloy, with a spring-loaded gate on one side. The *spine* is the solid bar stock opposite the gate. The small protrusion on one end of the gate is the *nose*, which tells you which way the gate opens. A *small pin* on the gate latches into a groove on the nose end. The favored and now-common "keylock" design eliminates the pin. The gate and bar meet in a machined notch.

Weight

Lightweight carabiners have less material, particularly around the "basket," the rope-bearing surface in the bend below the gate. A wider basket means less friction and rope drag, so when these are concerns—from hard sport climbing, where you want the rope to run silky smooth, to big toprope setups, where a free running cord is vital for belaying and lowering—heavier, wide-bodied carabiners are the call.

Size

Carabiners run from full size (about 4 inches long and 2.5 inches wide) to featherweight models (3 × 2), with most designs falling somewhere in between. Larger carabiners are easier to clip when we're cold or pumped, so are favored for alpine and sport climbing, where you want to clip quickly and easily and go. For racking gear on your harness, lightweight models are preferred.

Strength

No matter the model or size, a certified carabiner has so much overkill built into the design that any unit in good shape should never break in normal, real-world climbing. In those exceedingly rare cases where carabiners *did* break, the unit was old and corroded, was leveraged sideways over a rock edge and was abruptly and violently loaded, or somehow got loaded with the gate open. While the strength rating for carabiners is basically a moot point, it indicates a given carabiner's durability. The smaller, ultra-lightweight carabiners are typically rated at 20 kN, roughly 4,500 pounds. Medium to large carabiners (average strength rating, 24 kN) are beefier and contain more material, making bigger Ds more suitable for rigging, for constant loadbearing, as well as for toproping and lowering.

All aluminum wears out pretty quickly; it's a matter of specific use. The toproping or belay/rappel carabiners, owing to constant rope friction, are first to go. All other carabiners, not so much. Newer models, like the Edelrid Bulletproof Carabiner, combines the lightness of aluminum with the toughness of steel, with a stainless sleeve at the basket. The belay/rappel locking model is favored by guides but hasn't caught on widely among recreational climbers. **Rule of thumb:** For big loads and constant friction/impact scenarios, go with the bigger, stronger units. Anything else is abusing the gear.

Color

Manufacturers anodize various colors onto carabiners, not for show but to match the color coding on the cam heads and connecting slings on SLCDs (spring-loaded camming devices, or simply cams), which constitute the bulk of your rack—and have for going on three decades. Gone are the days of riffling your harness or gear sling looking for the right piece. The red carabiner holds a #1 Camalot; the blue one, a #3. For ease of use and efficiency (*safety and simplicity*), having cam heads, connecting slings, and carabiners all in the same color was a game changer for every trad climber. Most brands offer some version of a "rack pack": three to five carabiners in a variety of colors consistent with the color coding on popular cams.

Life Span

Without regular washing and cleaning, if there's salt in the air or on the rock itself (sea cliffs, etc.), carabiners corrode and become unusable after a year of active use. Dirt, grit, and sand—common in desert areas and on many big walls—can quickly turn a buttery-action carabiner into a worn and creaky link that sometimes sticks open. The repeated falls and sudden stops common to working a sport route will eventually gouge the "top" of the carabiner (grinding on the bolt hanger), while below, the heavily tensioned rope frictions a U-shaped groove in the basket of the carabiner. This also occurs from repeated lowering during toprope sessions. We can't reverse corrosion, but we can limit its effect by regularly washing carabiners with soap and warm water. Combined with a graphite lubricant, washing also addresses the sticky action caused by dirt and grit. Any carabiner dropped more than short distances down a rock face should probably be retired. Otherwise, evident wear and tear is the only indicator of when to retire a carabiner.

Carabiner Models

Ovals

The first carabiners were oval shapes. A century later, the modern oval remains the all-purpose tool. It works tolerably well for most scenarios—and is perfect for some. For toproping, large ovals are especially useful for connecting the climbing rope to the toprope anchor master point. When opposed and reversed, two ovals retain their symmetrical shape, greatly reducing rope drag. This configuration can also be used in lieu of a locking carabiner, or when you want extra security at a critical point in the anchor system. Owing to their uniform curves, ovals greatly reduce load shifting—when carabiners are connected together and shift, alarmingly under direct loading. This makes ovals a favorite for many aid climbers.

Wire-Gate

Wire-gate carabiners feature a tensioned wire serving as the gate, offering a wider opening (the wire is skinnier than bar stock) while eliminating "gate flutter," the vibration that sometimes happens to solid gate carabiners during a fall, or peak loading when, on rare occasions, the carabiner can open up. Despite their appearance, wire-gate carabiners are usually just as strong as solid-gate models. The wire replacing the bar-stock gate (found on all other designs) shaves 4–8 grams off the total weight. Not a huge amount individually; but for trad climbing, where a full-scale rack includes dozens of carabiners, grams multiply into ounces and into pounds. When you're cranking twenty pitches in a day, weight matters. Older wire-gates feature a notched nose, which can snag on the rope, a bolt hanger, your clothes, and such items. Recent designs have eliminated this notch with a wire-gate/keylock hybrid. Go with these if budget allows. Wire-gates made for sport climbing come with both bent and straight wire-gates. Wire-gates remain the carabiner of choice for many trad climbers.

Two oval carabiners with the gates opposed and reversed

Three oval carabiners opposed and reversed at a toprope anchor master point

Two pear-shaped locking carabiners with the gates opposed and reversed at a toprope anchor master point

D- and Pear-Shaped

D-shaped carabiners have the strongest configuration. When loaded along the major (long) axis, the weight naturally loads closest to the spine, making locking Ds a good choice for a belay/rappel carabiner. Locking pear-shaped carabiners (portly variations on the D), with their wide aperture on one side, are the favored carabiner when using both clove and Munter hitches. Pear-shaped carabiners are also useful to pair up at toprope anchor master points. When you oppose and reverse two pear-shaped lockers, the symmetry is maintained (unlike an asymmetrical D shape), and the climbing rope, if properly rigged, runs smooth as church music.

Asymmetric Ds (aka Offset Ds) work like regular Ds but are slightly smaller at one end to reduce weight. Most offset Ds feature larger gate openings than standard Ds, for ease in clipping the rope. The downside is slightly less room inside compared to similarly sized Ds or ovals. Inexpensive and versatile, offset Ds outsell all other designs by a wide margin.

Bent-Gate

Bent-gate carabiners were invented for sport climbing and are used on the rope-clipping end of a quickdraw. The lead rope is clipped by pressuring the line against the gate with your thumb or finger. The rope can slip on a straight-gate carabiner but catches in the crook of a concave (bent) gate, making clipping quick and easy.

- Generally speaking, a carabiner is only about one-third as strong when loaded with the gate open.
- Always load the carabiner in the proper direction—along the major, or long, axis.
- Do not cross-load a carabiner (on the minor axis) or load it in three directions (triaxial loading).

Danger! Never load a carabiner in three directions, as shown here.

By extending with a sling, the carabiner is now loaded in the strongest possible configuration, with the load on the spine.

Never load a carabiner over an edge—it's strength will be compromised, and if it's loaded with the gate open, the carabiner loses two-thirds of its strength.

- Do not load a carabiner over an edge of rock—this can open the gate when the carabiner is loaded, and two-thirds of the carabiner's strength will be lost.

Locking

The most common locking carabiner is the screwgate, where a thin collar screws shut over the nose of the carabiner. Screwed tight, the carabiner is locked closed, eliminating accidental gate openings. Always check your lockers to make sure they *are* locked. Press on the gate (squeeze test) to verify.

Autolock or **twistlock** carabiners have a spring-loaded gate that locks automatically. Several designs offer more complicated mechanisms that must be manipulated (like pushing the gate upward then twisting the gate to lock it, or pressing a button then twisting open the gate). Most climbers find these finicky to use. That said, for industrial

If you're forgetful about locking your carabiners, paint a red stripe at the base of the locking collar in the unlocked position.

Cases where a carabiner comes unclipped from the rope are rare but not unheard of. Whenever it is absolutely critical that the carabiner stays locked shut—connecting your belay device to your harness; when rope twist or other pressure on the rope might open the gate; or on that last piece of protection before a knee-knocking runout, to mention a few—go with a locker. Mega Ds and pear-shaped carabiners are designed as rigging tools, principally for connecting a belay device to your harness or belay anchors, and as connectors at master points for toproping. Medium-weight lockers are favored for all other uses. Pay the extra few dollars and get a premium locking D- or pear-shaped carabiner for your belay rig, as you use it all day long.

Toprope Masterpoint Carabiners

For professionals, the industry standard for attaching the climbing rope to the toprope anchor master point is either two locking or three oval carabiners, with the gates opposed and reversed. Many guides prefer three ovals because of the symmetry and

workers in the vertical rope access environment (rappelling and rope ascending on the faces of dams, buildings, and bridges), OSHA standards require autolocking carabiners, as does the tree-trimming industry.

Locking carabiners (left to right): Petzl William Triac, Petzl William Ball Lock, Black Diamond Twist-lock, Black Diamond Screwgate

wide base they present for the climbing rope. Many instructors who do extensive toproping prefer steel ovals over aluminum ones for durability and stability. Simply oppose and reverse the outside carabiners to the middle one. The wide radius created by the width of the three carabiners, plus the added weight of steel versus aluminum, provides a more stable platform for the rope and tends not to flip sideways as often as two locking carabiners—a situation that can pin the rope against the rock while lowering if the climber's (weighted) strand is on the outside, away from the rock.

If you frequently toprope, you'll see that aluminum carabiners wear rather quickly, developing noticeable grooves. The worn-off aluminum particles also get on the rope and the belayer's hands. When this happens, retire the carabiner. Steel is far more durable and wears much slower than aluminum. It's also much heavier, which largely limits steel carabiners to toprope setups.

Like most all climbing gear, carabiner selection depends on intended use. REI offers the following general guidelines:

Three steel ovals with the gates opposed and reversed at a toprope anchor master point

- **Belaying and rappelling:** Large, pear-shaped locking carabiner

- **Sport-climbing quickdraws:** Asymmetric Ds with straight-gates for clipping bolts; bent-gate and/or wire-gates for clipping the rope

- **Trad climbing quick-draws:** Asymmetrical Ds with wire-gates

- **Racking trad gear:** Asymmetrical Ds, Ds, or ovals

Slings

Slings (aka runners) are integral to every mode of roped climbing, and are especially crucial for trad and multipitch routes. Slings are commonly used for:

1. **Reducing rope drag.** Many sport climbs run arrow straight. Trad climbs often wander. As the leader clips the rope through available protection, the route might jag or zigzag, pass over a roof or around a corner, bending the rope into sharp angles and creating rope drag (high friction) at the protection points. To help the lead rope run in a straighter line, if only slightly, we "extend" the protection by attaching a sling, reducing the sharp angles and inevitable rope drag that can stop a leader cold.

2. **Making alpine quickdraws.** Single-length slings (commonly 24 inches, or 60 cm, long) can be doubled or triple-looped into alpine quickdraws that we un-loop and extend, as needed, to two or three times their carried length. Alpine draws give a leader options when clipping off passive protection like hexes and tapers (soon described).

3. **Rigging belay anchors,** and all that involves (examined in detail in chapter 10, "Anchor Systems"). Double-length slings are the first choice, and are either slung over the shoulder or tied into a tight bunching and clipped into the back of the harness.

4. **Tying off natural anchors** like trees, bushes, horns, and flakes of rock, etc.

Tensile Strength versus Loop Strength

Strength ratings are normally listed as tensile strength and loop strength. As with most all numbers concerning the strength of climbing gear and climbing systems, varying test results are typically summed and averaged. Exact figures might be lacking, but the testing gives us invaluable parameters for safe use. **Tensile strength** involves a straight pull on a single strand of webbing, cord, or rope, with no knots. Both ends of the material are wrapped around a smooth bar (4-inch diameter gives the most accurate test), and the rope is slow-pulled till it breaks. **Loop strength** starts with a loop, the ends joined together with a knot, splice, or bartacked stitching. In general, bartacked webbing loop strength is about 15 percent stronger than the same material tied with a water knot, depending on the quality and number of bartacks.

5. **Personal tethers.** Used for tethering to an anchor in situations when you need to untie from the climbing rope (e.g., rappelling).

6. **To carry equipment,** when racking gear on your harness is problematic—such as when worming through slots, chimneys, and body cracks. Here, the sling is worn over the shoulder, bandolier style.

Marcus Garcia on Cosmic Girl, Middle Cathedral Rock, Yosemite
PHOTO BY JOHN EVANS

Flat Nylon Webbing

Flat nylon webbing is woven solid, as opposed to tubular webbing (described next), which is woven into a flat, hose-like tube. Flat webbing is stiffer and more abrasion resistant than softer tubular webbing. The tensile breaking strength for most 1-inch flat webbing approaches 10,000 pounds, useful when astronomical strength is required—like for the waist loop on your harness. However, flat nylon webbing is stiff, handles poorly, and is rarely used by climbers except when sewn into accessories like harnesses and quickdraws (soon described).

Tubular Nylon Webbing

Since the late 1980s, standard slings consist of 24-inch-long loops of $^{11}/_{16}$-inch (18 mm) tubular nylon webbing, the ends connected with industrial-strength, bartacked stitching. Sewn slings are stronger and safer than webbing hand-tied into a loop (as they were since the nylon sling was first invented c. 1942). The stitching flattens the profile, reducing potential snagging, and there are no more worries about the knot loosening and coming untied.

Nylon webbing was first made for the military, to batten down gear on PT boats during World War II. *Mil-spec* webbing is still available in bulk (off a

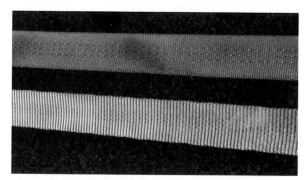

Top: Bluewater 1-inch climb-spec nylon webbing, rated at 18 kN tensile strength (4,047 lbs.); Bottom: REI 1-inch mil-spec nylon webbing, rated at 17.8 kN tensile strength (4,002 lbs.)

spool), though less popular for climbing owing to its rough-textured weave and pronounced ribbing. *Climb-spec* webbing sports a finer, higher-quality weave with a flat surface profile and a tightly woven edge, making it easy to handle and less vulnerable to tearing or slicing over sharp edges.

Climbing shops sell both mil-spec and climb-spec 1-inch tubular nylon webbing, taken off spools and cut with an electric heat knife (sealing the ends) to any length you wish. But beware! Webbing drawn off spools sometimes has splices where the ends are joined with masking tape. So closely inspect all webbing bought off spools. Several climbers didn't—with devastating results.

One advantage of cut-to-length webbing is that you can untie the knot then retie it around a tree, pass it through a tunnel in the rock, or thread it through bolt hangers for a rappel anchor. One-inch knotted slings are the call whenever rigging rappel anchors and leaving slings behind.

Life Span

When you purchase slings, read the manufacturer's user guidelines regarding maximum life span (usually 7 to 10 years), though climbing slings rarely last that long. Retire any nylon sling that (a) has been subjected to temperatures above 175°F; (b) is scorched or glazed from a rope being pulled across it; (c) shows signs of sun bleaching/degradation (faded color and/or stiffness); (d) has been exposed to acid or bleach.

Like nylon rope, the strength of nylon webbing is greatly compromised when wet or frozen. And remember, acid is the arch foe of nylon. According to Metolius, "Even fumes from a car battery can reduce the strength of your slings by as much as 90 percent." Direct contact ruins the sling every time.

Knots for Nylon Webbing

Nylon webbing is inherently slick and must be carefully tied. Poorly tied knots in nylon sling have resulted in many accidents. The standard knots for

Nylon Webbing Comparison (top to bottom): 1-inch tubular nylon webbing tied with water knot (Sterling Tech Tape, rated at 4,300 lbs. tensile strength); 18 mm Metolius Nylon Sling, rated at 22 kN loop strength (4,946 lbs.); 18 mm Black Diamond Runner, rated at 22 kN loop strength; $^{11}/_{16}$-inch Sterling tubular webbing, tied with a water knot (rated at 3,000 lbs. tensile strength).

tying nylon webbing into a loop are the water knot (aka ring bend) and the double fisherman's knot (aka grapevine knot). The water knot should be neatly tied, with the finished tails a minimum of 3 inches long. *Tighten the water knot carefully and firmly*, as it otherwise tends to loosen when not directly weighted.

A double fisherman's knot is tricky to tie neatly in nylon webbing and requires a longer piece of sling. Once weighted and pulled snug, the double fisherman's is very secure and will not loosen. It is also difficult if not impossible to untie after heavy loading. (See sidebar for knot illustrations.) A common mistake is to underestimate how much extra sling material is needed to form a 24-inch loop secured with a double fisherman's knot. Allow 26 inches of extra sling for the knot alone, 74 inches all told.

Knots for Webbing

The nylon webbing used in climbing slings usually has a slick, sateen finish that doesn't bite on itself when tied. Poorly tied knots in webbing have resulted in many accidents, often because the knot was not cinched tight enough and basically untied itself. Ergo, any knot tied in webbing requires caution.

The two basic knots for tying nylon webbing into a loop include: (1) the water knot (aka the ring bend) and (2) the double fisherman's knot (aka the grapevine knot).

For the both the water knot and the double fisherman's loop, your finished tails should be a minimum of 3 inches long. Always tighten the water knot with a few hard pulls. If slackly tied, the knot will quickly loosen.

Question: Why would you even use nylon webbing tied with a knot as opposed to a sewn runner, which is stronger than the same material tied with a knot?

Answer: To use for rappel anchors when tying slings around a tree, for example, or through bolt hangers. It is also sometimes useful to untie the knot, thread it through something (like a tunnel), and retie it.

The double fisherman's knot is a very secure way to tie nylon webbing into a loop, although it requires more material length than the water knot. The knot itself uses an additional 26 inches of sling, compared to the water knot, which takes about 19 additional inches of sling to tie. The double fisherman's is also nearly impossible to untie once it's been seriously weighted.

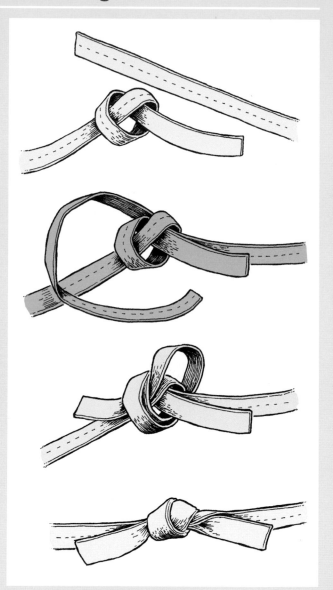

Tying the water knot (ring bend)

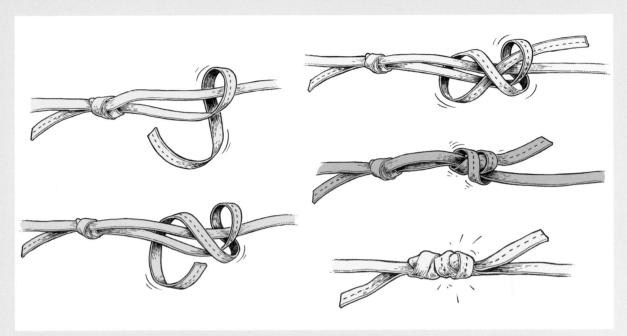

Tying nylon webbing with a double fisherman's (grapevine) knot

The water knot

Tech Webbing (aka Dyneema)

Tech webbing (known in Europe as "high-strength fibers") goes by various brand names: Dyneema, Spectra, Dynex, et al. It's all the same stuff—*ultra high molecular weight polyethylene* fiber (aka HMPE, or high-modulus polyethylene). Dyneema has become a generic name for all HMPE, and is used here.

When first introduced in the late 1980s, Dyneema was touted as the world's strongest fiber, "exhibiting strength-to-weight characteristics that far exceed steel." Dyneema is typically sold in various-length 10 mm loops connected with bartacked stitching.

Dyneema webbing is inherently slick, holds knots poorly, and is only available in sewn loops. *Do not cut a Dyneema sling and retie it with a water knot!* Dyneema has a lower melting point than nylon (around 300°F for Dyneema, 480°F for nylon). The lower melting point, along with its slick texture, makes Dyneema a poor choice for tying friction hitches like the prusik, klemheist, or autoblock. Better to go with 5 mm or 6 mm nylon cord.

In a pinch, if you need to use a sling to tie a friction hitch, use a nylon one over a Dyneema sling. Nylon grips better. The newer, thinner (10 mm) Dyneema slings will work for friction hitches; all models are blended with nylon (otherwise you have a pure white sling).

Manufacturers have always added nylon to Dyneema slings for added durability, usually in a border pattern. More recently, manufacturers have boosted the nylon percentage, which also lowers the price. Metolius's Monster Sling material features a 36 percent Dyneema, 64 percent nylon medley in their Open Loop Sling. BlueWater has followed with their Titan Sling. Edelrid introduced their innovative Techweb Sling, with a kernmantle

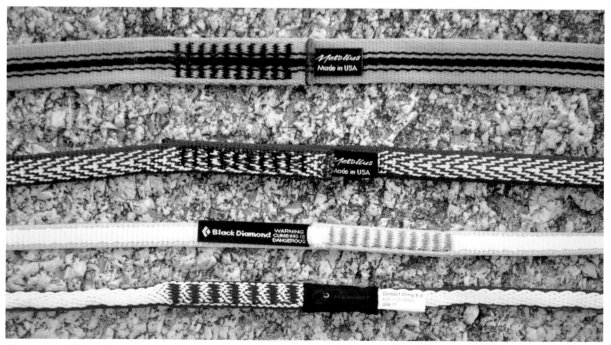

Dyneema Sling Comparison (top to bottom): Metolius 18 mm nylon sling (for comparison); 13 mm Monster Sling (nylon-Dyneema blend; 22 kN/4,946 lbs. loop strength); Black Diamond 10 mm Dynex Runner (22 kN loop strength); Mammut 8 mm Dyneema Contact Sling (22 kN loop strength)

Proper girth hitch configuration for joining two slings. Girth-hitching two Dyneema slings together can decrease their strength by 50 percent, but for most situations this is not a concern, since Dyneema loop strength is 5,000 pounds.

Dyneema and Spectra— The Actual Differences

Practically speaking, Spectra and Dyneema are the same thing, but the respective copyright and trademark holders would take issue with the climbing world combining the names. **Dyneema** is a registered trade name of the Dutch company DSM Dyneema, B.V. They have a factory in Greenville, North Carolina. **Spectra** is a registered trade name of the US firm Honeywell International Inc. Both products were independently developed by their respective manufacturers, and while their production details differ slightly, both are made of *ultra high molecular weight polyethylene (UHMWPE) fibers.* Per performance specs, Dyneema has a slightly higher breaking strength in the larger diameters. It displays slightly better wear characteristics in heavy-use areas, but has more elasticity than Honeywell's Spectra 1000.

A "basketed" sling is a stronger configuration than a girth-hitched sling.

construction consisting of a Dyneema core with a polyamide sheath. The Dyneema-nylon blend increases the strength-to-weight ratios over straight nylon and increases durability. But tech webbing is still much like wire cable, *with minimal stretch*, even with nylon blended into the weave.

Avoid tying knots in any tech webbing. It's nearly impossible to untie even a simple overhand knot in the newer, thinner Dyneema once a sling is seriously weighted (when the knot shrinks down to a pea). Wild Country warns that the material loses around 50 percent of its strength when tied in a simple overhand knot or girth-hitch. Not so with nylon. The best way to use a Dyneema sling is clipped to carabiners. If using them sling-to-sling, either basket one sling over another or use a properly tied girth-hitch.

Rope Slings

Rope slings have their advantages but are far less popular than webbing slings because they are much bulkier to carry. Specialized products like the Edelrid Aramid Cord Sling, made from high-strength, cut-resistant aramid fiber, are particularly useful for climbing on sharp limestone, where threads (threading the sling through little tunnels in the rock) are common.

The jury's still out about the advantages, real or imagined, of a rope sling over a Dyneema or nylon sling. Either way, the Aramid Cord Sling and other tech cord slings are useful for slinging natural protection like rock horns, flakes, and trees. But they are a possible liability when a dynamic connection is desired (like a tether)—again, tech cord is as static as rebar.

Products like Beal's Dynamic Sling address the problem of possible violent loading (unavoidable with all static slings and cord) by using 8.3 mm nylon climbing rope, with its modicum of dynamic stretch. Shorter versions (60 cm /24-inch) are useful for alpine draws. Longer lengths (120 cm /48-inch)

are good for anchor building and tethering/clipping into an anchor.

Swapping out webbing slings with *any* cordage, nylon or tech, is debatable, since cordage wears out quicker and is much bulkier. Of course standard nylon cord (7 mm or 8 mm), drawn off a spool and cut to order, is also an option, and much cheaper than manufactured cord slings, though factory-made designs have eliminated the knot and feature a durable splice, giving the runner a sleek profile. But there are few compelling reasons to choose cordage and rope over sling material for use as common runners.

Strength

Store-bought slings of both Dyneema and nylon are all rated to a minimum of 22kN of force, roughly 5,000 pounds. The maximum forces generated in real-world climbing rarely if ever approach this figure (even the hardest leader fall typically generates forces south of 9kN, or 2,000 lbs.). But that's on a dynamic nylon climbing rope. According to tests conducted by DMM Climbing, a 2-foot factor-1 fall directly onto a Dyneema sling generates 16.7 kN (3,600 lbs.) of force, enough to break carabiners and rupture kidneys. So the issue is not so much absolute strength but to avoid using tech slings in ways that needlessly imperil the roped safety system, as well as conditions that might compromise the strength of those slings. Considerations include:

1. Wear and tear; exposure to chemicals; UV degradation (sun bleaching). Regularly inspect your slings and retire them if remotely suspect.

2. Tying knots in Dyneema can reduce the strength by a whopping 50 percent. Avoid tying knots in Dyneema in critical applications (e.g., protection placements) where you'll want a full-strength runner.

3. For tethering, choose a nylon sling over a Dyneema sling, or use a lanyard-style tether made of nylon rope.

Water Resistance

Marketing copy has long claimed that Dyneema absorbs no water, while nylon slings are like sponges that can freeze solid on alpine routes, rendering them useless. Outdoor Gear Lab ran their own test and discovered that Dyneema and nylon slings absorbed roughly the same amount of water, and both froze iron stiff when exposed to below-freezing temperatures.

Dyneema fibers are waterproof, but water gets trapped in the weave, *between fibers*, and they freeze just like nylon. But nylon loses a significant amount of strength when wet or frozen, where Dyneema does not. Because of this, and the fact that it's far less bulky, Dyneema is the first choice for alpine climbers.

Runner Length

Pre-sewn nylon slings are commonly sold in $^{11}/_{16}$-inch (18 mm) width, bartacked into 24-inch or 48-inch loops with a rating of 22 kN (4,946 lbs.) loop strength. For trad climbing, a typical rack will include two double-length (48-inch) slings and half a dozen single-length (24-inch) runners—twice that many for given climbs.

Eight- to 12-inch sewn runners are available but rarely used because quickdraws, with their various-length "dogbones" (the sewn sling connecting the carabiners on the draw), can do the job as well if not better.

The 24-inch *single-length sling* (aka "shoulder length") is by far the most popular model—for extending a piece to thwart rope drag and for triple-looping for alpine draws. In a pinch, single-length slings can serve for anchor building and for tethering to both climbing and rappel anchors. They're normally slung single-strand and over the shoulder, and can double as gear slings when thrutching up body cracks, when gear racked on your harness will grind on the wall—and your side.

Trad and alpine climbers commonly carry at least a dozen single-length slings paired with wire-gate carabiners to save weight.

Double-length slings (120 cm/48-inch) are frequently used for equalizing two placements at a belay anchor (like a two-bolt anchor) to form a master point. Double-length slings are also handy as mega-extenders on protection, when pro is far off the center line, or whenever the terrain (like jutting roofs) warrants their use.

Companies offer sewn slings bigger than 48 inches, but few climbers find practical use for them except as cordelettes (discussed below) for anchor building. Most climbers use a hand-tied length of nylon or tech cord for this purpose.

Carrying Slings

Single-length slings are most often carried over the shoulder, old-school, bandolier style. Be sure to *loop all slings over one or the other shoulder* or you'll grope for the sling you need, which is crisscrossed under half a dozen of the wrong ones. Double- and triple-length slings can be chained-linked, tied, and/or twisted into compact balls and clipped onto the back or your harness. The quickest, simplest, most compact way to rack longer slings is to quadruple the sling into a 12- to 18-inch-long loop; hold each end and twist the sling, which will naturally spin into a tight ball; then clip both ends of the loops into a carabiner. To unfurl, simply hold an end and shake; the sling will instantly straighten out.

It's only useful to bunch a few slings before they dangle off your harness like bulbs on a Christmas tree. On long trad routes requiring many runners, most climbers carry some slings over the shoulder, bandolier style (*make sure not to shoulder the slings under a day pack*), and some rigged as alpine quickdraws.

Alpine Quickdraw

Single-length slings are commonly rigged as alpine quickdraws and racked on your harness for quick deployment.

1. To rig an alpine draw, use a single-length (24-inch) sling with two carabiners attached, and hold one in each hand.

2. Take one carabiner and thread the needle through the other carabiner . . .

3. . . . and even up the three loops.

4. Clip them back into the carabiner, and you have it. You can use the alpine draw in its shortened quickdraw length. Or, when you need to deploy its full length, clip into a piece, unclip the other carabiner from all three loops, then clip it back into any of the three loops. Pull down and you'll have the full-length sling. The big advantage of the alpine draw is that you can do all this with one hand—far easier than trying to use a sling that's around your neck and over your shoulder when you're on a steep climb where it's hard to let go.

A compact way to carry a double runner. Start by quadrupling the sling (top), then twist it tightly (middle), and clip both ends of the loop into a carabiner (bottom).

Wash It

Studies show that dirty slings are weaker than clean ones. The Mammut company suggests that "to maintain the quality and safety of your slings, you need to clean them regularly." Clean soiled slings in hand-hot water with a small amount of mild soap or in a "delicates" machine cycle up to 86°F (30°C). Rinse in clear water. Leave to dry in the shade.

Summary

Most climbers' sling collection resembles their carabiner rack—another hodgepodge of various brands and sizes. This works out because most slings work for most tasks. That said, 1-inch or $^{11}\!/_{16}$-inch-width tubular nylon webbing is the most versatile material for rigging rappel anchors. It can be cut to a desired length and tied with a water knot. Double-length (48-inch) sewn nylon slings are also handy for tethering into anchors and extending your rappel device away from your harness.

Nylon webbing is considerably cheaper than Dyneema, and custom lengths can be cut off spools available in many climbing shops. Unlike all tech-webbing, nylon webbing, as we've seen, will stretch and absorb impact forces during static falls (re: falling on your leash) with less shock-loading. While a knot tied in nylon sling makes it bulkier, the knot tightens under loading, absorbing impact forces in the process. Nylon is more heat and friction resistant than Dyneema, and is generally more durable over time. However, nylon webbing is far bulkier and heavier than Dyneema (to achieve comparable strength), so for long multipitch routes, when twenty slings are sometimes called for, Dyneema is usually the call, augmented with several nylon slings for rigging anchors and for clipping off your first piece of pro— off the ground or off the belay—as the stretchier nylon adds some shock absorption into the system.

In the end, once you understand the pros and cons, what matters most is matching slings to your intended objectives.

CHAPTER 6

Quickdraws

Quickdraws (commonly called draws) were first devised by legendary Yosemite climber Jim Bridwell at the start of the free climbing revolution (c. 1970). For decades, a leader clipped the lead rope into protection with two carabiners. In an attempt to decrease rope drag, a critical issue on harder free routes, Bridwell hand-tied a 3-inch-long loop of ⅜-inch tubular webbing, clipped two carabiners to each "end," and the quickdraw was born. The rope ran much freer through the protection points (mostly pitons) when extended with a quickdraw, and the rudimentary nuts (aka chocks) available back then were less likely to get lifted from the crack by the yanking action of a lead rope.

Quickdraw design evolved with advances in materials and manufacturing, and through the demands of both sport and trad climbing. In sport climbing, the connecting sling, called a "dogbone," went from a tied to a sewn section of tubular nylon sling. In the 1990s, flat webbing, both stronger and stiffer, replaced the tubular webbing as D-shaped carabiners were introduced. The protection-end of the dogbone was left open so the sling could freely pivot on the bolt. At the opposite (rope) end, a free-floating carabiner was tricky to grab and clip with one hand, so the sling was stitched tight around the rope-end carabiner, fixing its position in the dogbone. This made it easier to clasp and clip, and kept the D-shaped carabiner properly aligned in the draw, with the wider basket at the bottom. Over time, a rubberized keeper (sometimes an insert) was added

to the rope end to further secure the carabiner in place, while bent-gate carabiners, also at the rope end, made clipping the rope that much easier.

At the other end of the dogbone, lightweight sculpted, hot-forged carabiners became favorites. Modern top-end draws always use solid-gate, keylock carabiners, which cannot snag on slings, clothes, etc. The sport dogbone itself has evolved into a flat, semirigid 12- to 18-centimeter-wide unit that's as easy to grab as a suitcase handle—a plus, since grabbing draws (to clip in) is common practice while working difficult sport climbs.

With all this technology on board, modern sport draws are comparatively heavy, which is ironic in a sport where ounces make a difference. But the purpose of high-end draws is to facilitate easy clipping and to provide something (the dogbone) to grab while working the climb. By the time you "send" the route bottom to top, with no falls, in most cases the draws are already in place (like they are in every gym), hanging off the bolts. You need only clip them on your way to glory then clean them when lowering off.

Trad Draws

Big multipitch leads might require twelve to twenty pieces of protection, and nobody wants to lug even ten heavy sport draws up a trad climb. On long routes it's all about lightweight—from the gear you hump to the wall, including the water

Sasha Digiulian on Misty Wall, Yosemite
PHOTO BY JOHN EVANS

57

Quickdraws (left to right): dogbone with rubberized "keeper"; heavy-duty sport draw; lightweight Dyneema dogbone trad draw.

Quickdraws Consist Of:

Two carabiners attached to a length of semirigid sewn webbing known as a "dogbone." One carabiner clips protection in the rock, from bolts on sport climbs to cams, nuts, and pitons found on trad routes. The protection-end carabiner moves freely in a generous loop in the sewn dogbone, allowing the draw to freely pivot as the rope runs through. The carabiner on the opposite, rope end of the dogbone is checked in place by a rubber keeper sleeve or insert, better for clipping in the lead rope from strenuous positions, and for keeping the load-bearing carabiner properly aligned in case of a fall.

How Many Quickdraws Do You Need?

Beginners can usually get by with a dozen quickdraws. Few moderate sport climbs have more than twelve protection bolts, and whatever alpine draws you have can boost that number. Partners commonly combine racks as needed, so chances are good that between two or three beginners, you can scrub together enough draws to cover the vast majority of sport climbs, no matter the route or venue. Dedicated sport climbers might own two dozen draws, enough for any sport climb on Earth. Widths vary from thin (nearly impossible to grab) to wide (far easier to grab). The harder you climb, the wider draws you'll want because you'll frequently grab them—or fall off. Thin dogbones (averaging 10 mm) are for multipitch and alpine routes, where dozens of draws are sometimes required. So the lighter the better.

and grub and the crag pack you carry them in; the rope and tag line you climb on; and the cams, nuts, and draws that flesh out your rack. To lighten the already considerable load, standard trad quickdraws swap out the burly nylon webbing with a 10- to 12-centimeter-wide Dyneema dogbone, alarmingly thin and heroically strong, replacing the heavier full-size D carabiners with smaller, lightweight wire-gates—a svelte package, available from many companies, that typically weighs around 2.5 ounces apiece. While heavy sport draws are the priciest by a wide margin, lightweight trad draws are the cheapest by a similar margin.

Medium-Weight Quickdraws

While heavier and slightly more expensive than wire-gate trad draws, medium weight draws are far less expensive and more versatile than quality sport draws, and they perform well on everything from popular sport climbs to Yosemite big walls. In real-world climbing, medium weight draws are far and away the most popular models for new climbers seeking value and performance. The carabiners and dogbones can be purchased individually, so you can run any combination of carabiners, from double solid-gates, to double wire-gates, to a hybrid of solid on top and wire—or bent-gate Ds—on the bottom. For even greater savings, most companies sell packs of four to eight draws of various carabiner/dogbone configurations.

When to Retire a Quickdraw

Quickdraws wear out. The dogbone eventually becomes frayed or sun bleached. But the carabiners are usually the first to go, especially the load-bearing basket on the rope side of the draw. Constant tensioning and lowering wears a U-shaped groove in the aluminum, the edges of which can quickly sharpen up, which is hell on the sheath of your line. Sandy areas (like Joshua Tree, and the Aztec Sandstone found in Red Rock) and filthy ropes hasten this process.

Fixed draws are often found on classic routes at destination areas like Red River Gorge. Owing to the oblique angle of the lead rope—from the belayer to the first bolt—and the repeated lowering from failed attempts, the carabiners on these first draws are sometimes as perilously worn as the soft iron shuts found on top of older sport climbs. So keep an eye on those first draws.

Summary

Quickdraws are foundational gear for all modes of roped ascent. Thick draws work well for sport, less so for trad routes, but most any quickdraw will work across the face, just not as well as one designed for specific tasks and terrain. The rules for carabiners and slings hold for quickdraws: Wash (mild soap and warm water) whenever the action gets sticky in the gate of the carabiners, when the dogbone is clearly dirty, or every few months. Keep your draws away from extreme heat and all chemicals. With limitless funds, we'd all have specialized racks of thirty draws for every kind of route. Few of us are tycoons, but this rarely keeps us off a climb. If the fire is there, we make do with what we have. Or we beg and borrow what we need, especially so with quickdraws.

CHAPTER 7

Cordelettes

For *safety and simplicity*, redundancy, and low-potential for extension, the cordelette is the go-to system for rigging belay anchors, and it has been for more than two decades.

A standard, all-purpose cordelette consists of an 18- to 20-foot length of 7 mm nylon cord, tied into a giant loop and secured with a double fisherman's knot. Calibrate the generic size (18–20 ft.) to your own physique by choosing a length that allows you to double the cordelette within the span of your outstretched arms.

Nylon climbing cord is manufactured by many companies. When choosing, a good metric is Sterling's 7 mm diameter nylon cord, rated at 12.4 kN (2,788 lbs.) tensile strength, which tests out at more than 5,000 pounds when tied into a loop with a double fisherman's knot. At roughly 40 cents per foot, a 20-foot length of 7 mm nylon cordelette costs only $8.

The drawback with nylon cordelettes is not strength—quality nylon cordage is plenty strong—but that nylon cord is heavy and bulky, which makes it a second choice for multipitch routes. That's where tech cord like Dyneema and Technora find play.

Cordelettes made with a Dyneema core and nylon sheath have incredibly high strength and low stretch. As mentioned, pound for pound, Dyneema is stronger than steel (which is why the military uses it for body armor). Because Dyneema cordage is light, strong, and compact, Dyneema cordelettes

are preferred for top-end, multipitch climbing, where managing weight is essential. Dyneema's strength is appreciably reduced whenever tied with knots, but not nearly enough to discourage its use. (See sidebar.)

Bluewater markets the 5.5 mm diameter Titan Cord, with a Dyneema core and nylon sheath, rated at 13.7 kN (3,080 lbs.) tensile strength. The high strength, low elongation, and light weight provide solid characteristics. Dyneema does not lose significant strength with repetitive flexing and offers a huge increase in abrasion and cut resistance over other materials. But that's the Dyneema in the core, not the nylon sheath that contacts the stone. Bluewater Titan Cord can be cut and sealed with a hot knife. Bluewater recommends a triple fisherman's knot for tying 5.5 mm Titan into loops.

A recent and popular trend involves high-tech cords using aramid fibers (namely, Technora) for the core, jacketed with a nylon or polyester sheath. (Nylon is softer than polyester, while polyester is faster drying and slightly more abrasion resistant.) Aramid fiber has extraordinary tensile strength, with low stretch and an extremely high carbonizing (melting) point (900°F), making it difficult to cut and melt.(Cut aramid cordage with cable cutters, then milk the nylon sheath over the end and seal by melting the nylon with a lighter.) The Sterling 6 mm PowerCord also features a Technora core and nylon sheath, with a single-strand breaking strength of around 19 kN (4,271 lbs.); the 5 mm Tech Cord

Pamela Shanti Pack leads Heave Ho, Indian Creek, Utah.
PHOTO BY JOHN EVANS

By customizing your cordelette to a length you can double in your outstretched arms, you'll facilitate its use for many applications.

Moot Points

The endless discussions about a cordelette "equalizing" a multipiece belay anchor (most belay anchors are multipiece, notwithstanding being tied to a ponderosa pine tree or a giant block), and the need for the greatest possible strength for the ropes, carabiners, slings, and cordelettes is largely beside the point, having little to nothing to do with the root causes of most climbing accidents.

Micro wired nuts are always suspect, because a tiny dollop of brass, steel, or aluminum threaded with a guitar string–size wire is inherently weak. But once our equipment reaches a certain size, it does not break under normal circumstances. No rigging perfectly equalizes an anchor array. A cordelette properly rigged to "good enough" anchors *distributes* the loading between anchor points well enough that neither the cordelette nor the anchor it's rigged to will simply break or be ripped from the wall.

Many climbing accidents occur while lowering a leader, rappelling, or descending with a load, etc. Ninety-nine percent of accidents that happen to a team while belaying, leading, and following (that is, while actually climbing) occur because a leader couldn't find adequate protection, didn't set a reliable cam or nut, or placed protection in suspect rock and then fell. In none of these cases does rigging or gear strength play a meaningful role.

The takeaway is that a cordelette tied on appropriate-size nylon or tech cord in reasonable condition and properly rigged to reliable anchor points *is never going to simply fail or break*. That means what makes the "best" cordelette boils down to manageability (the cords "hand"), weight, bulk, and, for some, price.

Bends

A bend is a knot that joins two ropes or lengths of cord together. These knots are used to tie your cordelette into a loop, and also to tie two ropes together for toproping or rappelling.

Figure Eight Bend

A variation of the figure eight follow-through, this knot is commonly used to tie two ropes together. It has superior strength and is easy to untie after it has been weighted. It is simply a retraced figure eight. On 9 mm to 11 mm diameter rope, tie it with the tails a minimum of 5 inches long.

The figure eight bend

Bends

Double Fisherman's Knot

This is the preferred knot for joining nylon cord into a loop to make a cordelette. Also a very secure knot to tie two ropes together for a double-rope rappel, but it's a bear cat to untie after weighting.

The double fisherman's knot

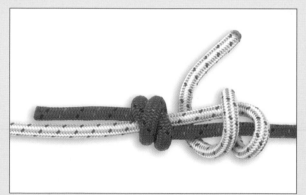

Tying the double fisherman's knot (aka grapevine knot). When tying 7 mm nylon cord, leave the tails about 3 inches long.

Triple Fisherman's Knot

For 5 mm and 6 mm diameter high-tech cord (e.g., Spectra, Dyneema, Technora), a triple fisherman's knot tests slightly stronger than the double fisherman's. Practically speaking, once this knot is seriously weighted, the knot cinches so tightly on itself that it is basically permanent. You usually can lightly tap the knot with a hammer while rolling the knot on a hard (cement) surface and eventually loosen the knot, though damaging the cord in the process.

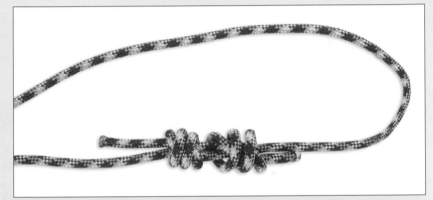

To tie a triple fisherman's knot, make three wraps before feeding the cord back through.

Completed triple fisherman's knot

sold by Maxim/New England Ropes, with a 100 percent Technora core and polyester sheath, rates at a whopping 5,000 pounds of tensile strength.

A few words of caution about Technora: Flex cycle tests were performed on cordelettes. The cord sample was passed through a hole in a steel fixture, flexed 90 degrees over an edge, and loaded with a 40-pound weight. The steel fixture was rotated back and forth 180 degrees for 1,000 bending cycles, then the cord's tensile strength was tested (single-strand pull test) at the section that had been flexed. The Technora sample showed a loss of nearly 60 percent of its strength, while Sterling 7 mm nylon cord and 1-inch tubular nylon webbing showed no strength loss at all. Bluewater Titan Cord (Dyneema core/nylon sheath) showed a few hundred pounds of strength loss—nowhere near the loss of Technora. Even so, this poses no danger—at least for a while—owing to the astronomical strength of Technora. This, combined with its supple hand and knotability, makes Technora cordelettes a favorite for many guides. But know going in that Technora cordelettes have a life span and, erring toward safety, should probably be retired after no more than one year of continuous use. At roughly $1.65 per foot, this is by far the most expensive cord ($33 for 20 feet), but there's no price tag for your life.

Cord Comparison (top to bottom): Bluewater 5 mm Titan Cord tied with triple fisherman's knot (Dyneema core/nylon sheath; tensile strength 13.7 kN/3,080 lbs.); Sterling 6 mm PowerCord tied with triple fisherman's knot (Technora core/nylon sheath; tensile strength 19 kN/4,271 lbs.); Sterling 7 mm nylon cordelette tied with double fisherman's knot (nylon core/nylon sheath; tensile strength 12.4 kN/2,788 lbs.)

One method for carrying your cordelette is to start by quadrupling it (left), then tie a figure eight knot (right).

On Dyneema- or Technora-core cords, a triple fisherman's knot tests slightly stronger than a double fisherman's knot. In nylon cord, tests reveal no difference in loop strength when tied with a double or triple fisherman's. A double fisherman's remains the standard knot for joining nylon cord.

High-tech cords cost roughly twice as much as nylon. For an affordable, *safe and simple* cordelette that's ideal for beginners, consider old-school nylon. Seven-millimeter-diameter nylon cord is a good choice. When weight and bulk are important, as they are on long trad routes, tech cord is far and away the call.

Hitches

To tie friction hitches like the prusik, klemheist, and autoblock (see chapters 10 and 11), use 5 mm or 6 mm diameter nylon cord (nylon core, nylon sheath). Products differ, so buy the softest, most pliable cord available. A stiff cord won't grip as well when used for friction hitches. Also, be aware of the difference between 5 mm *nylon accessory cord* (typically rated at 5.2 kN/1,169 lbs.) and 5 mm *high-tenacity cord* like Bluewater Titan cord (rated at 13.7 kN/3,080 lbs.). *Never use 5 mm nylon accessory cord for your cordelette.*

Less bulky and easily deployed, this coiling method is handy for multipitch climbing.

Figure Eight Loop

The *figure eight loop* is used for (1) tying off the end of a rope and (2) tying a loop in the middle, or bight, of a rope. It is commonly called a "figure eight on a bight."

How to tie a figure eight loop

Finished figure eight loop clipped to an anchor

Summary

A few companies offer premade cordelettes in 18- to 20-foot lengths, bartacked into a loop—and impossible to "untie." These are rarely seen. Most climbers buy the cord off a spool and tie their own to the desired length. The double or triple fisherman's knot is standard for joining the rope ends, though once it's heavily weighted, the knot is welded into the rope and untying is usually impossible. Nylon cord cordelettes are the least expensive and most versatile, but also the heaviest and bulkiest. Tech cord (principally Dyneema and Technora) are light, compact, and favored for multipitch and alpine climbing. As long as you understand the particulars of tech cord (no stretch; Technora wears out rather quickly), its advantages are significant. But a simple, inexpensive nylon cordelette remains a *safe and simple* option, and is recommended for beginning climbers. The many ways of rigging a cordelette are covered in chapter 10, "Anchor Systems."

Life Span

Warning signs that it's time to retire your cordelette:

- Rips or holes in the sheath of the cord
- Brittle or melted areas
- Soft or lumpy sections in the core
- Significant sun bleaching
- Discoloration from chemical contact
- Six-plus months of continuous use of a Technora cordelette

Primary Anchors

Rock Assessment

We look back to the Yosemite pioneers, sixty-plus years ago, climbing Half Dome and El Capitan with braided gold line ropes and homemade pitons, and are amazed they survived. Yet statistics show that the accident rate in the 1950s and 1960s was lower than it is today. During the entire "Golden Age" (roughly 1957 to 1968) of Yosemite climbing, there is no recorded case of catastrophic anchor failure. We're right to wonder: *How so?*

In 1960, when big wall climbing hit its stride, modern materials and equipment were not yet imagined. Rigging techniques were simplistic, sometimes sketchy by modern standards. So how did climbers safely scale the biggest walls in the land with such primitive gear? Because the holding power of chromoly steel pitons (the only man-made protection then available), driven into solid granite, was so robust that it hardly mattered how you clipped or tied them off. If that piton was bomber, so were you. *Safe and simple.*

So goes the Golden Rule for the entire roped safety system: Security begins with bombproof primary anchors, from the protection we place to the anchors we build. If those anchors are solid, so are we—provided we follow a few basic steps. If our anchors are bad, no matter the rigging, we're climbing on borrowed time.

Catastrophic anchor failures have occurred, not because the gear placements were bad or the

The Golden Rule

The Golden Rule is to always strive after bomb-proof primary anchors, from the protection we place to the anchors we build. Security in roped climbing hinges on solid anchors, without which climbing is Russian roulette.

The S.I.E.T. (School for International Expedition Training) puts it this way: "The foundation of any anchor is a well-placed piece of pro. Strong, bomber pieces are really, really important. Nothing else matters if your pieces are junk."

Nothing else matters. Not the strength of our cams, carabiners, and webbing; the capacities of our belay device; or the genius of our rigging. It all boils down to the holding power of our primary placements, which starts with one basic issue: rock quality.

In trad climbing, where the roped safety system is hand-built on the spot, if the rock you're building on is unsound, you have no chance. You might *climb* the rock, but if you're counting on the protection or the belay anchor to save the day should you fall, the rock must be good enough to withstand the potential dynamic forces, which occasionally can approach 2,000 pounds.

rigging was flawed but because the rock was grainy, loose, or soft; and when violently loaded, the gear broke the surrounding rock away and the anchors

Rita Young Shin leads Kebab (5.11+), Indian Creek, Utah.
PHOTO BY JOHN EVANS

ripped out. Edge case failures have also occurred (*very* rare); that is, weak components, well placed in good rock, subjected to fall factor 2 loads and failing in series.

When placing gear, the ideal crack is what guides call "a crack in the planet," a deep, straight-in fissure that runs perpendicular (at a right angle) to the plane of the rock face. In an ideal world, the crack cleaves a massive, solid face of granite.

In general, avoid detached blocks and flakes. A detached block is a chunk of rock unattached to the main rock structure, either sitting on top of the cliff, like a boulder, or part of the main rock face but completely fractured, with cracks on all sides.

To assess a block, first consider its size. Is it as big as your refrigerator, your car, your house?

> The primary concern when placing protection and building anchor systems is the quality (structural integrity) of the rock. Any anchor is only as good as the rock it is set in.

First Rule of Anchor Building

Determining rock structure and knowing what to watch out for are basic skills in building secure anchors. Ron Funderburke of the AAC (American Alpine Club) says: "Indisputably, anchors fail because the load exceeds the force that the anchor can withstand." If the rock can't "withstand" much force, neither can the anchor. Simple as that.

Placing gear in the crack beneath a smaller block is asking for trouble. When the piece is weighted, it exerts an outward prying effect on the block. Even large blocks can shift easily, as we've all experienced when slogging over moraine fields or boulder-hopping around massive blocks, only to have one shift under body weight.

Avoid small blocks and those resting on an inclined slab. Adopt a rule from Yosemite Search and Rescue protocol: For a detached granite block to be used as a sole, monolithic anchor, it must be at least as big as a full-size refrigerator, situated lengthwise on a flat surface.

Examine how the block is situated. Is it keyed into a hollow or slot where it cannot slide out? Does it rest on a flat surface, or is it perched on an inclined slab? Exercise caution whenever using detached blocks as part of your anchor system, especially smaller blocks.

Flakes should also be avoided. Flakes—formed by a crack in the rock that runs parallel to the main face—run from wafer thin to several yards thick. Flakes are inherently unstable, and any gear placement, when loaded, will exert that outward prying effect that can fracture and sometimes dislodge the flake from the wall. In naturally weak rock, like sandstone, a thin rock

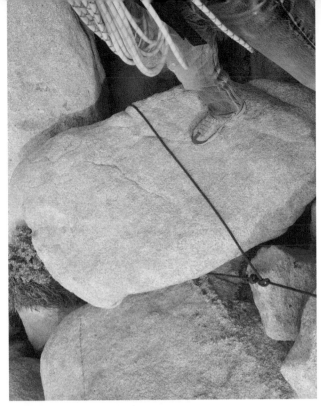

This block is not as big as a fridge but is incorporated into a larger anchor system because its position is low and it's locked in by surrounding blocks.

This large horn of rock is "attached to the planet" rather than a detached block resting "on top of the planet." The rigging rope is tied around the horn using a bowline with a bight.

Bowline Knots

The bowline is useful to tie the rope around something, like a tree, block of rock, or tunnel in the rock.

Even a perfectly snug bowline easily loosens through weighting and unweighting, so *always tie half a double fisherman's knot to back it up*. Since the bowline is easy to untie after weighting, it's used regularly by professional riggers. But beware! An unsecured bowline used as a tie-in knot (without the backup knot) has resulted in many accidents when it came untied. For this reason, the figure eight follow-through remains the widely preferred tie-in knot.

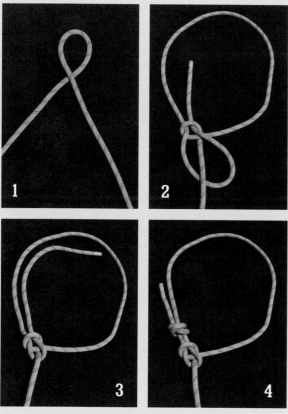

Tying the bowline. The bowline must always be tied with a backup, shown here with half a double fisherman's knot for the backup (photo 4).

The bowline knot with fisherman's backup

Rethreaded bowline. Tie a regular bowline, but leave the tail long enough to go all the way back around the object you're tying around, then retrace the start of the knot, like you would on a figure eight follow-through, finishing with a fisherman's backup. This is a great knot for tying a rope around a tree or through a tunnel, because you end up with two loops, adding strength and redundancy to your rigging.

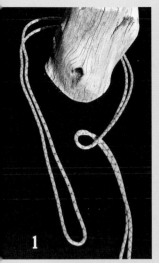

1

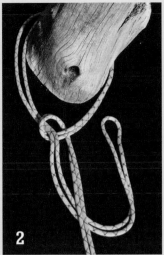

2

3

4

Tying a bowline with a bight (not to be confused with the bowline on a bight, aka the double-loop bowline). The big advantage of the bowline with a bight is that you can tie around an object anywhere down the length of the rope without having to pull the tail all the way through. It's essentially the same configuration as a simple bowline, but tied with two strands of rope—handy for tying off trees when using the Joshua Tree System for a toprope rig. Back it up with an overhand (photo 4).

Toprope setup using the Joshua Tree System on rock horns. The top horn is tied with a simple bowline, backed up with half a double fisherman's knot. The bottom horn is tied using a bowline with a bight, backed up with an overhand. The master point is tied with a BHK (big honking knot). This is a great system to use on two trees.

A camming device placed behind a thin flake. Once the cam is loaded, it will pry outward, potentially breaking the flake. How much force is required to break the flake is hard to determine—but in this case, probably not much.

A "rappel anchor" at Tahquitz Rock in Southern California. This flake is clearly ready to exfoliate. Only a lunatic would rappel off this time bomb. Again, almost every case of catastrophic anchor failure is due to poor rock structure.

Exfoliation is a natural process occurring on granite formations and is the key to dome formation. Flakes of granite are like layers of an onion. Outer layers occasionally peel off due to weathering and gravity, exposing a new layer beneath.

A solid rock bollard attached to the main cliff. Although only a sole monolithic anchor point, the rigging is redundant. The cordellete is doubled and tied with a figure eight loop.

This detached flake is a great example of bad rock structure.

This three-piece anchor has bad macrostructure. A force on the pieces could move the entire block, since it's cracked on all sides. Remember: **The number-one cause of catastrophic anchor failure is bad macrostructure.**

flake is a hazard to avoid. Many flakes take only a few pounds of direct force to send them, and you, sailing. There's a reason the base of many cliffs are strewn with rock debris. Next time, notice that most of that debris is flakes.

When setting anchors, look at any flake with skepticism. How thick is it? How well is it attached to the main rock structure or cliff face? Test its soundness by cautious thumps with the palm of your hand. Does it vibrate? Sound hollow? Play the geologist and scrutinize the rock and its various features, looking for trouble areas.

Macro to Micro Rock Assessment

Evaluate rock structure by toggling from macro to micro. Macro is the big picture. Start there,

accessing the entire rock face. Is it a solid monolith? Are there "cracks in the planet"? Or are the cracks an intricate matrix crisscrossing sections of choss (bad rock) and the occasional solid section. Are you dealing with blocks or flakes? Can you avoid using them? These are the questions you need to answer to know what you're dealing with.

Microstructure is what's *inside* the crack you're using. Is the inner surface of the crack rotten, grainy, dirty, or flaky? Are there hollow spots or hollow flakes inside? Microstructure can affect the integrity of your placements as much as the overall

Never blindly place gear in cracks without first scrutinizing the big picture: the overall structure and integrity of the rock itself.

Bad microstructure: The right side of this nut rests on a fragile flake.

This cam placement looks great—nice and tight in a parallel-sided crack. But how good is the rock? Close inspection reveals a microstructure problem on the crack's left wall, rendering the placement less than ideal.

macrostructure. If there are hidden weaknesses, a loaded anchor will expose them.

Natural Anchors

Natural anchors range from trees and shrubs to rock features such as horns and chickenheads. One of the greatest assets of solid natural anchors is that they are *safe and simple* and also multidirectional, meaning you can weight them from any side or angle and they hold fast.

Trees are plentiful in some areas, rare in others, like the high desert. How do you assess the reliability and strength of a tree? A strength study conducted in the Pacific Northwest sampled twelve different tree species. Key takeaways: (1) Trees routinely subjected to high winds are stronger. (2) Trees with a minimum diameter of 7 inches (a circumference of 22 inches), in areas commonly subjected to winds from 35 to 55 mph, tested between 10 kN and 25 kN at 2 feet up from their base. (3) For 7-inch-diameter trees routinely subjected to *higher* winds (60 to 90 mph), the strength ratings were higher: 30 kN to 60 kN.

OK. A properly girth-hitched nylon sling.

Good. A double-length (48-inch) nylon sling tied with an over-hand knot makes the sling itself redundant.

Good. A figure eight follow-through knot used to tie the anchor rope directly to the tree.

To trust a single tree as a sole anchor, the tree should be a minimum 9 inches in diameter (28-inch circumference), which is roughly the size of your helmet, and also meet the following criteria:

- The tree is living and structurally sound.
- The trunk and base are vertically aligned.
- The tree is rooted in soil (not in sand or gravel) with no voids.
- The trunk is symmetrical at its base.

When setting up a toprope anchor, whenever possible, use two separate trees in the anchor system. If only one tree is available, back it up with another gear placement. Double up the backup if it's less than a colossal tree, healthy and well rooted.

Look for large spikes or horns of rock attached to the main rock structure to tie off as part of your anchor. A tunnel in a solid rock structure is called a *thread*, accomplished by threading a sling or cord, or

tying a rope, through the tunnel. Threads are abundant in limestone but rare in granite.

Again, use detached blocks with discretion. A common practice it to tie off the block around its entire mass rather than using the pinch or contact point where the block touches another rock surface, or where two blocks contact each other. This way, even if the block shifts slightly, you're still anchored to the mass of the block itself. Whenever tying off

Whenever tying off a tree directly with the rope, always check the bark for sap. You will never get the sap out of the line, and it will gum up your belay device and stick to your clothes. Better to sling the tree with runners and keep the rope pristine. To avoid leverage, tie off or sling the tree low down on the trunk.

A "thread" is a sling or cord threaded through a tunnel, rare in granite but common in limestone. Here a Bluewater Titan cordelette (3,080 lbs. tensile strength) is doubled, looped through the thread, then tied off with an overhand knot, creating a strong, four-loop master point. It's worth repeating: It all boils down to the structural integrity of the rock, which here appears to have a small crack at its narrowest point. This thread is in granite, reliable as long as the direction of pull is down. This same thread in sandstone would be questionable.

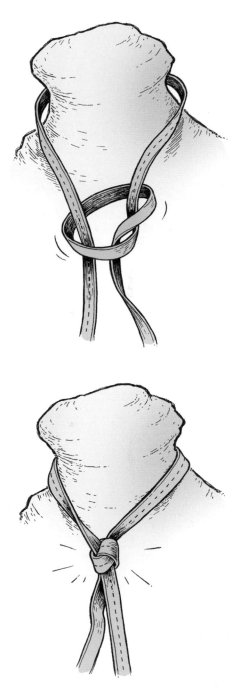

A slip hitch tying off a knob of rock

How to tie a slip hitch. The slip hitch can be tightened by pulling on one strand, making it more secure than a girth hitch for tying off knobs and chickenheads.

Double-length nylon sling, girth-hitched on a horn. If used for protection, the action of the rope might loosen the sling—better to use a slip hitch or choke the sling back on itself.

Choking the sling back on itself weakens it by 30 to 40 percent, but increases the chances of the sling staying put.

Sling girth-hitched on a fist-size chockstone. As long as the pull is straight down, this stone is wedged like a giant hex, and likely is as strong as any nut placement. A pull up and out, however, might easily dislodge it.

A monolithic tree anchor. This massive live pine tree at Tahquitz Rock in Southern California is 60 feet tall and well rooted at its base. The rigging is redundant, since the cordelette has been looped around the tree and tied off with a figure eight loop.

blocks, watch for sharp edges that may fray or cut your rigging rope. Use padding or an edge protector as needed.

Sometimes a single, bombproof natural anchor (guides refer to this as a "monolith") is safely used for a rappel or toprope anchor—like a 3-foot-diameter ponderosa pine tree, or a freezer-size knob of rock that's part of the main rock structure. When rigging a massive tree for a rappel anchor, use two separate slings with two rappel rings to gain redundancy in your anchor system, at least in the rigging. When rigging a belay or toprope anchor, loop two strands of the cordelette around the tree, then tie a figure eight knot for a two-loop master point. Clip in with two carabiners, opposed and reversed, and you have redundancy in your anchor rigging (although technically, a single tree is nonredundant). Always use caution and judgment when using a nonredundant natural anchor.

Nuts: The Evolution of Chockcraft

A chockstone is simply a rock wedged in a crack. Naturally occurring chockstones can be as small as a pebble or as big as a house. The practice of using chockstones for anchor points dates back to the origins of the sport. In the late 1800s in the British Isles, rock climbers began using natural chockstones for anchors by slinging a cord around them and attaching their rope to the sling with a carabiner. The use of *artificial chockstones*—called chocks or, more commonly, nuts—began in the early 1960s at Clogwyn Du'r Arddu, an iconic cliff in North Wales. The hike up to the crag followed a railroad track, and some ambling climber picked up a machine nut along the way and trousered it. Up on the cliff he threaded a small cord through the nut before wedging it in a constriction in a thin crack. Thus the subtle art of chockcraft was born.

In American rock climbing, pitons were used almost exclusively for protection and anchors until the early 1970s. In Europe, pitons were made of soft iron. Once hammered into a crack they were nearly impossible to remove and reuse, so they generally

A selection of chocks from the 1970s. Nuts have evolved over the years, though most are still based on these basic designs.

A selection of modern-day nuts

Original Salathé pitons
PHOTO BY DEAN FIDELMAN

Wayne Merry on Pancake Flake, Nose Route, El Capitan (c. 1958)
PHOTO BY WARREN HARDING, CINDY MERRY COLLECTION

were left in situ, or fixed. Legendary American climber John Salathé, a wrought-iron worker by trade, developed the first hard steel pitons, forged from Model A axle stock (so the legend goes), which he used for his groundbreaking ascents in Yosemite Valley during the 1940s. These high carbon steel pitons could be driven and then removed and reused, over and over again.

From 1957 to 1965, Yvon Chouinard perfected the shape and quality of chrome moly steel pitons, improving on Salathé's designs, debuting the knifeblade, horizontal ("Lost Arrow"), and RURP (realized ultimate reality piton). These pins revolutionized big wall climbing in Yosemite during the "Golden Age" of the 1960s, when hundreds of

placements were required to scale monoliths like El Capitan, Half Dome, Sentinel, and Washington Column. Once placed, hard steel pins could be *cleaned* (removed) by the second, leaving the climbing route devoid of gear and preserving the challenge for the next climbing team.

Throughout the 1960s, Yosemite climbing standards led the world. But this came at a price. Chrome moly pitons were harder than the densest granite, and on popular climbs (*trade routes*) their repeated pounding and removal permanently damaged the cracks, leaving ghastly "pin scars." Cracks were getting "beat out." The National Park Service closed down a few climbs because of piton damage. Something had to give.

Royal Robbins on the Dihedral Wall,
El Capitan, 1964 PHOTO COURTESY NORTH
AMERICAN HISTORY ARCHIVES

Piton scars on a Yosemite crack

In 1966 seminal American climber Royal Robbins visited England, saw the effectiveness of nuts, and exported the idea to Yosemite. His 1967 ascent of The Nutcracker, one of the Valley's most popular climbs, was done entirely with nuts—Royal's way of showing that nuts were a viable alternative to pitons. Climbing the route today, you'll notice piton scars, a testament to how slow American climbers were to embrace the new, gentler technology of chockcraft—a big change from bashing hard steel pitons into cracks with heavy blows from a hammer.

Not until Yvon Chouinard introduced chocks to American rock climbers in his 1972 equipment catalog and Doug Robinson espoused chockcraft in his germinal treatise, "The Whole Natural Art of Protection," did the American climbing community firmly embrace "clean climbing"—a much-needed new approach where climbing anchors were placed and removed by hand, without defacing the rock.

Today there are thin-crack climbs in Yosemite where for hundreds of feet every finger jam is in an ancient piton scar, although now instead of using pitons, nuts can be slotted into the V-shaped bottom of the old pin scars.

Artificial chocks, or simply nuts, now come in a dazzling array of shapes and sizes, the largest ones capable of holding more than 2,000 pounds and

The ingenious tricam, invented by Jeff Lowe in 1980, is essentially a single cam that can be used either passively or actively. Since it has a tapered

Yvon Chouinard proudly displays his new-fangled "clean climbing" gear—stoppers and hexes—at Tahquitz Rock, California, in the early '70s. PHOTO BY TOM FROST, COURTESY NORTH AMERICAN HISTORICAL ARCHIVES

the tiniest micronuts designed to hold body weight only. First introduced by Chouinard Equipment in 1971, the hexentric, commonly called a hex, is a six-sided nut with four distinct attitudes of placement. It was followed by the stopper in 1972, with its simple but effective tapered trapezoidal shape. Although many new designs have since been introduced, most are variations on these two (hex and stopper) classic and timeless designs, which are as viable today as they were decades ago.

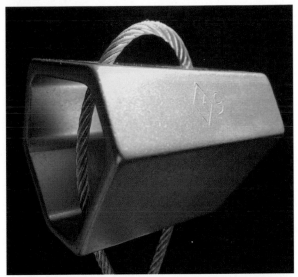

The classic designs of the hex (top) and the stopper (bottom) have changed little since their inception in the early 1970s.

A well-placed tricam in camming (active) mode

A well-placed tricam in passive mode

This tricam, placed in the camming mode, has no room for the camming action to occur. A D-grade placement at best.

design, with a point on one end, it can be wedged like a nut (a passive placement) or used like a cam (an active placement), where a mechanical action (i.e., camming) takes place. The camming action occurs when the sling is loaded on the back, or spine, of the cam, between two rails that contact the rock on one side of the crack, creating a force that pivots like a fulcrum onto the pointed end on the other side of the crack. The design is useful for many horizontal crack situations, but its main drawback is that it's often difficult to remove with one hand once it has been well set or weighted.

While most climbers would never consider carrying tricams on their rack, considering them kook items for gear nuts, tricam advocates like Ron Funderburke, former safety officer for the American Alpine Club, bristle at anyone "throwing shade on the most useful and misunderstood piece of equipment in modern climbing." Writes Ron: "A tricam is the most versatile piece of equipment on your rack and [is] especially useful when anchor building. When the cams have been depleted by the lead, the anchor builder can use tricams where the same sized cam would have been needed. In that context, they will likely not need to place or remove anything one-handed." Point taken.

Nut Placement

When placing any nut, return to the First Consideration: What is the integrity of the rock. Nuts have low holding power in soft sandstone and rotten, flaky rock. They work as protection through the downward force exerted by the rope when weighted, pulling the nut deeper into the constriction in which it is lodged. If the constriction is choss, it sheers away and the nut fails. A few considerations:

- Avoid placing nuts in cracks under or around detached blocks, or in cracks behind loose flakes.

- Look for "straight-in" cracks ("cracks in the planet") in solid rock, where the crack runs perpendicular to the plane of the rock face.
- Once a good crack system is found, look for obvious constrictions in the crack itself. A "bottleneck" placement describes where the crack tapers drastically and the proper size nut is fitted into the narrowing constriction.
- With a basic tapered nut, like the stopper, the preferred placement is in the narrow configuration. This position has the most

Stopper in a bottleneck placement. There is simply no way that a downward force could pull the stopper through this bottleneck. Something would have to give—the rock itself, the nut, or the cable.

This stopper is set in solid rock and has flush surface contact on both sides. Few nut placements are perfect; this one is close.

Good surface contact on both sides of this endwise placement, although the crack is slightly flared. Grade: B-.

Fail. Poor surface contact, particularly on the left side. Insufficient narrowing of the crack below the placement. Might hold body weight, but not a leader fall. Grade: F.

Marginal. This stopper is in a good bottleneck but lacks flush contact on the left side. A slight outward pull will pluck it from its placement. Grade: C-.

Good. The left side of this nut is nearly 100 percent flush, and the curve of the nut on its right side fits the curve of the crack. Grade: A.

Excellent. This nut has good surface contact on both sides, plus the lip on the right side of the crack protects against any outward force. Per endwise placements, on a scale of 1 to 10, this one's a 10.

Hugh Banner invented the offset nut in the 1970s, creating a shape that is tapered in two directions.

This DMM alloy offset fits nearly perfectly into this mildly flaring crack.

The Black Diamond Micro Stopper. This design, where the cable is soldered directly into the nut, fits well in shallow cracks due to its narrower profile.

Opposing nuts. Slider nuts, like the ball nut, are based on this concept. I'd only use this technique if I had nothing else to fit the crack, but it could work in a pinch.

This #3 micro stopper has excellent surface contact. Its breaking strength is rated at 5 kN (1,123 lbs.), roughly half that of a large stopper of 10 kN (2,248 lbs.).

surface contact and stability. The wider, endwise placement works for narrow slots and shallow cracks, but has less surface contact and is generally less stable.

A #6 micro stopper has a breaking strength of 8 kN (1,789 lbs.), although in a bottleneck, this placement lacks surface contact on its right side and, because of the stiff wire, is susceptible to being plucked out by an outward force. Here, the next smaller size would fit better. When I'm (BG) leading, I carry groups of small nuts on an oval carabiner, about a half dozen of similar size per carabiner, and use them like a set of keys. If one doesn't fit, I'll go to the next size, keeping them all on the carabiner. Once I find my placement, I'll unclip the carabiner and put a quickdraw on the placement.

Two nuts in a horizontal crack, rigged in opposition with clove hitches

Excellent. This hex placement has near-perfect flushness on both faces of the nut in a solid straight-in crack. Loading the nut's cable will kick in the camming action of the hex.

Bomber. This perfectly flush end-wise placement couldn't get any better.

It lacks surface contact on its left side, and the crack is a bit flared. Grade: D-.

Relatively flush on both sides, but the rock microstructure is grainy, with large crystals, and the right wall of the crack flares out a bit. Grade: C+.

A nice, flush fit. The concern is the rock structure, and the possibility of the rock itself fracturing.

The typical nut placement is in a vertical crack. Horizontal cracks will work if there is a narrowing at the lip of the crack and you can slide a nut in from the side then pull it into the constriction.

The real art of chockcraft comes into play with the subtler placements. Look for any slight variations in the walls of the crack. Aim for maximum surface contact between the metal faces of the chock and the walls of the crack.

When the walls of the crack are parallel, using the camming action of a tricam or hex is the best option for an active nut placement, although this is territory that camming devices (discussed shortly) were designed for. Unless you can see a V-shaped taper (however subtle) in the crack, chances are you will never find a reliable passive nut placement—it's that simple.

The direction of pull is a critical concern when placing any nut. In what direction will the chock be loaded? *Most placements can withstand a pull in only one, general direction.* While the nut may be able to withstand a load of 2,000 pounds in that one direction, the slightest oblique tug might jerk the nut out of its placement. When incorporating a nut placement into an anchor array, look at the ultimate direction your anchor system will be loaded, and equalize your placement in a line toward the master point (more on this later).

Properly setting a nut is important. Many novice climbers make a great nut placement but fail to set (or *seat*) it properly. A nut merely stuffed into a crack can easily get levered out by the pull of the rope. Set a nut with a few stout tugs in the direction of anticipated loading. If needed, attach a sling to the nut with a carabiner, and yank on the sling till the nut is wedged fast. This makes removal more difficult, but setting the nut is a crucial practice that many novices miss.

Cleaning a nut can be as easy as yanking it in the opposite direction from the intended direction of pull. Be careful with stubborn nuts, which can suddenly pop out and hit you in the face or teeth, or send your hand bashing into the rock, scraping your knuckles. A better approach is to use the nut tool, giving the nut a tap opposite from the direction of loading. A common way to loosen larger nuts is to tap the nut with a carabiner, metal to metal.

The art of chockcraft is an acquired skill. Experienced climbers out to refine their chockcraft are advised to spend a day at a traditional area like Devils Tower or Indian Creek armed with only a handful of passive nuts (hexes and stoppers), climbing some of the old classics that were put up before the

Assessing Nut Placement

When assessing any nut placement, there are three key elements:

1. Rock Structure
2. Direction of Pull
3. Surface Contact

A good acronym to use for nut placement is **SOS:**

S Structural integrity of the rock
O Orientation (direction of pull)
S Surface contact

The nut tool is indispensable for removing chocks. Here are two models: Black Diamond (top); Metolius (bottom).

To remove a nut with a nut tool, first inspect the placement and determine its intended direction of pull, then tap in the opposite direction.

advent of spring-loaded camming devices. Doing so forces us all to focus intensely on the subtleties of chockcraft.

If you're inexperienced at placing nuts, hire a guide for a day of anchoring practice. Getting your placements critiqued by a professional is the fastest way to gain skill and confidence. In the way old days of climbing clubs, a novice got towed up a host of climbs and learned through direct experience. This is still possible, and do so whenever you can. But as a general rule, the better the climber, the less time they have for tutoring, or even partnering with beginners. That's where a guide comes in.

Every nut placement is different—some less than perfect, some bomber, some worthless. A leader, even on easy routes, needs to know what's good and what's not, and what constitutes a placement you can trust. By whatever means you can learn this skill—through classes, bumming a "ride" on someone else's rope (common), boning up on the subject through reading and asking questions—do so.

Cams

The art of protection changed forever in 1978 with the invention of spring-loaded camming devices, or simply cams. The first models were called "Friends," and allowed quick and reliable protection in even perfectly parallel cracks. Of the four most significant inventions in the climbing world over the past forty years—sticky rubber shoes, camming devices, modern belay devices, and lightweight harnesses—none changed the trad climbing game more than cams. Once climbers got familiar with this technology, and got a feel for sizes and placements (usually in short order), scaling massive rock walls became a vastly more efficient and secure adventure.

Gone were the days of hanging off sketchy jams or sloping edges and frantically trying to stuff a glob of aluminum into a parallel-sided crack, the bane of passive chocks. Now, with cams, you *wanted* a parallel section of crack, and could usually set a reliable friend in nothing flat. In a few short years, excepting a small selection of wired tapers, hexes and all the other passive nuts became novelties used for special situations, or not at all. Many modern climbers don't even own any hexes, tricams, et al. These days, the protection game is all about cams.

Spring-loaded camming devices (SLCDs), or, in common terms, cams

The original Wild Country Friend was one of
the greatest innovations in rock climbing.

The Metolius Power Cam has color-coded dots
that help you assess your placement. Green is the
recommended range. Yellow means caution; you're
slightly out of optimal range. Red means danger;
you're making a potentially bad placement.

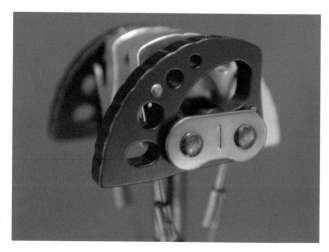

The Black Diamond Camalot was the first
double-axle design.

The idea of the SLCD, or "camming device" for short, is simple in concept yet complex in design. Ray Jardine's original Friend was a rigid aluminum shaft connected by an axle housing four independent aluminum spring-loaded cams ("lobes"). The cams retracted via a trigger bar that slid up and down a slot in the shaft. The unit was fitted into a parallel-sided crack with the cams retracted; when weight was applied to a sling tied into a hole in the bottom of the shaft, the cams were activated in response to the load. The downward force in the direction of the shaft was transferred outward at the cams, which generated an outward force against the walls of the crack, keying the cam in place.

The disadvantage of Ray's design was that a rigid shaft could not flex in the direction of pull, a problem for placements in horizontal cracks.

Today there is a huge array of SLCDs, and almost all these designs have replaced the rigid aluminum shafts with flexible wire cable. Another refinement is the double-axle design found on the Camalot, which allows for a greater range of cam placement. In addition to units with four cam lobes, there are TCUs (three-cam units) and off-set cams (for flared cracks). Each design variation

The Metolius offset TCU (three-cam unit) works well in slightly flaring cracks.

adds another wrinkle to the constants shared by all "active" protection devices. Each unit has three or four lobes that contract when the trigger is pulled, and then expand to fill a given section of crack when the trigger is released. Every lobe on every cam is spring-loaded to hold the cam in the crack when the unit is unweighted.

With a billion-plus-dollar market out there, every conceivable technology has been brought to bear on modern camming devices, which are marvels to see and miraculous to use. It is not a stretch to say that in a majority of cases, camming devices work like magic.

Placing an SLCD

When placing an SLCD, first consider the rock quality. In an ideal placement in solid granite, a Black Diamond Camalot can hold as much as 14 kN (3,147 lbs.). But as with all protection devices, cams can fail if the rock is soft, brittle, or loose. And they can easily pull out if placed behind a small, loose block or thin flake. Never rely on a camming device to hold in very soft sandstone, or in rotten or flaky rock.

Cam manufacturer Metolius advises:

> Rock fails in two basic ways: Either a relatively large piece breaks off or the surface layer is crushed under the pressure of the cam lobe, allowing the cam to "track out." You must assess the integrity of the rock and choose the soundest possible location for your placements. Look for fractures in and around the walls of a potential placement that could denote weakness, as well as pebbles, crystals, grain or micro-flakes that could snap off. Be extremely suspicious of placements behind flakes or blocks."

Since they rely on a friction coefficient (aluminum on rock), camming devices are not as strong in super-slick or polished rock, or rock that is wet or icy. Look for straight-in cracks in dry, solid rock.

This placement looks good, but how strong is that flake forming the crack's left side? Dubious. Grade: F.

Camalot placed for protection on a lead climb. The crack and the placement look good, but how strong is the flake? In general, avoid flakes and seek straight-in cracks that bisect the plane of the rock face at a 90-degree angle.

When placing a cam, look for a uniformly parallel section of crack, or where the walls of the crack form a subtle pocket. Avoid widening cracks, where the crack is wider above the cams; the camming device will naturally wiggle upward as the

The inside cams of this Black Diamond Camalot are open beyond the acceptable range, and the widening crack above the device will allow the cams to easily "walk" into the wider section of the crack with any to and fro motion on the piece, rendering the placement unstable and susceptible to failure. Grade: D-.

Excellent. All the cams are in the recommended ideal range (50–90 percent retraction), and the placement is in a parallel-sided crack in solid rock. When placing Camalots, strive for 50 percent and tighter. Fifty percent retraction is when the bases of the lobes on the cams are at a 45-degree angle relative to the vertical axis (the direction on the stem), or when the bases of the cams form a 90-degree angle relative to each other. Grade: A.

cam is activated (known as "walking"). Walking is most exaggerated when the cam is repeatedly weighted and unweighted, as in toproping. In a crack where the walls are uniformly parallel, or where the crack narrows slightly above the cams, if there is any walking, the cams will not open any wider and will stay within acceptable retraction range. As a test, grab the sling and yank and pull on it to see what walking, if any, occurs. This is an exaggerated test; when you actually use the piece, the force will be more constant. Any SLCD will

Metolius cams' colored-coded dots assist in assessing your placement. Green is the recommended range (75–100 percent retracted). Yellow means caution; you're slightly out of optimal range—the next larger size cam should be a good fit. Red means danger; you're making a bad (too-open) placement. The grade for this Metolius Master Cam placement: A.

"walk" if you vigorously yank it back and forth. The key is to be mindful of walking. Extending the piece with a sling can help reduce walking.

Another key to a solid placement is the range of retraction on the cams. Black Diamond recommends that the Camalot be placed in the lower to mid-expansion range (50–90 percent retraction is ideal). Wild Country advises the following for its

Good. *This Metolius Power Cam displays optimal green "range finder" dots in a solid, parallel-sided crack. Grade: A.*

Poor. *Although the range of retraction is acceptable, this Metolius Power Cam could easily walk up into the wider pod in the crack above, rendering the placement unstable. Also, the outside right cam has poor surface contact and is too close to the edge of the crack. Grade: D-.*

Metolius recommends that in a horizontal crack, the outside cams should be placed on the bottom of the crack for maximum stability.

Too tight. This Camalot is around 90 percent retracted. Any tighter, and it may be very difficult to remove. There is also some loss of holding power in the last 10 percent (90–100 percent retracted) on a Camalot.

Very poor. The two cam lobes on the right side of the crack are outside the acceptable range for a Camalot (too wide), and each set of cam lobes (inside and outside) are not symmetrically retracted. Cams are barely retracted and nowhere near the recommended range. The piece can easily walk, and fail completely. Grade: F.

A larger size cam would be better, but this Metolius Power Cam is in a pocket in the crack that lends some stability to the placement, even though it is borderline on the red "range finder" dots, signifying a marginal placement. Grade: C-.

increasingly rare, single-axle designs: "It is vitally important that all the cams make contact with the sides of the rock, preferably in the middle half of their expansion range (i.e., the cams should be one-quarter to three-quarters open)." Metolius recommends selecting "the largest size cam that will fit without getting stuck. Cams should not be placed near the wide end of their expansion range.

"When a cam is loaded, it expands as the slack is removed from the system and the cam lobes compress into the rock. The harder the cam is loaded

Not ideal. Although Camalots will work in slightly flaring cracks, a parallel-sided crack is what we're looking for. Here, even though the crack is flared and the inside cams are retracted tighter than the outside ones, all four cams have good surface contact and are in the acceptable range of retraction. Grade: C-.

Bad. The crack is way too flared for this Metolius Power Cam, and the cam on the right side has very poor surface contact with the rock. Grade: F.

in the direction of pull (ideally straight down), the more the lobes are forced against the rock. A nearly tipped-out cam won't have enough expansion left to accommodate this process. A loose cam is also more prone to walking and has little range left to adjust."

Good. This Metolius cam is in the tighter aspect of its range. It's also in a slight pocket where the crack narrows above the cam, making it even more secure. Green means good to go. Grade: A-.

The same crack with two different placements. In the left-hand photo, the left outside cam is too close to the edge of the crack. By flipping the cam around (right photo), the outside cam is now on the right wall, and the inside cam (now on the left wall) is deeper in the crack. Since the inside and outside sets of cams are offset, flipping the camming device one way or the other can often render a better placement, particularly in shallow cracks in corners.

While the placement itself looks good, the rock structure is questionable. How strong is that chunk of rock forming the right side of the crack? If the cam were to sustain a high load, would the rock fracture? Maybe not in sound granite like this, but in weaker rock, like sandstone, it probably would. Best not to test it. Remember, the most important thing to consider when placing cams is the structural integrity of the rock. Grade: D-.

Surface to Surface

Ideally, with all cam placements, we want the entire surface of the cam lobe to achieve flush contact with the surface of the crack, like when two parallel planes (imagine two books stacked against each other) lie flush together. If you tip the left book even slightly off the book to the right, only the edge of the books will touch. This is the challenge with flaring/tapering cracks: They don't present a plane of contact that is parallel with the face of the cam lobes. The difference between 5 degrees and 30 degrees off flush amounts to the same thing (try the experiment with stacked books, and see): Only the edges of the cam and the rock will touch. Surface area, lobe to rock, provides the holding power. Anything less is questionable.

To illustrate what constitutes an acceptable range of retraction for the lobes of a camming device, consider the double-axel Black Diamond Camalot. What does 50–90 percent retracting actually look like for the Camalot? Before the trigger is pulled, the unit is at 0 percent retraction. Imagine squeezing the trigger so that the cams are retracted as far as they'll go—100 percent retraction. In a very tight placement at maximum retraction, the Camalot will be difficult to remove, and you risk losing a costly piece of gear. In the last 10 percent of the retraction range (90 to 100 percent retracted), the Camalot also loses some of its holding power—another reason to avoid going too tight on a placement.

The starting point for a good placement is at 50 percent retraction, when you pull the cams halfway tight, when the base of each cam is at a 45-degree angle relative to the vertical axis of the Camalot. If the cams are symmetrically retracted, they are set at a 90-degree angle relative to each other. A common novice mistake is to place a Camalot near the outer limit of its range (0–50 percent retraction). This yields a very unstable placement if the unit moves

in the crack, which commonly happens if the crack widens above the cams and the piece is repeatedly weighted and unweighted. Again, the optimal Camalot placement is when the cams are at least halfway tight (50 percent retracted).

From the beginning position, pull the trigger till the range on the cams is half the starting size, then go smaller and tighter from there. Scrutinize the unit after placement to visually confirm that the cams are within acceptable range.

Metolius cams have color coding that assists your assessment. The company gives this advice:

> Verify that you have chosen the best size by making sure that the green Range Finder dots are lined up where the cam lobes touch the walls of the placement. Yellow dot alignment is okay too, but you must exercise more caution with the placement because the cam will be less stable, hence more prone to walking, and it will have less expansion range left to accommodate walking to a wider position. If the cam you choose aligns in the yellow zone, the next larger size will align perfectly in the green zone. Use that cam instead, if it's still on your rack. Never use a placement in the red zone unless it's the only placement available.

Bottom line: Size matters. One size too big or too small might work in a pinch, just not nearly as well as a unit that better fits the crack at 50 percent retraction.

Metolius Cams

The difference between Metolius cams and other SLCDs (like Camalots or Wild Country single-axel cams) is that Metolius's recommended range is 75–100 percent retracted. Point is, while general principles apply to all cam use, you need to know the specs for each brand, which differ slightly.

Cam Removal

Ultralight cams, now favored by most climbers, *start* at around $75 for the smallest units, so losing a cam feels like losing your wallet. It is also almost inevitable if you climb long enough, and is the best incentive to develop your cam cleaning skills, and to avoid jamming a fully retracted cam into a crack. Cleaning most cam placements simply involves pulling the trigger mechanism, retracting the cam lobes, and wiggling the unit out.

Removal usually becomes difficult when, for whatever reason, you can't retract the cams far enough to loosen the unit—even if only one lobe is hung up—and wrangle it out of the crack. Expect to find these kinds of placements, because you will. After a while you will get a feel for how to work the trigger while jockeying the cam around, trying to toggle the piece around so you can get some play in the lobes and wiggle it free. Yanking on the trigger while jockeying the unit, if done just so, can often free what seems like a helplessly stuck piece. It's a learned skill that most climbers pick up quickly—or end up with an empty rack.

Summary

Cams can initially seem daunting and complex, and they are—in design; yet most cams are fairly easy to place. Once you get familiar with triggering the lobes and making and cleaning placements, the mysteries dissolve and you're left with a few key concepts, which give you a working formula: The better the rock, the better the placement. Solid placements favor a parallel-sided section of crack, with no sudden widening above or below the unit (to inhibit walking). Seek even positioning and flush contact (aluminum to rock) of the lobes, with the unit deployed in the medium to semi-tight range. While anything but foolproof, cams that meet this simple criterion are usually good enough. TCUs and offset cams are trickier to use, but active climbers can master their use with experience.

Study the literature that comes with any camming device you purchase, and learn what the manufacturer recommends for the acceptable range of retraction and the various placement criteria. Most manufacturers also have PDF files on camming device guidelines that you can download from the company's website. The data in those files comes from exhaustive testing. It's worth knowing the results.

In practical terms, what the study of anchors and protection boils down to is our ability to efficiently place solid pieces, and our confidence to lead and belay off those pieces. This presents a Catch-22 to beginning trad climbers: You can't know for sure about your placements till you fall on them, and you don't want to fall on them till you're sure they will hold. Because we fall far less on trad routes than sport climbing, gaining confidence simply by doing routes—half the time holding our breaths for fear of the gear blowing out—is a slow and nervy process. Canadian climber Sonnie Trotter, one of the best in the business, offers probably the finest method to hasten your ability to place solid anchors and to confidently know as much. Writes Sonnie:

> My best advice (to get fluent with trad gear) is to do a lot of aid climbing. I don't mean using pitons, beaks, and a hammer; I'm talking about easy, clean aid, like leading splitter cracks, thin, wide, steep, and steeper. When I was 19, I was climbing 5.14 sport routes but only trad climbing 5.11 because *I had no faith in gear, or in my ability to place it well.* Aid climbing gave me the confidence I needed, and I soon began climbing at my limit on gear-protected routes. It doesn't have to be hard aid—it can be a 5.9 route—but instead of freeing it, aid it. Treat this like mental training; the idea is not just to get to the top, but to place as much gear as you possibly can. This exercise forces you to weight every single piece of gear, and by doing this, you

In addition to parallel-sided cracks, Camalots also work well in pods or pockets, as shown here. Make sure the cams are in the recommended range. Grade: A-.

This Camalot has issues. It violates a rule stated in the Black Diamond literature under "Bad Placements": "Never place a unit so that the cams are offset (e.g., with two cams extended and with two cams retracted. It may not hold a fall." Also, the left outer cam is dangerously close to the edge of the crack. Grade: F.

Marking Gear

Climbing gear is expensive. It constantly gets mixed in with your partner's gear because almost nobody has all the equipment needed for all the routes you'll climb. We invariably end up leading with a composite rack culled from whomever shares our rope. You sort stuff out when you're tired, hungry, and over it all, and stuff goes missing. Pricy stuff. Favorite stuff. Stuff that blends in with most anyone's rack—unless it is marked. That's why you always mark everything—slings, cams, nuts, and carabiners.

Avoid marking hardware by stamping, engraving, or filing, as it can weaken the metal, albeit ever so slightly. So you apply a bit of colored tape (don't; it gums up the works), paint (comes off quickly), or nail polish (better than paint). With nail polish you can create a simple, unique dot or color pattern that will easily identify your gear. Apply to areas where abrasion is low, or where rope drag won't wear off the paint or polish in a rope length (e.g., the spine of a carabiner instead of the rope basket). I (BG) mark my slings by using a colored ink marker on the small label of the sling, not the sling itself, as some inks contain acid that can weaken nylon. Best to avoid marking your slings with ink.

Using a rigid-stem camming device in a horizontal placement risks breaking the metal stem. Remedy this with the "gunks tie-off."

Bad. Not the placement itself, but the poor microstructure. The left wall of the crack is rotten, ready to exfoliate if the cam is loaded with any great force, like in a leader fall. Fall on this one, and it likely will rip out. Grade: D-.

start to truly trust your placements and realize what works, what doesn't, and why. You shouldn't need any special gear; a standard double rack (nuts and cams) should suffice.

The "gunks tie-off"—named for the Shawangunks in New York, a trad area renowned for steep face climbs protected by mainly horizontal cracks—is a pretied loop of high-tensile cord through the hole in the stem closest to the cam head.

*Caroline Gleich places
a cam on Sasquatch
(5.9+), Little Cottonwood
Canyon, Utah.*

PHOTO BY JOHN EVANS

By far the best option for a horizontal cam placement is a flexible-stemmed unit that bends and can withstand a downward force. A leader fall may bend the stem, but the ability of the stem to flex may save the day.

Assessing SLCD Placements

When assessing a camming device placement, the key elements are:

1. **Rock structure.** Evaluate both macro- and microstructural integrity.

2. **Placement** in parallel-sided cracks.

3. **Orientation**—placed in the direction of pull.

4. **Range of retraction** to manufacturer's guidelines (e.g., 50 to 90 percent for Camalots).

5. **Test for walking.** Tug on the placement and wiggle it slightly; beware of widening cracks.

A good acronym to use for all cam placement is **SPORT:**

S Structural integrity of the rock
P Placement in parallel-sided crack
O Orientation (direction of pull)
R Range of retraction
T Test for walking

Fixed Anchors

Pitons

A piton is a steel spike that is hammered into a crack for an anchor. The blade of the piton enters the crack, leaving the protruding eye through which you clip a carabiner. Piton anchors are rare these days, but occasionally you'll come across fixed pitons (also called pins) at the top of a crag or on multipitch trad routes. Follow these steps before using any fixed pin.

First, assess the rock structure and look at the crack where the piton is set. Is it behind a block or flake, or is it set in a straight-in crack with good structure? A bomber piton is driven to the eye, and should not be corroded or cracked. (Look closely at the eye of the piton for cracks, which are often found here.) A hammer is needed to effectively test a fixed pin. Give the piton a light tap—it should not wiggle or rotate *at all*; rather it should give off a high-pitched ring as the hammer springs off the pin. Sans hammer—which few climbers ever carry—clip a sling into the pin and vigorously yank in the direction of loading. You can also tap it with a carabiner or small rock.

Over time, pitons loosen because of weather, mainly thermal expansion and contraction, particularly in winter. Water expands when it freezes, loosening the piton. Often a piton, welded to the eye and initially bombproof, can be plucked out with your fingers after only a few seasons. Use all fixed pins with skepticism—and always back them up.

Climbers at Verdon Gorge, France

Piton Placement

To practice piton placement, grab a hammer, a few pitons and slings, and venture to a chossy outcrop or section of rock where nobody climbs or goes. All you need are a few cracks. Most every area has such a place—probably more than a few. The process is fairly straightforward. Select a piton that corresponds to the dimensions of the crack, one that when slotted by hand, goes in roughly 75 percent of its length before hammering. Then drive it home. Go for that shrill ringing sound. To test your work, clip a sling into the piton, step into the sling, and gingerly weight it. Remove (*cleaning*) the pin by knocking it up and down along the axis of the crack till it works loose. You might be surprised that pitons that seem bomber come out with just a few hammer blows. It takes some fiddling to learn what is and is not a bomber placement. The best way to learn piton placement is to jump on a beginning wall climb that is primarily aid, or artificial, climbing. Most every destination area has these break-in aid climbs. Most of them go clean (nuts and cams only), but a few, usually featuring thin cracks, are still nail-ups requiring pitons. By the time you reach the summit of an aid climb (that requires pitons), you'll know all about "ironmongery."

Pitons (left to right): knifeblade, horizontal, angle

Pound it in the rest of the way. A shrill ringing, like a scale on a xylophone, denotes solid rock and a well-seated pin.

To place a pin, insert it into the crack. Ideally, it should go in about two-thirds of its length before pounding.

An angle piton driven all the way into the rock in a straight-in crack. An ideal pin placement.

Bolts

In a gym, the security of the bolts is a given. They are directly attached to the steel superstructure supporting the wall itself. Outdoors, protection bolts and anchors are set in the rock, which varies dramatically area to area in quality and holding power. Most bolts we encounter outdoors are good enough. Some are not, depending in part when a route was first ascended, how carefully the bolt was placed, and the density of the rock it is set in. What's more, bolts are frequently found on big multipitch routes—some old, some new—especially at belay stations. Bottom line is there are safety concerns for understanding bolts, since we're so frequently hanging our lives on them.

History

In the 1960s and 1970s, bolts were placed by hand drilling—an exhausting process where a drill bit was inserted into a steel drill holder that you pounded with a hammer, twisting the holder as you slugged away, painstakingly drilling a hole into the rock. Once the hole was deep enough, a bolt stud, with a hanger attached, was hammered into the hole.

The most common bolt (up to the late 1970s) was the ¼-inch Rawl Drive contraction bolt, designed to secure anchors in masonry and concrete, and used in construction projects. A contraction bolt has a split shaft that is wider than the diameter of the hole. When pounded into the hole, the two bowed shaft pieces are forced to straighten slightly, contracting under tension in the hole. Contraction bolts work well in hard granite; but in soft rock like sandstone, the split shaft doesn't contract much, and there is little tension to keep it seated in the hole, resulting in weak pullout strength (i.e., pulling straight out on the bolt).

Another problem with ¼-inch bolts is that they came in various lengths, some as short as ¾ inch. Once placed in the rock, there was no way for future climbers to visually determine bolt length.

Rawl Drive bolts come in two basic styles: buttonhead and threaded. The buttonhead has a mushroomlike head and is pounded into the hole with the hanger preattached. The threaded Rawl Drive has threads with a nut on the end to hold the hanger in place—a weaker configuration, since the threads can weaken the shear strength of the shaft if the hanger rides on the threads. More significantly, the pullout strength of threaded bolts is only as strong as the holding power of the nut on the threads—a dangerous problem if the bolt is hammered too deeply and the nut is caught at the very quick of the threads.

The shear strength on a brand-new ¼-inch Rawl Drive bolt is roughly 2,000 pounds, but the problem with contraction bolts is not shear strength but pullout strength, which varies dramatically depending on the rock. In soft sandstone, the pullout strength of a ¼-inch contraction bolt is extremely low. Such bolts are always unsafe.

The buttonhead Rawl Drive bolts were also available in ⁵⁄₁₆-inch diameters, far more reliable as long as they were placed in fine-grained granite.

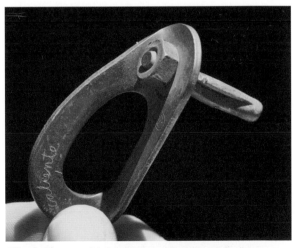

The infamous ¼-inch threaded Rawl Drive contraction bolt, complete with the SMC "death hanger." This coffin nail was removed and replaced from a route on Suicide Rock, California.

With shear and pullout strength exceeding 4,000 pounds, the ⁵⁄₁₆-inch buttonhead was for many years the bolt of choice for first ascensionists who hand-drilled bolts. Unfortunately, hand-drilling a ⁵⁄₁₆-inch hole was so taxing, sometimes taking a half hour or more in hard stone, that most climbers went with the ¼-incher and hoped for the best. It's a wonder that more of these didn't fail.

The ⁵⁄₁₆-inch buttonhead Rawl Drive has been discontinued, but the ⅜-inch buttonhead is still on the market, with a 7,000 pound shear strength and a pullout strength of more than 4,000 pounds—when set in bulletproof rock. The problem with buttonhead Rawl Drive bolts is that they're made of carbon steel, which corrodes over time. What was bomber in the 1990s was suspect a decade later. At least one ⁵⁄₁₆-inch buttonhead failure (due to corrosion) led to a climbing fatality.

The biggest danger with the old ¼-inch bolts is not the stud but the hangers. From the early 1970s on toward the turn of the twentieth century,

hangers made for rock climbing were manufactured primarily by the SMC company, with an "SMC" brand stamped on them. There were two series of hangers—one good, the other very bad. The bad hangers were nicknamed the SMC "death hangers," since some of them failed under body weight after only a few seasons. These hangers have a distinctive corrosive discoloration—a yellowish or bronze tint—whereas the "good" SMC hangers, made from stainless steel, show no signs of corrosion and still appear silvery bright, even after thirty years.

Learn the difference between these two hangers—one good, one very bad. They were manufactured by the SMC company and stamped "SMC" on the hanger. On the left is the infamous SMC "death hanger"—slightly thinner and, since it was made of carbon steel, corroded with a yellowish, bronze, or rust tint. The good SMC hanger on the right is made of stainless steel, and shows no sign of corrosion after thirty years set the rock. Another identifying feature is that on the "bad" hanger, the letters "SMC" are stamped horizontally, while on the "good" hanger, "SMC" is stamped vertically.

Buttonhead Rawl Drive contraction bolts (left to right): ⅜-, ⁵⁄₁₆-, and ¼-inch sizes

A 5/16-inch buttonhead Rawl contraction bolt with good SMC hanger. In a sound placement in solid granite, when new these bolts were rated at more than 4,000 pounds shear strength. But since they're made of carbon steel, they've corroded over time and are now considered suspect.

A relic from the 1970s, this 1/4-inch Rawl Drive buttonhead still looks good after many years, as does the "good" SMC hanger, with no signs of corrosion. Brand-new, these bolts had a shear strength of 2,000 pounds, roughly that of a medium wired stopper; but since the bolt is made of carbon rather than stainless steel, corrosion eventually degrades them. Many are ticking time bombs. Often when I'll (BG) pry one out to replace it, the resistance is the same as pulling a nail out of plywood, especially in soft rock, where the bolt's split shaft had minimal contraction.

Another subtle but noticeable difference is in the thickness of the hangers: The "bad" hangers are roughly the thickness of a dime; the "good" ones, as thick as a quarter. Another way to distinguish between them is to look closely at the SMC stamp on the hanger itself. On the "good" hangers "SMC" is stamped vertically; on the "bad" ones "SMC" runs horizontally.

Another dangerous relic from the 1970s is the Leeper hanger. More than 9,000 of these hangers were manufactured by Ed Leeper of Colorado; they were subsequently recalled because of stress-corrosion problems, since they were not made of stainless steel. These hangers are easily identifiable because of their strange geometric shape and rusty condition.

Climbers establishing new routes (and placing bolts) haven't used any of this archaic bolting gear in decades, though you will likely find a few vintage bolts on old (pre-1980) trade routes. Most have

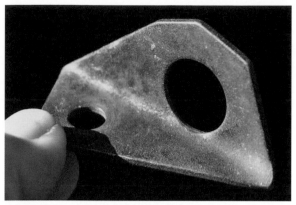

The Leeper hanger, recalled in the 1970s, is easily identified by its trapezoidal shape and rusty finish.

Bad corrosion on a ³/₈-inch-diameter threaded Rawl Drive bolt, with a badly corroded Leeper hanger to match

The ³/₈-inch threaded wedge expansion bolt is another commonly seen bolt. Check to make sure the nut is tightly screwed down to secure the hanger on these bolts.

been replaced by modern hardware, but not all, so knowing the specs and concerns regarding the old bolts is essential for all trad climbers.

A "spinner" is a bolt placement where the hanger moves freely and you can spin it around the bolt in a circle. Here, the hole wasn't drilled deeply enough, so when this ⁵⁄₁₆-inch buttonhead was pounded in, it hit the back of the hole before the buttonhead came up flush against the hanger.

Modern Bolts

Sport climbing boomed in the 1980s, when climbers began placing bolts on rappel using cordless rotary hammer power drills. Since these bolts were certain to absorb numerous falls, climbers sought out the strongest available bolts. The standard quickly became ⅜-inch diameter for solid rock (like granite), and ½-inch diameter for softer rock (like sandstone)—the same standards we have today.

The go-to bolt for sport climbing has long been the "five-piece Rawl" (now sold as the DeWalt Power-Bolt). This expansion bolt has a shaft with a hex head on one end and threads on the other end (the end that goes in the hole), with a cone-shaped piece screwed onto the threads. The shaft has a two-part split sleeve. As the hex head is tightened, the cone climbs up the threads and under the sleeves, which presses the sleeves outward, "expanding" the bolt in the hole. The more you tighten it, the wider the sleeve gets. *Safe and simple,* when properly placed in solid rock.

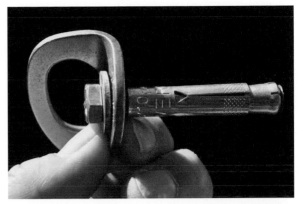

The ⅜-inch-diameter stainless DeWalt Power-Bolt expansion bolt matched with a stainless steel hanger is considered the current minimum standard. In good granite these bolts rate at around 7,000 pounds shear strength and 5,000 pounds pullout strength. Most climbers who replace old bolts now use ½-inch-diameter stainless steel Power-Bolts (10,000 lbs. shear strength). If you're installing bolts, use a stainless steel bolt matched with stainless steel hanger to avoid corrosion or reactions from mixing metals.

The performance and strength of the Power-Bolt hinges on the tolerance (diameter) of the hole and the strength of the rock. In good rock, the ⅜-inch Power-Bolt is rated at more than 7,000 pounds shear strength, with a pullout strength of roughly 5,000 pounds.

Another widely used bolt is the wedge anchor, with a shaft that widens slightly at its base, fitted with a two-part sleeve. The opposite end has threads. Once a hanger is fitted and a nut is screwed onto the threaded end, so the end of the shaft is flush with the top end of the nut, the bolt is pounded into the hole. The hole should be drilled deeply enough that the shaft does not contact the bottom of the hole. When the hanger is flush to the rock, the nut is tightened, backing the bolt out of the hole as the two-part sleeve tightens onto the wedged shaft. The drawback of this design is that the hanger often loosens over time on the threaded end.

Since thousands of bolts have been set in rock for more than twenty-five years, the reliable life span of bolts and bolt types is becoming clear. Many older, carbon steel bolts are seriously corroded, which happens quicker in the mountains than in the desert. But the point is moot. *A stainless steel bolt with a stainless steel hanger is the way to go.* Mixing metals (carbon steel and stainless steel) can accelerate deterioration because of galvanic corrosion (a reaction between different metals).

In marine areas (sea cliffs), even stainless steel bolts and hangers corrode rapidly. By trial and error, climbers have found that in salty environs, the only bolts that last are titanium glue-in anchors—essentially a U-shaped titanium bolt that is epoxied into the hole.

In very soft sandstone and decomposed granite, even expansion bolts fail to tighten up properly. Here we go with glue-in bolts—typically a ⅜-inch (10 mm) or ½-inch (12 mm) diameter stainless steel eye bolt that is epoxied into the hole. The key to installing glue-ins is to make sure the hole is scrupulously cleaned to ensure a good epoxy bond

The DeWalt company website (anchors.dewalt.com) offers an excellent tutorial ("mechanical anchors") on the various types of bolts and their strength in different concrete densities.

between the metal and the rock. Use a wire-bristle brush and blow tube until *all* the drill dust is gone.

Since most bolts are designed for construction work, the DeWalt company lists strength ratings based on the density of concrete in which the

A well-engineered rappel anchor. Both bolts are ⅜-inch stainless Power-Bolts with stainless steel Petzl hangers, along with a stainless steel chain, quick link, and ring. Everything was painted before installation to match the color of the rock.

Bolt Guidelines

- The hanger should not be deformed, cracked, or miscolored.
- The bolt hanger should set solidly and flush against the rock.
- The hanger should not move, even under direct force, like pulling the hanger sideways with a carabiner.
- Beware of "spinners," where on a protruding bolt, the hanger spins like a roulette wheel. In most cases, the hole was not drilled deeply enough. When hammered home, the bolt bottomed out in the hole before the hanger could be tightened flush against the rock.
- Beware of loose hangers, or bolts that wiggle in the hole. If the bolt has a hex head or a nut on threads, tightening with a wrench may help. Most likely the bolt can't be fixed and needs to be replaced.
- All ¼-inch bolts are unreliable, particularly in softer rock. Many can be removed with the same resistance as a nail being pulled out of plywood.
- To replace a ¼-inch bolt, (1) pry it out of its hole; (2) redrill the same hole to a ½-inch diameter; and (3) install a ½-inch-diameter stainless steel Power-Bolt (10,000 lbs. shear strength) with a stainless steel hanger.
- Paint all hangers (before installation) the same color as the rock so the bolt is unobtrusive— visual ecology.
- Whenever possible, be a mensch and replace time bomb bolts with solid ones that will last a lifetime.

The American Safe Climbing Association (ASCA) donates the necessary (and expensive) hardware to climbers who upgrade aging bolt anchors with modern stainless steel bolts and hangers. Support the ASCA by visiting safeclimbing.org.

All these old bolts at Joshua Tree were replaced with brand-new stainless steel hardware, courtesy of the ASCA.

bolt anchor is typically placed. Concrete is given a psi (pounds per square inch) rating. For example, "2,000 psi concrete" means it would take a weight of 2,000 pounds to crush a square inch of concrete. Dense granite equals about 6,000 psi concrete; soft sandstone, 1,000 psi concrete.

Once a bolt is installed, it's impossible to see what's going on beneath the surface (such as the length of the bolt). The only thing visible is the head of the bolt, which makes it difficult to ID the bolt type. What you *can* do is evaluate the condition of the bolt, as far as you can tell.

Rust is an obvious red flag. Never trust SMC "death hangers," Leeper hangers, homemade aluminum hangers, and any bolt or hanger that's clearly corroded. Look closely and identify the diameter of the bolt. A ⅜-inch–diameter bolt is the minimum standard, along with a stainless steel hanger. A bolt with threads and a nut holding the hanger in place is generally not as strong as the hex head types.

The rock should not show cracks spiderwebbing out from the bolt—a more common problem with contraction bolts than expansion bolts.

Anchor Systems

Anchor systems are essentially *rigging systems*. Using slings, loops of cord, knots, and carabiners, we link two, three, and sometimes more primary nuts, cams, and bolts, and hub these assets together at a master point, which absorbs the loading. Primary anchors are the critical component of any anchor system, which is why we studied them first. We take that knowledge as a given as we now move to integrating solid primary anchors into a solid anchor system via rigging. This sounds involved, and it is, but the picture clears when we briefly review why anchor systems came about.

Modern anchor systems arose with the clean climbing revolution (c. early 1970s), when the conventional means of protection changed from driving hard steel pitons into cracks to hand-placing passive, aluminum nuts wherever you could. Problem was, the first generation of clean climbing hardware was limited to hexes, stoppers, and variants of the two. Often you couldn't make placements remotely as solid as the pitons that nuts had replaced. The commitment to clean climbing, especially in regards to building anchors, was nearly a decade ahead of the technology to dependably achieve it. This changed once and for all in 1978 with the arrival of camming devices. In the meantime, the critical need to milk maximum holding power from limited clean climbing tools led to rapid innovations in rigging.

Before clean climbing caught on, piton anchors (always more than one piece) were coupled on the

Hubbing multiple assets together at a master point distributes the loading, as in this four-piece anchor rigged with a 7 mm diameter nylon cordelette.

Rita Young Shin on Cosmic Girl, Middle Cathedral Rock, Yosemite
PHOTO BY JOHN EVANS

121

climbing rope with clove hitches and overhand knots. Clean climbers, however, anxiously sought some means of spreading the load so that any fall factor was collectively distributed across what sometimes was a cluster of dubious nuts. The fear was that the leader would fall and, in one ghastly cascade, the nuts would launch from the crack "like cloves from a holiday ham," as climber John Sherman once put it.

Various anchoring systems quickly evolved, as did beliefs and philosophies about what rigging qualities were critical and what the rigging was actually achieving. Comprehensive lab testing was limited. "Field testing" was helpful, but rigging theory was in large part subjective—and sometimes straight-up false.

As equipment improved and systems were refined, decades of lab testing, informed by the practical realities found on the cliffside, slowly transformed anchor systems into a data-based performance art—still an art, because creativity is often required. After nearly fifty years, solid principles and protocols, proven countless times from the Pinnacles to Patagonia, are finally becoming standardized.

The NARDSS Principle

The NARDSS principle is a simple, easy-to-remember acronym used for evaluating any anchor system. We've gone through many different acronyms, updated by continued lab results and field testing, to finally determine the most essential qualities of a solid belay anchor, which are summarized by NARDSS.

"NARDSS" stands for "No Extension, Angles, Redundant, Distributes Load, Solid, and Simple." These six qualities are closely analyzed later on. For now, a short-form description looks like this:

No Extension means that if any one piece in the anchor system fails, no significant amount of slack will develop before the load abruptly shifts to the remaining pieces (often called "shock loading," mostly a muddied term). The rule of thumb is to limit any possible extension in your anchor system to no more than half the length of a single (24-inch) sling—12 inches.

Angles addresses the *load multiplication* that occurs when the outside arms of a rigging system (which form a V) are too far apart. If you keep the *angles* of the V under 60 degrees, you split the load roughly 50/50. Rule of thumb: The angle between the arms in any belay anchor should never exceed 90 degrees.

Redundant means there is no place in the anchor system where you rely on a single piece of equipment, be it a strand of cord, a sling, or a carabiner. There is *always* a backup. For bolt anchors, the minimum is two bolts, preferably ⅜-inch diameter. For gear anchors, the minimum number (and the industry standard for guides) is three cams and/or

Acronym	Meaning
RENE	Redundant, Equalized, No Extension
SRENE	Solid, Redundant, Equalized, No Extension
ERNEST	Equalized, Redundant, No Extension, Solid, Timely
EARNEST	Equalized, Angles, Redundant, No Extension, Solid, Timely
LEADSTER	Limit Extension, Angles, Direction, Solid, Timely, Equalized, Redundant
NERDSS	No Extension, Redundant, Distribution, Solid, Simple

NARDSS derives from the evolution of other acronyms (listed in the table above) developed as reference points for anchor building, which list the most critical concerns as indicated by decades of lab testing and the practical realities encountered on the cliffside.

nuts. If the rock quality is questionable, using two different rock features (e.g., two different crack systems) adds redundancy.

Distributes Load means that when the master point is loaded, the loading is *distributed* among the various components of the anchor. "Distributed" has come to replace "equalized," which in years past suggested that the load was evenly spread across the points in the anchor array, something never achieved in real-world climbing. The practical aim is load distribution, knowing the load is never evenly divided. A *pre-distributed* anchor means the system can accept loading in one specific direction. A *self-adjusting* anchor can adjust to loading within a range of directional changes (multidirectional).

Solid refers to the structural integrity of the rock, which we evaluate from macro to micro.

Distributed, Not *Equalized*

Even in theory, to approach true equalization with a pre-distributed rigging system (examined in detail below), the various arms of your rigging system must be exactly the same length, which is impossible to achieve with a knotted sling (even sewn slings must be knotted to form a master point) or loop of cord. Even static material like Dyneema stretches a little bit. When weighted, any knots in the rigging tighten differently, absorbing a little force and adding unpredictable lengths to the arms in the rigging. Testing (as well as engineering models) clearly shows that *the shortest arm in the rigging system will bear most of the weight most of the time.* Self-adjusting rigging systems (e.g., the quad and sliding X) feature a dynamic master point. But the load-bearing carabiner tends to *bind* on the sling/cord owing to friction as the loading spikes from one arm of the rigging to another. Until pulleys replace (if ever) carabiners at the master point, true equalization will remain an elusive goal.

A toprope setup composed of two bolts pre-distributed with a double-length (48-inch) nylon sling tied with an overhand knot. The two pear-shaped locking carabiners are opposed and reversed. This simple setup is redundant, tied off for a load in one direction, and rigged for minimal extension. Here, a nylon sling is a better choice than Dyneema, since it has a modicum of stretch and the knot will be easier to untie. If using a Dyneema sling for this setup, go with a figure eight instead of an overhand knot. It's easier to untie after it's weighted.

"Solid" also refers to the security of the placement itself—that is, have you placed the piece like it was designed to be placed? Solid placements in solid rock. That's what "solid" means, and is the foundation of all anchors all of the time.

Simple harks back to this book's introduction and Occam's razor, or the *law of parsimony*—that the simplest solution is most likely the best one. This

What Is Shock-loading?

There is much disagreement about what "shock-loading" actually means, so definitions vary. For example, once testing proved that equalization was never fully achieved in anchor systems, *no-extension* became the critical factor for many climbers. By limiting the possible extension in the system, some maintained that if one anchor point failed, a belay system with limited extension reduced the shock-loading that occurred when the load "extended" from a failed arm in the system to the next arm in the chain, which held. However, testing proved that the load never multiplied through this small extension *but, in most cases, was reduced because the placement absorbed some force—sometimes a lot—before it failed.* Even if the failed piece absorbed no force whatsoever, the force only traveled a few inches before impacting the next arm in the chain. And because the force is transmitted through a dynamic climbing rope that stretches, "shock-loading," in this scenario, is an ambiguous term.

As a measurable phenomenon, true shock-loading is much more likely within a closed, static system—like what happens when a climber is clipped directly to an anchor with a static tether, climbs a few feet above the anchor, and falls directly onto it. There is no dynamic link in the anchor chain. It's a direct load absorbed by a static tether hitched to a static anchor. The result is a true shock load, because the entire dynamic force almost instantly decelerates, which generates forces great enough to break carabiners and vertebrae. When the same load is absorbed by dynamic rope, because the rope stretches, the fall force happens slower, and sudden loading doesn't generate such astronomical peak forces. In this regard, "shock-loading" more ac-curately describes the sudden and violent loading that occurs in a closed static system involving tech cord and webbing (Dyneema) directly attached to other static links like carabiners and bolts.

Fact is, whenever you fall onto a piece of protection, or suddenly and dramatically weight the anchor, "shock-loading" might be an appropriate word, even though the protection was placed and the anchor built to sustain this "shock." However, the term is misleading in the way it was often used (and we are belaboring this point because you are sure to hear it): that when one anchor point blows out in an anchor array, the load *multiplies* before it cascades (usually a matter of inches) onto the next point in the anchor array. Testing shows the opposite happens, to varying degrees, per the reasons stated above.

This point is driven home by reviewing the loading stats when using a Yates "Screamer," an ingenious device consisting of a loop of sling doubled back on itself with rows of bartacked stitching. The Screamer is rigged like a quickdraw, with carabiners at each end of the loop—one end clipped onto a marginal protection point, with the rope clipped through the other end. When fallen upon, the bartacks rip out, directly absorbing energy owing to this stitch-ripping effect. The Screamer also allows your rope to absorb more energy from the fall by slightly increasing the time interval of the fall. It is absurd to think the load would multiply as the stitches rip out, and, in fact, lab tests conducted by Black Diamond comparing a regular quickdraw and a Screamer, both connected to a bomb-proof anchor point, show the Screamer lowers the peak loading force by 17.7 percent. Enough said.

is especially useful when building anchors, which otherwise can get needlessly cluttered and complex. "Simple" means "timely." We need to place protection and build anchors quickly and efficiently, because time on a big multipitch route is something that needs to be managed.

Pre-Equalized Is Out. Self-Adjusting Is In.

In the early 1980s, I (JL) wrote the first anchor book well before testing demonstrated what various rigging systems were and were not doing (mostly in terms of loading). Decades of tests, conducted in many countries by many experts, made clear that some of the anchoring terms I originally coined were misleading and inaccurate, none so much as "equalization," for the reasons stated earlier. For a while, we reframed "equalization" to mean "load distribution," or "load sharing" (which point to the same thing), not wanting to abandon the term, for reasons no longer valid. Now the time has come. Going forward, "equalization" is gone, replaced by "load sharing" or "load distribution" (depending on the context). "Pre-Equalized" is out. "Self-Adjusting" is in. Some sources suggest "self-tightening," but this pertains to what the sling is doing, not what is happening within the overall anchor system. So "Self-Adjusting" it is.

Vectors (angles)

The "A" (angles) in NARDSS points to a dangerous, unobvious rigging error most of us will make unless we understand the factors and forces involved.

A vector is a quantity of both direction and force. Picture a highliner—call him Poncho—balancing out on the middle of a taut line. If Poncho weighs 200 pounds, the load at each end, where the line is attached, will be roughly 1,000 pounds. Why is this, and how does it apply to anchor building?

When an anchor is distributed between two primary placements, the sling, cord, or rope coming from each placement (down to a master point) forms a V. When the inside angle of the V approaches 180 degrees, the forces at both anchor points multiply dramatically. For instance, if the V angle reaches 120 degrees, a 100–pound load at the master point will be 100 pounds at *both* anchor points. When we keep the V angle under 60 degrees, we split the load roughly 50/50.

A good rule of thumb is: The widest acceptable angle between arms in any belay anchor (V angle) is 90 degrees. Also, avoid rigging a sling between two anchors in a triangular configuration (called the American Triangle). Even at 90 degrees, a triangle places 1.3 times the force at each anchor point. Keep this in mind when rigging any anchors.

American Triangle

Load per anchor with 100 lbs. of force

Bottom Angle	V Rigging	Triangle Rigging
30 degrees	52 lbs.	82 lbs.
60 degrees	58 lbs.	100 lbs.
90 degrees	71 lbs.	131 lbs.
120 degrees	100 lbs.	193 lbs.
150 degrees	193 lbs.	380 lbs.

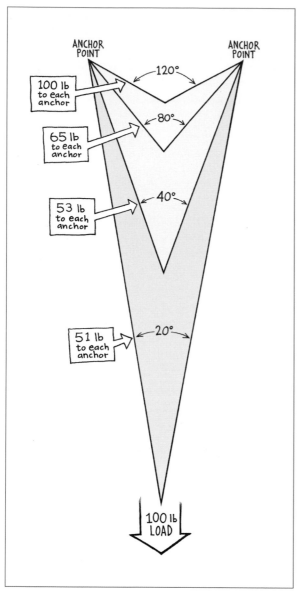

This diagram illustrates how a 100-pound load is distributed between two anchor points at various angles. Keep the angle between two anchors as narrow as possible, striving to keep it under 60 degrees. At 120 degrees the load is 100 percent at each anchor! Think of 0–60 degrees as ideal, 60–90 degrees a caution zone, and over 90 degrees a danger zone.

The American Triangle rigged at a rappel anchor. Avoid rigging with a triangle configuration—it adds unnecessary force to your anchor points. Stick to a V configuration for lower loads.

Redundancy

Next to the "S" (Solid), the "R" (Redundant) in NARDSS is paramount.

When NASA studied redundant systems on their spacecraft, they concluded that if one particular system had a failure rate of 1 in 1,000, then by backing it up with a redundant system, the failure rate (for both to fail) was more like 1 in 1 million (1,000 × 1,000).

When climbing anchors, the calculus is not so simple, but every credible source agrees that redundancy is part of a minimum standard for climbing anchors.

Redundancy Means . . .

When you evaluate your anchor, from the master point to the various components, there is no place in the anchor system where you're relying on a single element—be it one nut, cam, cord, sling, carabiner, etc. There is *always* a backup.

Exceptions to the redundancy rule might be a monolithic anchor (like a 2-foot-diameter ponderosa pine tree), but you can still achieve redundancy in the rigging. *Redundancy is important, but it does not guarantee a fail-safe anchor.* Always remember the basic ingredients: solid placements in solid rock. Six poor placements in chossy rock still result in a questionable anchor.

Develop the skill to quickly assess any anchor system based on NARDSS criteria: *No Extension, Angles, Redundant, Distributes Load, Solid, and Simple.* Evaluating redundancy alone does not get you there.

What Is a Kilonewton (kN)?

The "newton" was named for Sir Isaac Newton in recognition of his groundbreaking Second Law of Motion. A newton measures mass in motion.

One newton is the force required to accelerate 1 kilogram of mass at the rate of 1 meter per second squared, or roughly the force of gravity acting on a small mass (like an apple) on planet Earth. One kilonewton (kN) is equal to 1,000 newtons.

Think of it in terms of pounds and how much load a piece can sustain. One kN is equal to 101.97 kilograms of load; 1 kilogram is equal to 2.205 pounds, so 1 kN is equal to 224.8 pounds of force. A sling that's rated to 22 kN could theoretically hold 2,243 kilograms (4,946 lbs.). It's not that simple, however, since a kN rating signifies the maximum impact force the sling can withstand, which is a force of gravity rating (force = mass × acceleration). It's easier to grasp the fact that, yes, you could hang your car from that sling.

Principles of Load Distribution

Pre-Distributed: The Cordelette System

If we looked at every belay anchor rigged by every climber worldwide over the past ten years, well over 90 percent of those anchors would feature some version of a cordelette. In short, the cordelette remains the go-to anchoring system for most every mode of ascent, as it has since the late 1990s.

The cordelette is a load-sharing rigging system. Once the cordelette is tied in the anticipated direction of loading, all forces are, to varying degrees, *distributed* between the various arms of the system. The weakness is that the cordelette is unidirectional. If the load shifts slightly in any

Four-piece toprope anchor pre-distributed with a 6 mm Sterling PowerCord cordelette

Simple two-bolt toprope anchor rigged with a doubled 18-foot length of 7 mm nylon Sterling cordelette. The cordelette is doubled to start with, producing four strands at the master point loop. The climbing rope is clipped into three oval carabiners, opposed and reversed. The bolts have Fixe Ring Hangers. The welded rings are rated at 10,000 pounds breaking strength.

Demonstration of pre-distributed cordelette with three anchor placements, tied with a 7 mm nylon cord. A clove hitch has been tied to the top-left piece to keep the double fisherman's knot away from the end loops. This is a simple, effective rig as long as the direction of load is predetermined, which it usually is when toproping.

direction, the entire load goes onto one placement and one arm of the cordelette (albeit with minimal extension). Not so with self-adjusting systems, which moderately adjust with changes in the direction of loading. In most cases, you can readily

determine the direction of loading on your anchor system, so more-complex self-adjusting rigs are unnecessary.

A cordelette anchor is essentially a system of backups: If one piece fails, the load transfers almost

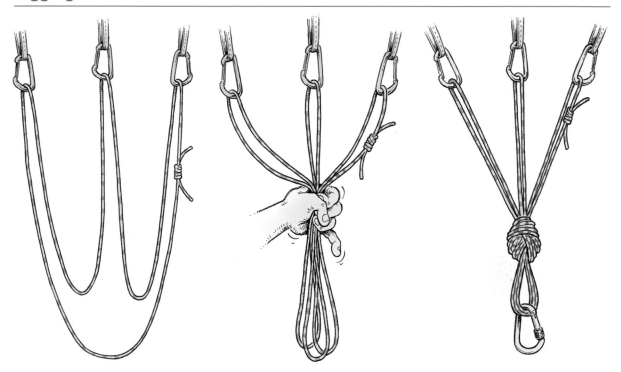

An 18- to 20-foot-long cordelette is usually long enough to cover three or four anchor points, as long as they are not spaced too far apart. If necessary, extend the anchor points with a couple of slings to get all the carabiners within working range. Clip a single strand of the cordelette into each carabiner, then pull down between the pieces and gather the loops (with three pieces you'll have three loops). Clip a carabiner into the loops before you tie the knot, which makes it easier to equalize all the strand lengths. Tie a figure eight knot to create your master point, which should be roughly 3–4 inches in diameter. If you don't have enough cord to tie a figure eight, an overhand knot eats less cord.

instantly to the remaining pieces with minimal extension, since the master point knot limits this.

The beauty of the pre-distributed cordelette system is its *simplicity, security,* versatility, and efficiency. You can quickly rig two, three, or four placements. Two side-by-side bolts are the most conventional fixed anchor. An easy and bomber rig is to start by doubling the cordelette, then clip the doubled strand into both bolts with locking carabiners. Pull down between the bolts, gather all strands, and tie an overhand knot. This gives you four strands of cord at the master point.

To rig three or four placements, clip the cordelette into all the placements, then pull down between the pieces and gather the loops together. Clip a carabiner through the loops and pull in the anticipated loading direction, then tie a figure eight knot with the carabiner attached, to help even out all the strands. Should you come up short and need more length, tie off the loops with an overhand knot, which eats less cord—a slightly weaker knot, yes, but this is not a factor, since you'll have at least three or four loops at your master point.

The drawback of the cordelette system (left) is that if the direction of the anticipated load changes, one piece in the anchor takes all the load (right). Think of the cordelette system as a system of back-ups: If the one piece fails, the load goes onto the next piece, with relatively minimal extension in the system. For toproping anchors and top belaying, since the load on the anchor system is relatively low, the cordelette system has the advantage of being easy to use and simple to rig.

Another popular method is to take a regular length (24-inch) sling and clip it into (and extending) the piece that's farthest from the master point. This gives you more length to work with on the cordelette.

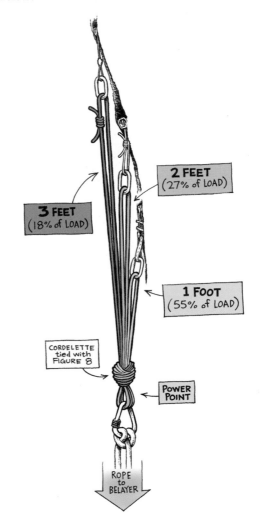

3 FEET
(18% of LOAD)

2 FEET
(27% of LOAD)

1 FOOT
(55% of LOAD)

CORDELETTE
tied with
FIGURE 8

POWER
POINT

ROPE
to
BELAYER

Three-piece anchor rigged with a 7 mm nylon cordelette. Since nylon cord stretches, the very short bottom arm will absorb most of the force in this setup. If you're using a high-tensile cord (Dyneema or Technora), this stretch is largely negated since the material is basically static. Guide Chris Baumann offers this tip when rigging a nylon cordelette with a long arm: "Lean in to the shortest arm before you tie the knot, creating a tiny bit of slack in the shorter arms." In this case, if you had "leaned" a little to the left before tying the knot, the short arm would have a bit of slack, allowing the top arms to load and stretch before the shorter arm is loaded.

Using a nylon cordelette to connect anchors in a vertical crack results in an anchor that does not truly equalize the forces; but if all the placements are bomber, it is a simple, easy rigging method that is essentially a series of backups to the piece that absorbs the brunt of the loading, with minimal extension should any one piece fail.

Here a 7 mm nylon cordelette has been untied and used in its full length. Many guides tie their cordelettes with a knot that can be easily untied so that, if necessary, they can use the full length. A good knot to tie a cordelette into its original loop is a flat overhand (make sure the tails are at least 8 inches long, or back it up with a second overhand tied right on top of the first one), or a figure eight bend, tied with the tails at least 3 inches long. The figure eight bend is stronger, but it's a bear cat to untie once weighted. When untied, the cordelette can distribute the load to three or more widely spaced pieces, where the standard, fixed-loop cordelette is too short. To rig three points, tie a figure eight loop on each end, clip these into the two outside pieces, then clip a strand to the middle piece. Pull down the cord between the pieces and you'll end up with a loop to the middle piece and a single strand to each outside piece. Tie a figure eight loop to fashion a two-loop master point.

Three-piece cordelette anchor. Note how the cams have been positioned so that the stems are not bent over the lip of the crack.

Self-Adjusting Systems: The Sliding X

The sliding X (aka magic X) is a system many climbers shun unless the few advantages it offers are needed. That said, the sliding X is a simple system, easy to rig, and has its place in certain circumstances—it takes some close analysis to understand what those are.

The sliding X was devised to distribute loading onto two anchor points by way of a sling, creating a mini-anchor system that self-adjusts as the load shifts direction. When using a sliding X between two pieces, count this as one placement in terms of redundancy, since it involves a single sling.

The sliding X is most commonly used to distribute the load between two suspect pieces, the thinking being that it's better that any weighting be shared by two sketchy pieces instead of one. But even if the load is perfectly divided, which it never is, the combined strength of both placements does not necessarily equal the amount of loading a fall might place on the system.

For example, on a two-point sliding X rig with two small stoppers, a #3 stopper (5 kN / 1,124 lbs.) on the left, and a #2 stopper (2 kN / 450 lbs.) on the right, it seems logical that the actual loading the rig could sustain before failing would be 7 kN (5 kN + 2 kN). But the overall strength is less, since with a force of more than twice the breaking strength of the right side (4 kN), the #2 stopper fails. If the remaining force is greater than 5 kN, the left-side stopper

Lanyard-Style Slings, aka "Rabbit Runners"

Many pro guides tie their cordelettes into a loop with a flat overhand, easier to untie and rig like a rabbit runner after tying figure eight or overhand loops on each end.

 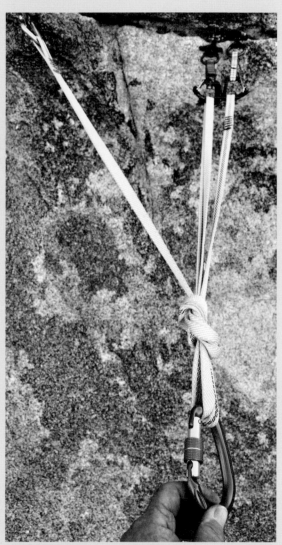

Mountain Tools Dyneema Webolette. The rabbit runner is a lanyard-style sling with bartacked loops on either end. Mountain Tools markets their Dyneema "Webolette," coining the mnemonic "V + W + 8 = on belay," describing how to rig a three-piece belay anchor: Clip the two outside pieces with the end loops, clip the middle piece, pull down all the strands, and tie a figure eight loop for the master point.

also fails. This is not so much a knock on the sliding X, as confirmation that no rigging can ever compensate for vulnerable primary placements.

When rigging the sliding X with a long sling (like a sewn, 48-inch double-length sling), minimize extension by tying overhand limiter knots just above the clip-in point. Should a piece fail, the system will adjust with limited extension.

Testing by the Black Diamond company showed that a simple sliding X, rigged on a Dyneema sling, was so strong that it exceeded the capacity of their testing machine (8,000 lbs.). But no testing was done to confirm any shock-loading if one anchor point failed.

DMM tested for shock-loading, rigging the system so one anchor point failed (on a two-point sliding X anchor rigged with a 24-inch Dyneema sling), then reran the test when both anchor points held. The surprising results revealed that even using

static Dyneema, "shock-loading" (where the anchor extended half the length of a 24-inch sling, or 1 foot) is something of a misnomer, as the impact force was lower than on the rig that *did not* fail, since when one side failed, some force was absorbed.

DMM also noted that with a sliding X rig, "the forces on the anchor points will only be uniform if both angles between the direction of the load, and each of the slings, are identical. Strictly speaking, it would be better described *as self-tensioning*."

Many tests, replicated by many labs conducted over the past twenty-five years, suggest that the maximum possible force anyone can generate in a climbing fall is 9 kN (2,023 lbs.). So as long as each piece in your two-point sliding X rig is 9 kN or stronger (e.g., a #.4 Camalot or larger), there's no worry about any inherent weakness in the rigging. As the saying goes, *climbing gear does not break*. In fact, micro wired nuts *do* break, but you get the idea. With all that said, the Golden Rule still holds:

Binding

The goal of self-adjusting rigging systems is for the master point to freely shift (along the bottom of the sling/cord) with changes in the direction of pull/loading, while keeping that loading distributed between anchor points. Under specific circumstances, the quad (discussed shortly) can approach true equalization. Less so the sliding X. A weighted master point carabiner is not a pulley; it's a curved aluminum bar. When weighted and pulled across slings/cord, the carabiner will always generate friction and *bind*—to lesser or greater degrees. With a quad fashioned from thin, slick-textured Dyneema and rigged with an anodized, pear-shaped carabiner, the binding is usually minimal. With the sliding X, the sling or cord is essentially hitched around the master point carabiner, so the binding is sometimes significant, especially with nylon sling. Under ideal conditions, the quad and the sliding X go a ways toward true equalization, but neither get all the way there.

When rigging a sliding X, make sure you clip into the loop you've created by twisting the sling.

Rigging a Sliding X

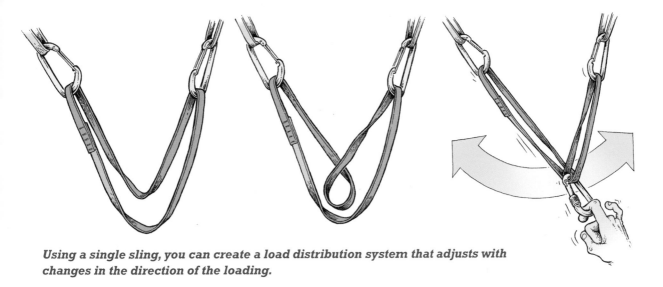

Using a single sling, you can create a load distribution system that adjusts with changes in the direction of the loading.

Even with sophisticated load-distributing systems, the key is to rig off solid primary placements in solid rock.

To set up a simple self-adjusting anchor system from two bolts, use two single-length slings formed into a sliding X. This creates a redundant rig with minimal extension. Guides often use this setup when they're rigging a toprope anchor off two bolts, with the plan to toprope several climbs off the same anchor, which will load the anchor in various directions: a route on the left, one directly below the anchor, and a climb to the right.

A simple two-bolt anchor rigged for toproping with a sliding X using two separate slings and three oval carabiners at the master point for a redundant, self-adjusting system. The drawback here is that if one bolt fails, the system will extend to the length of the slings. As a general rule, limit the maximum extension in your anchor system to half the length of a single (24-inch) sling, which is what you have here.

A sliding X (with limiter knots) is especially useful for load sharing between two questionable placements, with the sliding X clipped off to one arm of a cordelette or quad (discussed shortly); and to rig a belay off two bomber, side-by-side placements, usually bolts. You can rig this second setup faster than any other belay system. And remember, the sliding X, rigged on a Dyneema sling, is stronger than a testing machine. Lacking a shelf—as found on cordelette systems—the sliding X is not as convenient for multipitch anchors.

Two pieces rigged with a sliding X. An overhand knot is tied on the long arm of the sling to limit extension. If the top piece fails, the sling moves only a few inches. This rig is not redundant, since the master point is a single loop of twisted sling.

A tricky belay anchor on Mechanic's Route, Tahquitz Rock, California. The top two pieces are rigged with a sliding X, with an overhand knot tied to limit any extension to the top piece. The double-length red nylon sling is tied with a figure eight to create redundancy at the master point.

A two-cam anchor on Tahquitz Rock, rigged with a sliding X using two separate slings. While making three separate placements is a dogmatic goal for gear anchors, consider one of the most common anchors on face climbs: two bolts. Here we have perfect rock structure—immaculate, fine-grained granite—and two perfect Camalot placements. Should we trust this anchor? Absolutely. Each Camalot has a breaking strength of 12 kN (2,698 lbs.), each sling is rated at 22 kN (nearly 5,000 lbs.), and two opposed and reversed carabiners are stronger than that. Know your equipment, its breaking strengths, and how it all adds up. A good rule of thumb is for your anchor to be no weaker than 24 kN (5,395 lbs.).

Two-bolt toprope anchor rigged with a sliding X and extension-limiting knots. By using a double-length (48-inch) nylon sling tied with two overhand knots, the sling itself becomes redundant at the master point, since it has two loops of webbing.

Stacked Xs. Redundant by way of two extension-limiting knots tied in the purple sling.

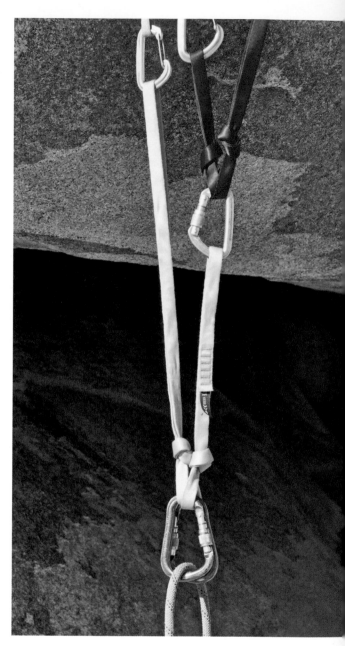

Stacked Xs. By tying two overhand knots on both the red and yellow double-length nylon slings, this three-piece anchor has redundancy and minimal extension throughout the system.

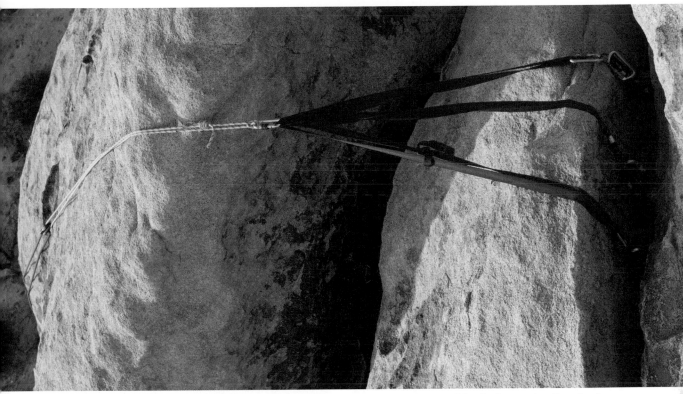

This toprope anchor is self-adjusting but lacks redundancy in three critical elements: the single, rewoven 1-inch tubular nylon sling; the single yellow cordelette; and the single locking carabiner that connects them. While plenty strong, the lack of redundancy is a liability for unmonitored toprope anchors like this one, all the more so if it's heavily used. The soft nylon cordelette will abrade over the edge, and no one will see it happening. Also, if one of the three pieces fails, you'd get major movement in the red sling and sudden loading on the two remaining pieces.

Summary on the Sliding X

You can sport climb every weekend for a year and never see a leader rigging an anchor with a sliding X—or even hear one mentioned. In the real trad world, however, the sliding X is commonly used. If you ever climb with someone who fully understands its strengths and weaknesses, and is experienced in setting it up, you might be surprised at the versatility, speed, and simplicity of this system when used by expert hands. It's also one of the most thoroughly tested rigging systems we have. The sliding

X is especially handy when, for whatever reason, you don't have a cordelette and want to rig a self-adjusting anchor.

The X binds on the rigging, sometimes a lot. It's not redundant on a single sling unless two extension-limiting knots are tied. Without limiter knots, extension is a concern. Its main benefit is often as a component in a larger anchor system. There are few anchoring scenarios when a self-adjusting anchor is called for that a quad is not the favored option. But when speed is critical and the placements are almighty strong, the sliding X is *simple, safe*, and solid. And when distributing the load between two questionable anchors, the sliding X remains a valuable tool, there for us if we need it.

The Quad: Evolution of the Cordelette

The quad was first devised—by exhaustive trial and error by Jim Ewing (safety engineer at Sterling Ropes)—during drop testing prior to writing the third edition of *Climbing Anchors*, back in 2006. Our aim was to see what possible rigging configuration got closest to true equalization between two anchor points, and the quad came closest by a wide margin. The quad has since gained popularity as a rigging system for multipitch anchors, and is the go-to rig for many guides. The quad is unsurpassed for rigging two-bolt toprope anchors. When using anodized carabiners on tightly wound tech cord,

A two-bolt toprope anchor rigged with a 7 mm cordelette and the quad system. The cordelette is clipped directly to the bolt hangers with locking carabiners, bypassing the cheap hardware store lap links (only rated at around 1,000 lbs.).

Detail of a quad rig master point rigged for toproping, with three oval carabiners opposed and reversed

To rig a quad on two bolts, start by doubling your cordelette, then grab the middle with your fist. Tie an overhand knot on each side of your fist, and you're ready to rig. Clip the double-strand loops into the bolts with locking carabiners, then clip only three of the four strands at the master point, leaving one loop outside your master point carabiners. This ensures that if one bolt fails, you are clipped into a pocket on the master point.

A quad rig using Sterling 6 mm PowerCord and three steel oval carabiners for a toprope setup

Detail of quad rig with two locking carabiners opposed and reversed

the quad approaches true equalization with minimal extension and great strength. *Simple and safe.*

Another rigging system that resulted from Jim Ewing's testing was the equalette, which also featured a dynamic master point (self-distributing) and the capacity to load-share over three, even four, placements, and it found some favor for a while. However, a quad (as we will see) offers the same merits as the equalette, plus is easier to rig, so the equalette has largely gone away.

Rigging a three-point anchor with the quad. First, double the cordelette (left). Clip a single loop into two points, and pull the cordelette down in the direction of anticipated loading. Even the loops, then tie an overhand knot (center). Tie a similar overhand knot and clip to the third piece (right). Ideally, the third piece should be your strongest placement. Now you have two redundant master points.

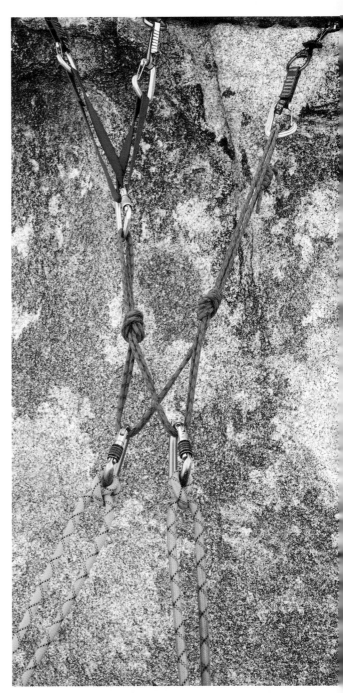

By splitting the four strands, two and two, the quad offers two separate, redundant master points, great for belaying from single- or multi-pitch anchors. To use the quad on a multipitch anchor, split the end loops two and two, giving you two separate but redundant master points. The quad can easily be rigged from two or three anchor points.

A three-piece anchor using a combination of quad and sliding X rigging

The Equalette

To tie an equalette rig, form a U shape with your cordelette and grab the bottom of the U, positioning the fisherman's knot about 18 inches away from the bottom of the U. Tie an overhand knot on both sides of your fist, about 10 inches apart. At the master point you'll have two separate loops. Clip into each loop with a separate locking carabiner.

The equalette gives you four strands, or "arms," running from the master point to various pieces in your anchor matrix. These four arms can be attached to the pieces with clove hitches or loop knots.

Although quite effective in load distribution, the equalette never gained popularity because of a big drawback—the lack of a singular, defined master point.

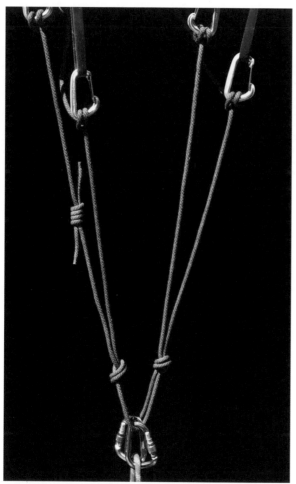

The equalette rigged with a 7 mm diameter nylon cordelette

Detail of an equalette master point using two locking carabiners opposed and reversed

The Joshua Tree System

Joshua Tree National Park features hundreds of crags and domes spread across a vast swath of high desert. It is one of the most popular winter climbing areas in the world, with well over 9,000 routes. The setups are often time-consuming and gear intensive because most anchors require placements set well back from the cliff edge, and bolted anchors are rare. Out of necessity we developed a system to rig toprope anchors that is *simple, safe,* and redundant, using a length of low-stretch rope. We call it the Joshua Tree System, and almost every local climber can vouchsafe its efficiency.

For the rigging rope, a minimum of 10 mm diameter is best for durability—always a concern on the rough quartz monzonite rock. For most situations, a 60-foot length is ideal. A proven rigging rope, popular with guides, is the 10 mm Sterling Safety Pro, with a stretch of about 4 percent for a toprope fall. The Safety Pro handles well, has superior abrasion resistance, and is useful for fixing lines, tethering, and rappelling. Avoid using a dynamic rope for toprope rigging. Its stretch will let it seesaw back and forth over edges (as it's weighted and unweighted in turn), which quickly blows out the sheath, as many have learned the hard way.

To rig the Joshua Tree System, visualize a V configuration, with two separate anchors at the top of the V and your master point at the bottom, or V point. The master point is tied with a BHK ("big honking knot"), essentially an overhand knot tied on a doubled bight, which gives you two-loop redundancy at the master point.

The rigging line is called an *extension,* or *extendo rope.* The two separate strands of rope that run from the master point to anchors A and B compose the "legs" of the extension rope.

Strive to keep the angle of the V under 60 degrees—and certainly at least less than 90 degrees. Once you have determined where the climb is and where you want your master point, visualize the V, and begin setting your anchors. If you climb at areas with many trees at the clifftop, you're in luck;

Tying the BHK ("Big Honking Knot")

Start by taking a doubled bight about 4 feet long.

Tie an overhand knot on all four strands.

Thread the two loops back through the loop you've created . . .

. . . or incorporate the loop into the master point carabiners.

the Joshua Tree System will greatly simplify your rigging. All you need is the rigging rope itself—no slings or cordelettes required.

Tie one end of your rigging rope around one tree with a simple bowline. Run the rope over the edge, and tie a BHK. I usually weight a bight of rope with a few carabiners and let it dangle about 4 feet over the edge, knowing that when I pull it back up and tie the BHK, the master point will be about 4 feet higher, which is the length of doubled bight taken up by tying the BHK. Next, tie around the second tree with a bowline with a bight, and you're done.

With gear anchors, the combinations are endless, but a solid minimum is at least three bombproof placements. Typical setups feature two gear placements on each end of the V. If you learn to tie double loop knots, you generally can eliminate slings and cordelettes. *Simplicity.*

For safety, as you approach the cliff edge, protect yourself by tethering with a double-length (48-inch) $^{11}/_{16}$-inch nylon sling. Pick the leg of the V you feel is stronger, or the one that's redundant (two pieces), and tether to that strand by tying a klemheist knot around it and attaching the other end of the sling to your harness belay loop with a locking

Tying the Klemheist Knot on a Sling

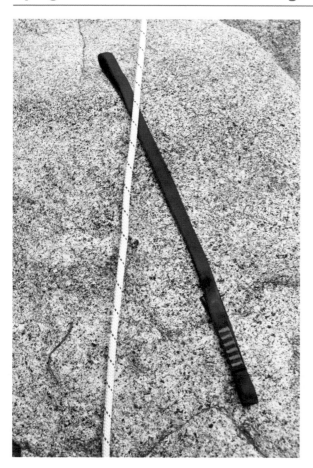 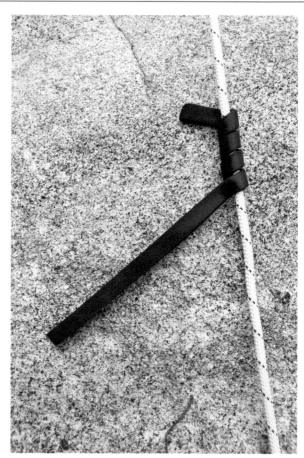

carabiner. A nylon sling is preferable to a Dyneema one, since a nylon friction hitch grips better and has a bit of stretch, whereas Dyneema is slicker, static (like a wire cable), and has minimal stretch. Now you can slide the klemheist knot up and down the rigging rope to safeguard yourself as you work near the edge.

Tie a BHK (see photos) so that your master point dangles just over the lip of the cliff edge, *positioned directly above your chosen climb.* Attach your climbing rope with carabiners (either two opposed and reversed locking or three ovals opposed and reversed) and run the rope back to anchor B,

attaching it with a clove hitch to a locking carabiner. This allows you to adjust the tension and fine-tune the load distribution. Use edge protectors at the lip to protect your rope from abrasion and cutting if sharp edges are present.

Learn to tie double loop knots, like the double-loop figure eight and the double-loop bowline, plus the in-line figure eight. These knots eliminate many slings and cordelettes from your system, bringing simplicity and efficiency to your rigging. When using the Joshua Tree System, start with two bomber pieces at the end of one leg of your extension rope. Next, equalize them with a double loop

Overview of the Joshua Tree System. The left leg of the extension rope is attached with a double-loop bowline to two cams; the right leg is clove-hitched to a single, bomber cam. A BHK is tied for the master point, with three opposed and reversed oval carabiners ready for the climbing rope.

Using a tether for safety while rigging a toprope. One end of a double-length nylon sling is attached to the rigging rope with a klemheist knot; the other end of the sling is attached to the harness belay loop with a locking carabiner.

Another version of the Joshua Tree System. Here, both legs have two cams rigged with sliding Xs—an elaborate rig, but one that fully adjusts to any shift, however minor, in the direction of pull. In most setups, double loop knots are preferable; it's more efficient, and since you know the direction the anchor will be loaded, drastic vector changes are not a concern.

Tether detail. If you're working at the cliff's edge, protect yourself. This climber has rigged his BHK master point, all the while protected with a personal tether—a double-length nylon sling. He's secured one end to his harness with a locking carabiner; the other end is attached to the rigging rope via a klemheist knot.

The Joshua Tree System rigged with two double-loop figure eights

Close-up of the master point on the Joshua Tree System using a BHK and three steel oval carabiners with the gates opposed and reversed

knot. As you move toward the edge, and perhaps find more anchor placements, use the in-line eight to distribute these pieces to the system. The double loop knots and in-line eight are principal tools for every master rigger.

Unmonitored Anchor Systems

An *unmonitored* anchor system means that once rigged, you'll be at the base and unable to watch what is happening at the anchor—like the extension rope abrading over an edge. Take special care to prevent this by padding the edge (a pack or rope bag will work) or, better yet, using commercial edge protectors.

Toprope all day long with your extension rope rubbing on a sharp edge, and you'll end up with a core-shot rope like this one.

A commercial edge protector, like this one from Petzl, is a wise investment. Attach it to your rigging rope with a friction hitch.

Double-Loop Figure Eight

This knot is useful for rigging off two anchor points. Note that if the two loops are used together to form a master point, they are not redundant due to the rewoven configuration.

Tying the Double-Loop Figure Eight

1. Take a bight of rope and cross it back over itself, forming a loop.

2. Take two strands of the bight, wrap them around the standing part, then poke them through the loop.

3. To finish, take the loop at the very end of the bight and fold it down and around the entire knot you've just formed.

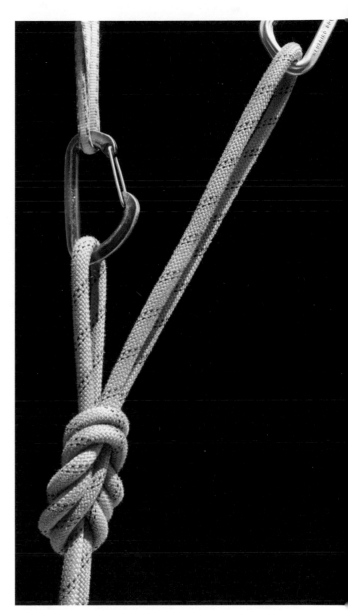

The double-loop figure eight is a great knot to equalize two gear placements. You can manipulate the knot by loosening one strand and feeding it through the body of the knot, shortening one loop and making the other loop larger.

Double-Loop Bowline (aka Bowline on a Bight)

This is another great knot for rigging off two anchor points. Also handy for clipping into a two-bolt anchor. Back it up with half a double fisherman's knot if the tail end is near the body of the knot, as it can shift a bit when weighted.

A note of caution when using the double-loop bowline: Do not clip into one of the loops and load the loop independently—and always load the knot in the correct orientation, via one of the two non-loop strands coming out from the body of the knot.

Tying the Double-Loop Bowline

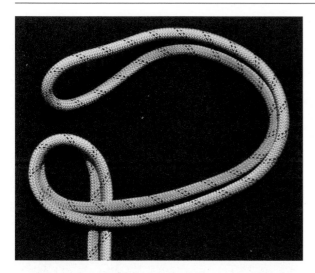

1. Take a bight of rope and cross it over the standing part.

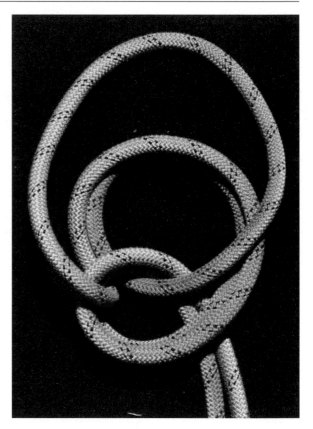

3. Configure the end of the bight in a loop above the rest of the knot.

2. Thread the bight through the loop you've just formed.

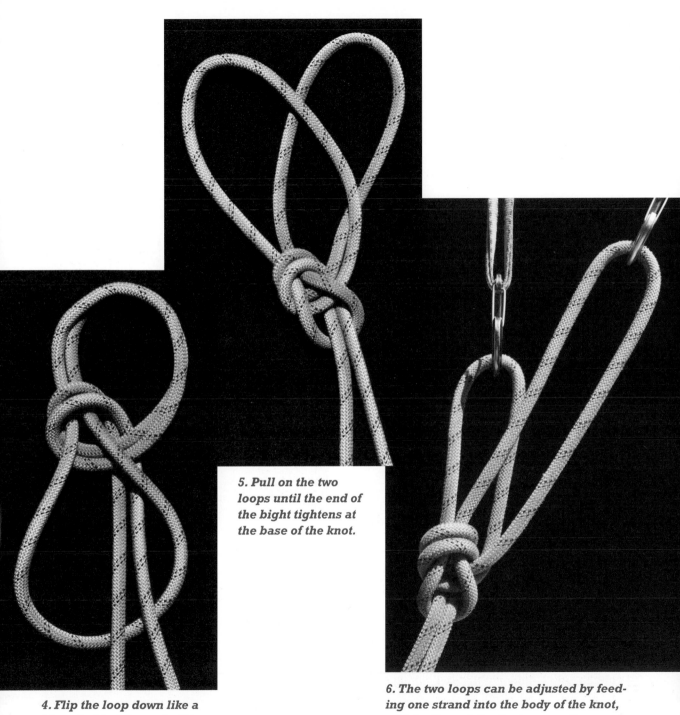

5. Pull on the two loops until the end of the bight tightens at the base of the knot.

4. Flip the loop down like a hinge behind the rest of the knot.

6. The two loops can be adjusted by feeding one strand into the body of the knot, which alternately shortens one loop and lengthens the other.

In-Line Figure Eight

The In-line Figure Eight resembles a clove hitch and is commonly used with an extension rope attached to a series of anchors in a line. Practice is required to master this knot, but some find it easier to use than a clove hitch.

Tying the In-line Figure Eight (aka Directional Figure Eight)

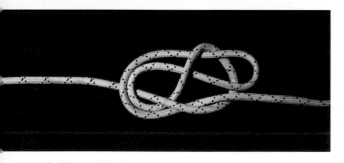

1. Cross the strands to form a simple loop.

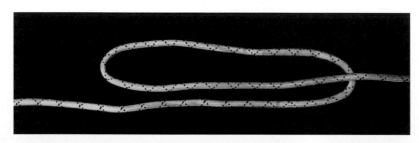

2. Cross a bight under the single strand.

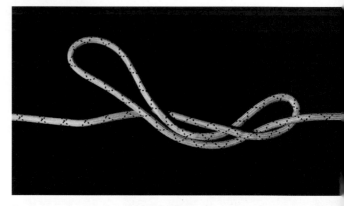

3. Cross the bight over the strand.

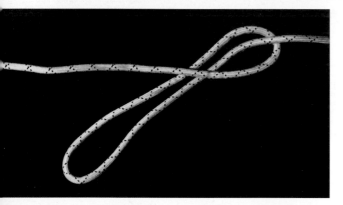

4. Thread the bight back through the loop you've just formed.

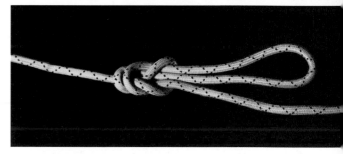

5. Finished in-line figure eight

Making the Transition from Rigging to Rappelling

After rigging the toprope, if you choose to rappel you'll need to transition from your extension rope to your rappel rope. For a personal tether, a solid option is a 48-inch length of ¹¹⁄₁₆-inch nylon sling. Tie a klemheist knot around one leg of the extension rope (pick the stronger leg) on one end of the sling, then attach the other end to your belay loop with a locking carabiner. Slide the klemheist knot down until you approach the edge. Just shy of the edge, pull up your doubled rappel rope, rig your rappel device, and back it up with an autoblock. Slide the klemheist knot down until it's just on top of the BHK. Make the transition over the edge, using the extension rope for balance, until you've weighted your rappel system. Double-check everything before removing your personal tether—then rap away.

Instructor Erin Guinn making a safe transition from rigging to rappelling. She's used a 48-inch nylon sling for her tether, attached to the rigging rope with a klemheist knot. She's backed up her rappel device with an autoblock knot clipped to her harness leg loop with a locking carabiner.

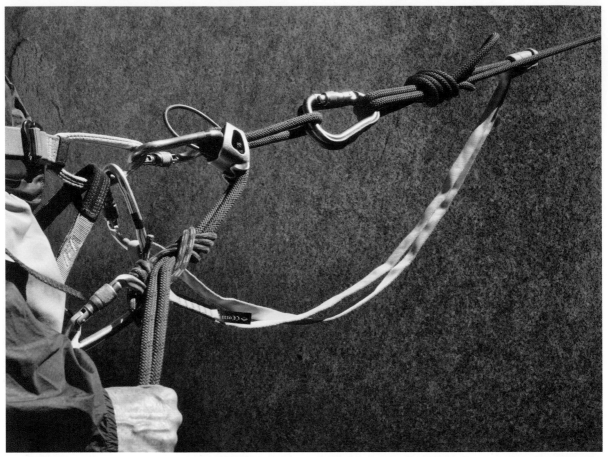

Transition rig detail. If you know you'll be rappelling, don't make your BHK loop too long, since you'll need to get around it without your tether coming tight. Before you unclip and remove your tether, weight your rappel system and double-check everything. Make sure your autoblock is engaged and not up against your rappel device, which would keep it from grabbing the rope.

As with any ritual, anchor system assessment initially feels long and wearisome when all you really want to do is climb. Trust that the process quickly becomes as second nature as putting on your clothes. As your experience grows, you'll relax into a fluid state of alert watchfulness, where obvious hazards and secure options are quickly seen, acknowledged, and shared with your partners as needed.

An experienced climber keeps their guard up—not just at the belay, but always. No one is omniscient. No one sees everything. But when a team of three, for example, keeps six eyes on the lookout *and* keeps communicating, you keep the game *simple and safe* and greatly reduce the chance of mishaps—on the lead, at the belay, and at every rousing turn on the High Lonesome.

Adam Radford prepares a rappel site, Joshua Tree National Park, California.

Anchor System Assessment in Review

Start with the macro and work toward the micro. How solid is the formation overall? On multipitch routes, some choss (bad rock) is expected. But if the formation is a "junker," bottom to top, no matter how well set the individual placements, catastrophic failure is possible. The ideal is the "crack in the planet"—a crack in diamond-hard rock that bisects the plane of the face at a right angle. Loose blocks, flakes, and fractured rock are all suspect. Be especially critical in assessing rock structure—it's the foundation for building your anchor.

Next, evaluate the overall anchor rigging. Is it redundant? Is the load well distributed, with no extension? To pass muster, the anchor system must satisfy the NARDSS principle.

Finally, scrutinize the microstructure of the rock. Are there loose flakes, hollow spots, or any rotten or disintegrating rock within the crack? Then look closely at each individual placement. If it's a nut, does it satisfy the SOS principle? If it's a camming device, is it in the manufacturer's recommended range of retraction? Does it satisfy the SPORT acronym requisites?

CHAPTER 11

Belaying

In chapter 3 we introduced the dizzying array of belay devices currently available. Now we examine how to use them.

There are few skills we need—or can ever hope—to master. Belaying is one of those skills. Belaying is a relatively simple technique, but one we must mindfully execute every second of every belay. *We call it the "roped safety system" owing to the many factors involved. Few of those factors are as critical to our safety as belaying.* Most people can learn the basics in 15 minutes and have the process down after a few outings. This chapter will first review and clarify the fundamentals, then push belaying into the wider context of outdoor climbing, with all its shades and flavors.

The Hip Belay

All trad climbers should know how to hip belay, the easiest method of clearly understanding (a) how to use your brake hand to arrest a fall and to lower a climber, and (b) that *your brake hand can never leave the rope*—the cardinal rule in all belaying, no matter the method or device you use.

What's more, there are rare instances where some experienced climbers might opt for hip belay, like when climbing big formations, where the angle often kicks back toward the top, the rock becomes broken and ledgy, and the rope drag becomes onerous from the friction of the rope dragging over acres of low-angled terrain. The same goes for easier alpine rock (e.g., exposed Class 3 and Class 4), where the rope runs over considerable terrain, and when the formation itself is used as a giant friction brake. Whenever the terrain is very easy (for you) and you're climbing at speed, a hip belay remains an option.

There's no question that a modern belay device is far more secure and user-friendly than a hip belay, but it's worth remembering that every Yosemite big wall was first climbed (and repeated countless times) using hip belays, *with no record of belay failures.* Yet the hip belay did have its drawbacks. Back in the era of hip belays—before the advent of belay devices—at the end of a climbing day our backs were singed with a black stripe along the waistline from pulling hundreds of feet of rope across our backs, and from lowering someone with the friction of the rope pulled taut around our back. In the modern era, where ropes are thinner and falls more numerous as free climbers push their limits, the hip belay is vastly obsolete; but it's still an option *in certain situations.*

The Big Three

Belaying involves three major elements: managing the slack in the rope, maintaining a brake hand on the brake strand of the rope, and stopping the fall. Belaying is a big responsibility; if you take on the task, you must remain competent and alert, and know the proper safety checks and belay signals.

John Mallory belays Tom Callahan on Separate Reality (5.12a), Yosemite, 1983.

Beef up the security of any hip belay by clipping the non-brake strand (the strand going *to* the climber) into a carabiner at the front of the belayer's harness, which keeps the rope at the belayer's waistline in the event of a fall. If tied in and anchored with the rope, the tie-in strand to the anchor should remain on the non–brake-hand side of the belayer's waist.

Belaying with a Munter Hitch

Like the hip belay, knowing how to belay with a Munter hitch is an important tool in every climber's repertoire, useful for impromptu situations—like

Rappelling on a doubled rope with a Munter hitch

The Munter hitch

when you're up on the cliff and fumble and drop your device (it happens). The only equipment required for a Munter belay is a single, locking carabiner, preferably a large pear-shaped model. The Munter hitch can be used for belaying a leader or a follower. A great attribute of the Munter hitch is its use for direct belays (belaying the follower directly off the anchor). Maximum friction is achieved when the brake strand is held parallel to the load strand. In a pinch, the Munter hitch can be used for rappelling, always with a locking carabiner. Make certain the gate is opposite the brake-strand side of the hitch so that the action of the rope doesn't unlock the gate.

Let's quickly review the three basic belay devices: manual, autoblock, and assisted.

The hip belay is the most elemental form of belay. To take in rope, start with the brake hand at your hip and the guide, or "feel," hand extended.

To take up slack, the brake hand goes out as the guide hand comes in.

The guide hand reaches above the brake hand and pinches the rope . . .

. . . so that the brake hand can slide back.

In the event of a fall, the brake hand brings the rope in front of the waist for maximum friction.

Manual Braking Devices

The most commonly used belay/rappel device is a manual braking device (MBD), the tube or slot devices we covered in chapter 3, "Belay Devices." There are many techniques acceptable to safely belay with an MBD, and they all effectively (a) manage the slack, (b) maintain a brake hand on

Petzl Reverso in lowering/brake position

the brake-strand side of the rope, and (c) generate enough friction to stop a fall and safely lower a climber.

Multipurpose Devices: Autoblocking Devices

Hybrid tube devices (e.g., the Black Diamond ATC Guide and the Petzl Reverso) have both a manual braking mode and an autoblocking mode, making them versatile choices for both belaying and rappelling in the regular manual mode or belaying directly off the anchor in the autoblocking mode. For multipitch climbing, they allow you to belay

Thin Line

Belay devices have evolved along with the ropes, which keep getting thinner. When buying a belay device, check the manufacturer's specifications and make sure it's appropriate for the diameter of your climbing rope.

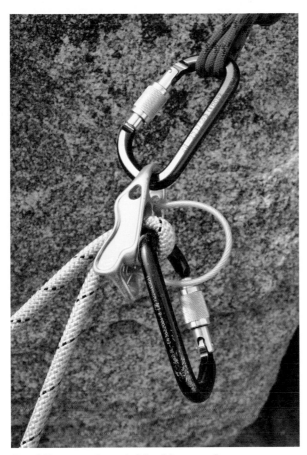

Petzl Reverso in autoblocking mode

Black Diamond ATC Guide in autoblocking mode

two followers at the same time. Their main disadvantage is the difficulty in lowering a climber when the rope is under tension.

Assisted Braking Devices

Assisted braking devices (ABDs), with self-locking cams, are de rigueur for sport climbing. The most popular model is the Petzl Grigri. These devices normally lock when suddenly weighted, as during a fall, but might not lock if there is a slow and accelerating pull, when the handle is pressed against the rock or a carabiner, when the belayer grabs the rope on the non-brake-hand side, or when the belayer

grabs the device incorrectly and holds the cam down, preventing it from locking.

Even though ABDs are self-locking, a brake hand should always be maintained on the brake side of the rope.

ABDs are far from foolproof, and many accidents have occurred when someone is being lowered, when the handle is pulled all the way open and the belayer loses control of the brake hand. The Petzl Grigri Plus addresses this problem with a built-in anti-panic function that, when lowering a climber, essentially locks the device when the handle is opened too quickly. Then, by pulling back even further, it allows you to override the anti-panic locking function.

Standard Climbing Signals

We stay alive through proper use of the universal climbing signals along with methodical safety checks. Both are integral to secure climbing. Ambiguous signals—usually a lack of communication between the climber and belayer—have injured, even killed, many climbers.

One infamous tragedy occurred in a toprope setup at a popular ice climbing area. The leader reached the anchor at top of the climb (top of the cliff) and yelled down, "I'm OK!" The belayer thought he heard "Off belay." The belayer unclipped the rope from the belay device and took the climber off belay, thinking he was going to walk off the top. The climber leaned back to be lowered and fell to his death.

This bears repeating: *Before, during, and after every climb, make certain to know, announce, and mutually confirm the exact status of the belay. Those who don't will pay dearly for their negligence.*

On a yo-yo (up-and-down) toprope climb, be especially vigilant at the transition from the climb up to the lower down. This is where most accidents occur due to bungled climbing signals. *There can be no ambiguity.*

Before lowering off an anchor, hold on to the strand of rope that goes back down to the belayer until you reconfirm that he or she heard your command and is in the brake position, ready to hold your weight, and start lowering. You normally can see the belayer, so after hearing the verbal command, look down and visually confirm that the belayer has their hand in the brake position and is alert and ready to safely lower you. A belayer at the ready assumes a distinctive posture as immediately recognizable as a basketball player ready to shoot a free throw. The verbal command verifies this, to remove all doubt.

When other teams are climbing nearby, include your partner's name in the signal (e.g., "Off belay, Maybelline") to prevent confusion. Although once, at a crowded multipitch crag, I (BG) saw a leader in the middle of a pitch get taken off belay when someone else yelled, "Off belay, Josh"—and there was more than one Josh on the cliffside. We can never be too vigilant, so heads up.

Standardized Climbing Signals

On belay? Climber to belayer, "Am I on belay?"

Belay on: Belayer to climber, "The belay is on."

Climbing: Climber to belayer, "I'm beginning the climb."

Climb on: Belayer to climber, "Go ahead and start climbing; I have you on belay."

Up rope: Climber to belayer, "There is too much slack in my rope. Take up some of the slack." (Too much slack in the belay rope will mean a longer fall. Remember that rope stretch also contributes to the total distance of a fall, especially when there is a lot of rope out in a toprope scenario.)

Slack: Climber to belayer, "Give me some slack; the rope is too tight."

Tension (or Take): Climber to belayer, "Take all the slack out of the rope and pull it tight; I am going to hang all my body weight on the rope." (This could be a situation where the climber simply wants to rest by hanging in the harness while weighting the rope, or a toprope situation where the climber is getting ready to be lowered back down a climb.)

Tension on (or I've got you): Belayer to climber, "I've taken the rope tight, and my brake hand is now locked off in the brake position, ready to hold all your weight."

Lower me: Climber to belayer, "I'm in the lowering position (feet wide, good stance, sitting in the harness, weighting the rope, and leaning back), and I'm ready to be lowered."

Lowering: Belayer to climber, "I'm proceeding to lower you."

Off belay: Climber to belayer, "I'm safe. You can unclip the rope from your belay device and take me off belay." (*Never take someone off belay unless you hear this signal.* The universal contract between belayer and climber is that the belayer must never take the climber off belay unless the climber gives the belayer the, "off belay" command.)

Belay off: Belayer to climber, "I've unclipped the rope from my belay device and have taken you off belay."

That's me! Climber to belayer, "You've taken up all the slack in the rope, and the rope is now tight to my harness."

Watch me! Climber to belayer, "Heads up! Be attentive with the belay—there is a good chance I'm going to fall right here!"

Falling! Climber to belayer, "I'm actually falling; go to your brake position and lock off the rope to catch my fall!" (A fall can happen so fast that the climber might not be able to shout this signal during a short fall, but it helps the belayer react more quickly, especially in situations where the belayer can't see the climber.)

ROCK! Climber to belayer and others below, "I've dislodged a rock and it's now free-falling below me—watch out below!" (The equivalent signal to "Fore!" in golf, "ROCK!" should also be yelled when the climber drops a piece of equipment, like a carabiner.)

Petzl Grigri in lowering mode

As with any belay device, the cardinal rule is: *The brake hand can never leave the rope!* If for some reason you need to take your brake hand off the rope, tie a backup knot (e.g., overhand loop) on the brake-strand side of the rope.

For direct belays, the Grigri allows an easy lower when the rope is under tension. When lowering with a direct belay using a Grigri, the brake strand should be redirected. Many experts use gloves when belaying with ABDs, which allow you to put more weight on your brake hand—all the better for smooth lowers.

Calista Holden with a good stance, braced against the cliff to resist an upward pull
PHOTO BY CHRIS BAUMANN

Belaying on a Toprope

Whenever toproping, attach (with a locking carabiner) the rope and belay device directly to the belay loop on your harness. The rope then runs directly from you, up through the top anchor, and back down to the climber. Your body is part of the anchor; the added friction at the toprope anchor makes it relatively easy to catch a fall, hold a climber hanging on the rope, and lower a climber back down. The belay device remains directly in front of you, where it's to operate. When the climber far outweighs the belayer, or when the belayer is balanced on uneven terrain, the belayer needs a ground anchor—just like in the gym (more on this below).

A direct belay (directly off the anchor) is not recommended for toprope belaying from the base.

1. The BUS (brake under slide) method of belaying on a toprope. Start by clipping the rope into the slot in the belay device closest to the spine side of the carabiner. If you're right-handed, orient the carabiner so that the gate is facing left, and vice versa if you're left-handed. Orient the rope so that the brake side is down.

2. To take up rope, pull the rope up with your brake hand (palm down) as you simultaneously pull the rope down with the other hand . . .

3. . . . then brake the rope down under your belay device.

4. Take your non-brake hand and grasp the rope below your brake hand . . .

5. . . . then slide your brake hand back up under the belay device, and return the non-brake hand to its starting position above the belay device. In a fall, remember your brake position is down (thumb up), keeping your hand in an ergonomically strong position.

Two-Rope Toprope Setups

When rigging long topropes of more than half a single rope length, tie two ropes together using a double fisherman's knot or figure eight bend. With such a huge amount of rope out between the climber and the belayer, rope stretch is a major concern, especially when using dynamic ropes. *Even a short toprope fall will stretch a dynamic rope about 10 percent, so tighten up the rope when belaying someone just off the ground, or just off a ledge.*

There are two methods used to deal with the knot joining the two ropes, and the annoying fact that on mega toprope sessions, you have to pass that knot through your belay device. The simple solution (also the best if there's no stance for the climber to stop at) avoids the knot pass altogether. With the knot joining the two ropes at the anchor, tie a figure eight loop and attach it to the climber's belay loop with two locking carabiners (gates opposed and reversed). When the climber reaches the anchor, the knot will be just above the belayer's device, so no knot pass is required.

A second solution is to use two belay devices. The climber ties into the end of the rope, as usual. The belayer anticipates the knot pass and has a second belay device, at the ready, clipped to his belay loop. When the knot reaches the belayer, the belayer alerts the climber to find a good stance then ties a backup knot (overhand loop) on the brake-hand side of the belay device. The belayer steps forward to create a bit of slack then clips the rope into the second belay device on the climber's side of the knot, leaving the first belay device clipped in. When the climber reaches the anchor, the belayer lowers him until the knot is almost to the belay device, and the process is reversed: The climber takes a stance, the belayer unclips the second belay device (first double-checking that the first belay device is still clipped in and has the backup knot), then unties the backup knot and lowers the climber as normal.

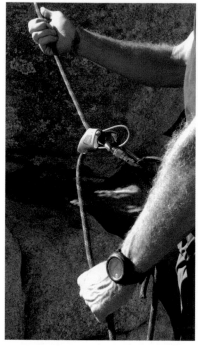

After you've mastered the BUS method, a more advanced technique is to brake under and switch the brake hand, alternating back and forth with either hand. As a professional guide or outing leader, in a day's belaying you can pull more than a thousand feet of rope, which can exhaust your shoulders, especially when there's rope drag. Most instructors prefer this method, as you can alternate arms/ shoulders rather than torching one arm or shoulder.

The Ground Anchor

Belaying accidents are common, and in many cases they have the same cause: no ground anchor.

When should you use a ground anchor? It's a wise choice when belaying a leader on a trad climb. Clip into your ground anchor with your rope, and allow about 3 feet of slack. If there's a high enough impact force to pull you tight against the anchor, this movement will serve as a counterweight to lessen the impact force on the protection the leader has fallen on. The ground anchor will keep you from losing control of the belay, or slamming into the cliff.

Whenever toproping, if both the climber and the belayer are roughly the same body weight and the terrain at the base of the cliff is flat, a ground anchor is unnecessary. But if the climber far outweighs the belayer, a ground anchor is required. If the climb is vertical or overhanging, more force will be exerted by the falling climber than a fall on a low-angle climb. Again, it is crucial to rig a ground anchor whenever the belayer is standing on uneven terrain, particularly if the belay stance is perched on top of boulders or is some distance from the base of the cliff.

Start with the belayer tying into the end of the rope. Not only does this "close" the rope system, but it allows the belayer to use the climbing rope to connect to a ground anchor with a clove hitch, which can be easily adjusted to suit the stance.

Belayer ground-anchored in uneven terrain. Remember your ABCs: The anchor, belayer, and climber's direction of pull should all come into a straight line. Her tie-in strand is on her brake-hand side, so she won't spin awkwardly once the system is loaded.

Natural anchors are obvious choices for ground anchors, such as a sling or cordelette around a tree or a large block. A single bomber cam or nut will also do, as long as it's set in the anticipated direction of pull.

Whenever belaying in a toprope scenario, anticipate the direction of pull, which is always in a line directly to the toprope anchor master point. Anchor and brace yourself accordingly. If you're belaying the leader, and she falls, you'll be pulled in a straight line between the ground anchor and the leader's first piece of protection. Ideally, the ground anchor will be low and directly behind or beneath you, or just slightly to the side. Remember your ABCs: anchor, belayer, climber. There should be a straight line between the anchor, the belayer, and the direction of pull created by the climber. If not, the impact force transmitted down the rope will yank you into a direct line, and that's when belayers are sometimes wrenched off their feet and lose control of their stance. When that happens, and it does, the belayer sometimes gets hurt and the falling leader does not.

In the single-pitch environment, it's critical to always close your rope system, either by tying into the end of the rope or by tying a stopper knot like this.

Belaying from the Top

Whether on a single-pitch or multipitch climb, when belaying the second (the follower), the belayer can choose from a variety of belay methods, depending on the situation.

Belaying Off the Harness: The Indirect Belay

For the indirect belay, the belayer clips the rope and belay device into a locking carabiner attached to the belay loop on her harness. The belayer is "in

Here the belay device is clipped into both the belayer's belay loop and the rope tie-in loop. If the climber below falls, his weight will go mostly onto the anchor, not the belayer. Avoid this method when belaying a leader, as the belay becomes less dynamic, increasing impact force on the leader's protection.

Belaying with an indirect belay. The belayer is in a good seated stance, with his rope clipped to the anchor's master point. The ATC XP belay device is attached to his belay loop. If the climber below falls, the belayer must absorb all the loading and bear the full weight of the falling climber onto his belay device/harness. The braking position will be awkward; and since the belayer is slightly out of line from the direction of pull to the anchors, he will get pulled into that line. The easy fix here is for the belayer to position himself in line (anchor-belayer-climber, or ABC) with the anticipated loading. Here, and in situations like this, many guides will use a direct belay and a Grigri.

1. The old-school "pinch and slide technique" is commonly used as an indirect belaying technique when belaying from the top of a cliff. Start with the brake hand (the right hand in these photos) next to the belay device, with the left hand extended out.

2. Pull the rope in with the left hand, and simultaneously pull rope out with the brake hand.

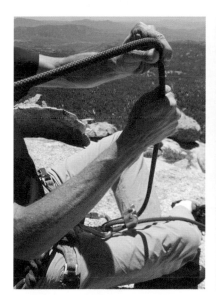

3. Move the brake hand back behind the braking plane (more than 90 degrees from the angle of the rope going to the climber), and pinch the rope above the brake hand with the left hand . . .

4. . . . then slide the brake hand down toward the belay device.

5. Move the left hand back to the extended position, and repeat the process. The cardinal rule, here and elsewhere: Always keep your brake hand on the rope.

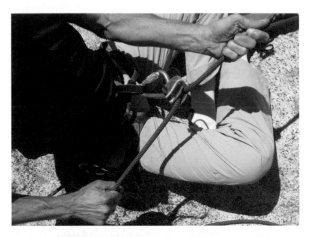

1. *Another belay method for an indirect belay from the top of the cliff is a variation of the BUS (brake under slide) method. Instead of braking down, the brake position is up and back. (The belayer's right hand is the brake hand in these photos.) Starting with the brake hand palm down, the brake hand pulls the rope out as the left hand pulls rope in.*

2. *Next, the brake hand pulls the rope back into a brake position.*

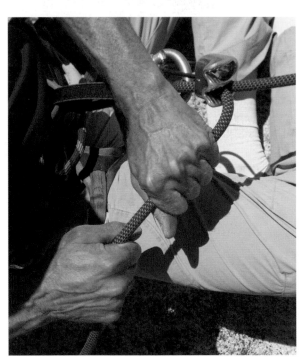

3. *The left hand grasps the rope, palm down on the brake strand, just below the belay device.*

4. *The brake hand slides back toward the device without releasing its grip on the rope. The left hand extends again and grabs the non-brake side of the rope to repeat the process.*

the system." If the climber falls, the belayer's body will help absorb the force of the fall. We call it *indirect*, since the force generated in a fall does not go directly onto the belay anchor.

For example, if the belayer is sitting with her legs braced against a ledge and the climber falls, the belayer can absorb the loading without transferring any load to the anchor, owing to the stability of the stance (leg's braced), the friction of the rope running over the rock, and the belay device itself.

When using the indirect belay, the anchor and stance are vital because if the belayer gets pulled off-balance or yanked sideways, she can possibly lose control of the belay. The belayer should always anticipate the direction of pull (loading) if a fall occurs, and position herself accordingly, taut to the anchor. Again, the belayer should remain in a direct line between the anchor and the climber—ABC (anchor-belayer-climber).

While the indirect belay is commonly used by most recreational climbers, it is rarely used by professional guides—for several reasons. First, the belayer is trapped "in the system." If a climber falls, the climber's weight hangs directly off the belay loop of the belayer, making it difficult for her to even move. Once in this position, it is awkward for the belayer to hold the fallen climber, particularly on a poor stance, as many are. Lowering the climber from the top of the cliff using an indirect belay can be difficult, even dangerous, if the cliff is steep and the climber far outweighs the belayer.

The indirect belay is also the worst method if the belayer needs to assist (like rigging a raising system) the climber below, since the belayer is trapped in the system and must perform a "belay escape" in order to get free and convert the system to a raise.

This sounds complicated—because it is. Even pros and guides might spend half a day at a seminar to even understand all these steps, and the rest of the day to perfect the "raise." The steps were in part detailed to illustrate a point: *If the anchor is reliable, an indirect belay is a poor choice for belaying a second.*

Then why even use an indirect belay? For those rare circumstances when the anchor is questionable and can't be trusted. You don't want to direct belay from a dicey anchor, but you can use a marginal anchor to bolster your stance by clove hitching your rope to the anchor's master point with a tight connection, then bracing yourself with your legs in the direction of pull so that your stance and the falling climber weighting the harness mutually absorb the force of the fall, *not the anchor.*

Escaping the Belay

If you are belaying with the belay device clipped to your harness (indirect belay) and need to escape from the system, follow these steps:

1. Tie off the belay device with a mule knot and overhand backup.

2. Tie a friction hitch (klemheist or prusik) on the load strand going to the climber.

3. Attach a locking carabiner to the friction hitch and tie a Munter/mule with the climbing rope (off the back side of the knot connecting you to the anchor).

4. Back up the system by tying the rope directly to the anchor (on the brake-hand side of your belay device).

5. Release your mule knot at your belay device, and transfer the load to the Munter/mule/friction hitch system.

You have now escaped the belay. What you do next depends on the situation. To set up a 3-to-1 raising system to assist your climber, attach a prusik knot at the anchor for a ratchet, then use the friction hitch on the load strand for a redirect to construct your 3-to-1.

1. When tying a mule knot, be aware that when the rope is under tension (holding a climber's weight), you'll need to keep a firm grip on the brake strand.

2. Keeping the load and brake strands parallel, form a loop on the brake strand by crossing it behind while still maintaining your grip with your brake hand.

3. With your non-brake hand, take a bight of rope and pass it through the loop you've created with the load strand in between the loop and the bight. Snug the mule knot up tight against the Munter hitch.

4. Pull some slack, and finish with an overhand loop backup.

1. Pass a bight of rope (from the brake-hand side) through the belay carabiner.

2. Tie a mule knot above the device on the load strand of the rope going to the climber.

3. Finish by tying an overhand backup on the load strand.

1. Pass a bight of rope through the carabiner and form a loop. If the device is under tension, pinching the rope against the device with the opposite hand will help lock it off.

2. Pass a bight of rope through the loop you've created, with the spine between the loop and the bight.

3. Finish with an overhand loop backup on the load strand in front of the device.

Prusik Knot

The prusik is technically a hitch, but it is referred to as a knot by most people. The prusik is used for rope ascending and as a component in rescue systems. Like all friction hitches—which let you temporarily attach a cord to a rope—the prusik knot grips the rope when weighted, and once unweighted, you can hand-slide it up or down. It can be loaded in either direction.

To tie a prusik, first make a "prusik cord" out of a 4-foot length of 5 mm or 6 mm diameter nylon cord tied into a loop with a double fisherman's knot, which gives you about a 16-inch loop. Buy the softest nylon climbing cord you can find, because a softer cord grips best. To tie the prusik, girth-hitch the rope with your cord, then pass the loop of cord back through the original girth-hitch two or three more times. Dress the knot to make sure all the strands are even and not twisted—a sloppy friction hitch will not grip as well. Test the knot before using it.

Thinner cord grips better, but below 5 mm in diameter, the cord will be too weak for many rescue applications. To slide the prusik after it has been weighted, loosen the "tongue," which is the one strand opposite all the wraps.

A four-wrap prusik

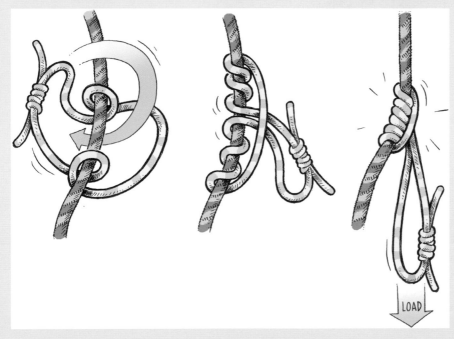

LOAD

Tying a prusik knot

The Redirected Belay

This redirected belay uses the additional friction caused by running the rope back through the anchor in order to assist in catching a fall. Clip your belay device into your belay loop, then run the rope back through a locking carabiner at the anchor master point. If you've rigged the anchor with a cordelette, you can also redirect the rope through a locking carabiner clipped to the "shelf," the loops in the cordelette just above the master point knot. If your partner falls, you'll be pulled toward the anchor, so brace yourself for a pull in that direction—it's often a stout one.

Because of rope friction through the redirect carabiner, you need only hold about two-thirds of the force generated in the fall. The redirect nearly doubles the force on the anchor (just like in a toprope rig), *so any redirected belay requires an absolutely bombproof anchor.* The friction of the rope running across the redirect carabiner makes for smooth lowering. The drawback with this technique is that if a lighter person is belaying a much heavier person, the falling force of the heavier climber can slam the lighter person into the redirect point. Like the indirect belay, if you need to assist or rescue the climber below, it's more complicated

The redirected belay. If the climber below falls, the force on the belayer will be directly in line to where the rope is redirected through the anchor. The friction of the rope running over the redirect carabiner will absorb some of the force.

and time-consuming to rig a raising system. If this is even a remote possibility, rig a direct belay, described next.

The Direct Belay

Many experienced climbers and most guides prefer a direct belay for belaying a follower. The belay device is clipped directly to the anchor. If the second falls, the anchor, not the belayer, bears the brunt of the loading from the climber's weight. The recommended devices for a direct belay are

Detail of a direct belay setup using a quad rig

The direct belay. A Grigri is clipped directly to the master point. As long as the anchor is bomber, this method is preferred by many professionals.

assisted braking devices, autoblocking devices, and a Munter hitch.

A non-autoblocking, tube-style manual braking device (like an ATC) is not recommended for use in a direct belay. Unless the manual braking device is positioned below your waist, it's awkward and sometimes impossible to pull the brake-hand side of the rope high enough to double it back on the device, essential to locking off the load. Even if you can, this puts your brake hand in an ergonomically weak and *dangerous* position to manage much loading. If the master point is above your waist level, the Munter hitch works well, since the braking position for maximum friction is when the two strands of rope are parallel to each other, with the brake position down below the carabiner, not above it.

Another method of rigging a quad for a direct belay

Direct belay with an ATC Guide in autoblocking mode using a quad rig

The best way to set up a direct belay is to use an ABD like a Grigri or an autoblocking device like the ATC Guide or Petzl Reverso attached directly to the master point on the anchor. The advantage of a Grigri or other ABD is that in the event of a fall, the Grigri simply locks off and the anchor holds the climber's weight.

While the direct belay with a user-friendly Grigri is the favored technique of many guides, there are several caveats. The Grigri's manufacturer, Petzl, offers these guidelines:

- "Do a function test as indicated in the Instructions for Use."

- "Make sure to avoid any blocking of the device, or of the cam, as this will negate the braking action on the rope."

- "This method of belaying the second is less than ideal: in this position, the GRIGRI's braking action on the rope is not optimal (especially with thin ropes). In addition, the risk of blocking the cam is greater. We therefore recommend a different technique, using a redirect point."

With this in mind, whenever using a Grigri in the direct belay mode, avoid thin ropes. For better braking, use a thicker (e.g., 10 mm) line. Be vigilant when the device is close to rock, as anything that presses against the handle (i.e., the rock) when the device is loaded will release the locking mechanism. Be sure to position the handle away from the rock.

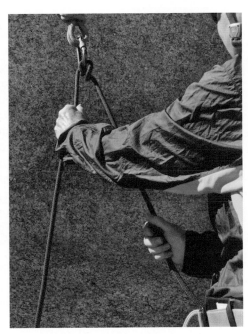

A direct belay with a Munter hitch. Here the belayer's right hand is her brake hand. The starting position (left photo, position 1) is with the brake hand at the top and the guide, or feel, hand at the bottom. Pull the rope down with the brake hand as the guide hand goes up. Feeding the rope up with the guide hand, rather than pulling the rope down tightly with the brake strand, puts fewer kinks in the cord—a real concern with the Munter hitch. The brake hand stays on the rope as the guide hand grabs below it. Then return to position 1. Unlike a manual braking tube device, maximum friction with a Munter hitch is achieved when the two rope strands are parallel.

Remember, an MBD or similar non-autoblocking device is *not recommended* for use in a direct belay if the master point is at or above the belayer's waist level, as the braking position is all wrong (way too high) to lock off a fallen climber.

The Rope Direct Belay

If the belay anchor is situated well back from where you can see your follower, and you want to belay from a stance where you can observe the follower climbing up from below, use the climbing rope and a rope-direct belay technique, which is essentially belaying off an extended master point.

Clip your climbing rope to the master point with two locking carabiners, opposed and reversed.

Then lower yourself to your preferred stance (you can remain on belay for this process) and tie a BHK. The master point loops on the BHK should be within arm's length so you can easily belay from these using an ABD. We call this method "rope direct" because you are essentially belaying directly off the anchor, albeit extended whatever distance is required to position you at the edge.

Using a device like a Grigri, you'll have the benefit of a quick and easy conversion to a raising system, as required, and it's straightforward to lower someone on this setup by redirecting the brake strand on the Grigri (see "Lowering" in this chapter).

Guides often use this rope direct method in single-pitch situations where the anchor is well away from the edge and they want to position themselves to better watch their clients, and perhaps lower them back down when they reach this point. It is essentially an extended master point, created by running the lead rope through carabiners at the anchor's master point (guides often prefer two lockers, opposed and reversed), lowering down to the preferred position, then tying an overhand knot on both strands, creating another two-loop master point. While the loop extending up to the anchor is not redundant, it's monitored, and it's your full rope strength.

Rope direct belay using the "Atomic Clip." This is a great method for a two-bolt anchor on a single-pitch climb, or a multipitch sport climb when you're swinging leads. Tie a double-loop bowline, equalize it to the two anchor points, then tie a figure eight loop off the back side of this knot. Tie the figure eight loop so that it's about arm's length above you, and belay with an ABD. To belay the leader, switch the belay device to your harness belay loop.

Another method of rope direct belay rigging, useful for belaying from the top on a single-pitch climb. The belayer is on the right strand of rope, attached to the master point with a clove hitch to a locking carabiner. Off the back side of the clove hitch, the rope is clipped back to a separate carabiner with a figure eight loop. Off this strand, the Grigri is clipped to another figure eight loop. Here the distance is fairly close to the anchor, but this rigging technique is most useful for greater distances between the anchor and your desired belay stance, limited only by the length of available line. The big advantage is visual contact with your climber in situations where the anchor is some distance back from the edge.

Lowering

It's often easier and quicker to lower someone back down a single-pitch climb than to have her rappel. Depending on your belay device, lowering a climber can range from simple to complicated, especially when you can't just buzz a climber down in one fluid go—like when the climber must lower over roofs or traverse around bushes or loose rock. Unexpected things happen on even the easiest lower-offs. Have this in mind when considering which belay device will work best for a given situation.

Lowering with a Grigri

For a majority of experienced climbers, their first choice is always to lower someone using a Grigri. Since it has a built-in autolock, there is no need to back it up. Petzl sells the Freino, a carabiner with a special gate on the side for the brake strand, which you clip into to facilitate lowering. Without the

A Grigri rigged for lowering with the brake strand redirected through a carabiner clipped to the master point

A Grigri in the lowering mode with the brake strand redirected using the Petzl Freino carabiner, which is specifically designed for this application

special carabiner, you can redirect the brake strand back up through a separate carabiner clipped to the master point (or, on a cordelette anchor, up to the shelf). The big advantage of the Grigri is that once the rope is clipped in, you can use it for lowering (just remember to redirect the brake strand!) or belaying (as the climber moves back up), and it's all set to rig a 3:1 hauling system if your climber needs a hoist.

Munter Hitch

Tied on a carabiner, the Munter hitch can serve for belaying, lowering, and rappelling. It can be tied off and released under tension, a benefit that makes it a key knot for rescue and assistance applications. The Munter can be tied off and secured with a mule knot.

Tying a Munter Hitch

1. Grasp a single strand of rope with both hands, with thumbs pointing toward each other.

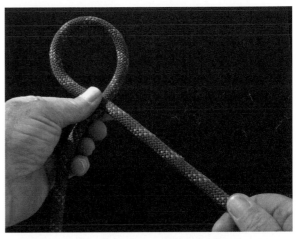

2. Cross the right-hand strand on top of the left-hand strand, hold the two strands where they cross with your left thumb and forefinger, then slide your right hand down about 6 inches.

3. Now bring the right strand up and behind the loop.

4. Clip a locking carabiner where the forefinger is shown here, below the top two strands.

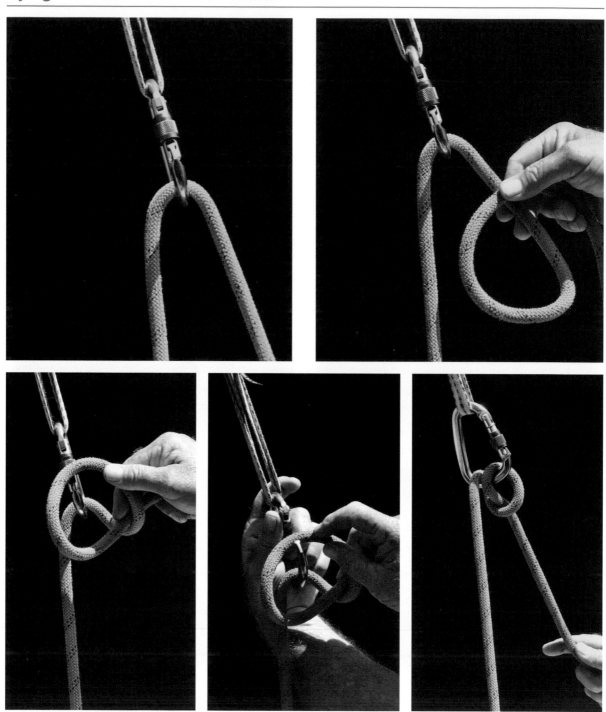

Lowering with a Munter Hitch

Flake the rope at your feet so that if it tangles—and it will—it's within reach to sort out. If you're anchored with a clove hitch, it's adjustable, so you can micro-adjust the length of your tie-in. If the stance at the anchor allows you to see down the cliff and watch the climber as you lower, clip another locking carabiner (a large, pear-shaped carabiner works best) to the master point and tie a Munter hitch. Back it up with an autoblock clipped to a locking carabiner at your belay loop, and you're ready to lower your climber.

Autoblock

Sometimes called the *third hand,* the autoblock is primarily used to back up your brake hand when rappelling, and also as a brake hand backup when lowering someone. The length of your autoblock loop is critical, since if it's too long it can ride up and contact your belay/rappel device, impeding its lock-off function. You'll want to construct and carry a dedicated autoblock cord for these specific applications.

Tie it with a 3-foot, 9-inch length of the softest 5 mm or 6 mm diameter nylon cord you can find, tied into a loop with a double fisherman's. For a rappel backup on a doubled 10 mm rope, go with three wraps. For a lowering backup with a single 10 mm rope, four wraps usually work best.

The autoblock with nylon cord

The Sterling Hollow Block, shown here wrapped in an autoblock configuration, is a 100 percent Technora sling designed specifically for use with friction hitches.

The belayer is ready to lower the climber with a Munter hitch on a locking carabiner clipped to the master point, backed up with an autoblock clipped to a locking carabiner attached to the belayer's belay loop.

Lowering with a Munter hitch and an autoblock. The belayer is holding an autoblock backup that's clipped with a locking carabiner to his belay loop.

Mule Knot

The mule knot is used to tie off a Munter hitch. The great advantage of the Munter/mule combination is that it can be tied off and released when the rope is weighted and under tension, making it one of the key knot combinations for many rescue scenarios.

Using an Autoblock Knot as a Backup When Lowering

Whenever you are lowering a climber with a manual braking device, it's best to back up your brake hand with an autoblock knot clipped to a locking carabiner attached to your belay loop. The autoblock adds an extra level of security, especially when there are tangles in your rope (common) that need sorting as you lower your climber.

For single-pitch climbs, if the stance at the anchor does not allow you to watch the climber as you lower him, to maintain visual contact, rig the rope direct belay system to position yourself at the edge. Always strive for visual contact with your second, whenever belaying or lowering.

Lowering with a Redirected Manual Braking Device

To lower a climber with an MBD (like an ATC), clip the device to your harness and redirect the climber's strand back through the anchor at the master point. This adds friction and makes it easier to hold the climber's weight, but nearly doubles the load on the anchor (pulley effect). Also, if the climber far outweighs the belayer, it's awkward and difficult to lower the climber, as the loading is sucking the belayer into the anchor.

A more workable technique is to clip the ATC directly to the anchor master point and redirect the brake strand back through a locking carabiner at a higher point in the anchor system (on a cordelette anchor, preferably to the shelf, which is all the loops in the cordellette just above the master point knot). This maintains the proper angle (for maximum

A manual braking device (Black Diamond ATC XP) rigged with a redirect for lowering. The climber's end is coming out of the left side of the belay device, and the brake strand is redirected up through a carabiner clipped to the shelf.

friction) on the brake strand. Back it up with an autoblock attached to your belay loop with a locking carabiner. Remember, *do not use a tube device for a direct belay* if the device is at your waist level or above, as the braking position is weak, awkward, and dangerous.

Lowering with an Autoblocking Device

Whenever you're using an autoblocking device (like the ATC Guide or Petzl Reverso) and belaying a second with a direct belay (in the autoblocking mode), if the second falls, the device locks off. Lowering from a locked device under tension is complicated, slow, and awkward compared to the ease of lowering with an ABD. Autoblocking devices

For very short lowers (inches), or to provide slack, you can simply grab the blocking carabiner and ratchet it up and down. Make sure you have a firm grip with your brake hand on the brake strand.

can release suddenly when you manually disengage the autoblocking function, so an autoblock backup is recommended for lowering operations. Tie the autoblock knot on the brake-hand strand, and clip it to your harness belay loop with a locking carabiner.

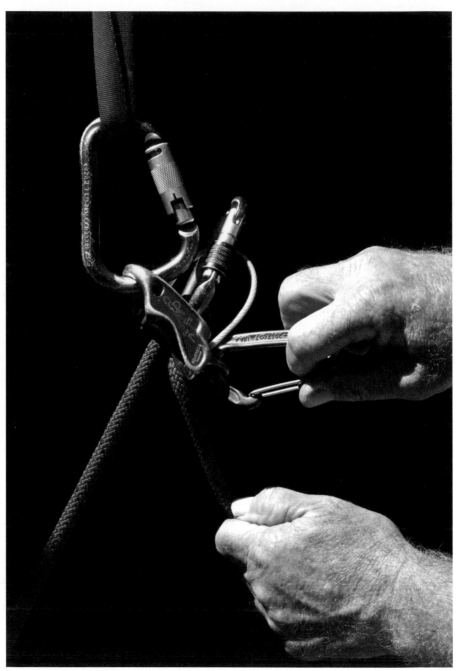

For a short lower of a few feet, you can use a small carabiner (it's good to have one dedicated in advance for this application) clipped to the small hole in the auto-blocking device. Auto-blocking devices can be unpredictable—and can release suddenly—so an autoblock backup is recommended. If it's a steep wall, additional friction (and control) can be achieved by redirecting the brake strand through a higher point at the anchor. Tie the autoblock knot on the brake-hand strand and clip it to your harness belay loop with a locking carabiner.

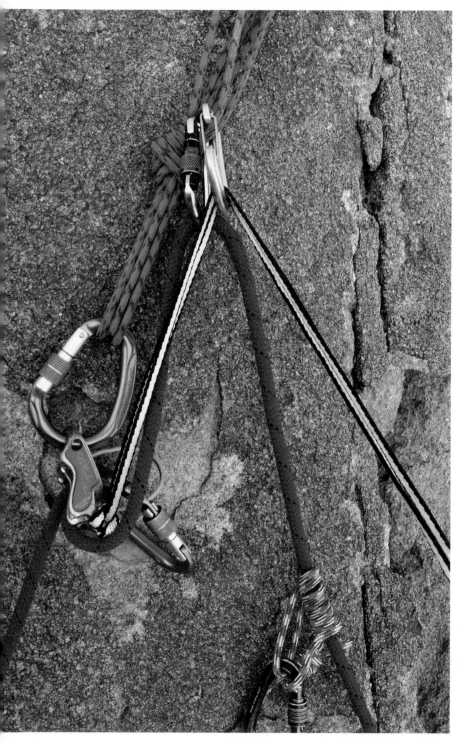

For longer lowers, if the climber is weighting the rope and the device is under tension, follow these steps:

1. Tie a catastrophe knot (overhand loop) on the brake-hand side of the rope.

2. Redirect the brake strand up to a higher point on the anchor (preferably the shelf). If it's a very steep or overhanging lower, additional friction can be obtained by tying a Munter hitch (a wide pear-shaped carabiner works best) at the redirect point.

3. Tie an autoblock knot on the brake-hand strand, and clip it to your harness belay loop with a locking carabiner.

4. Using a double-length (48-inch) Dyneema sling, thread it through the small hole in the device, then redirect it up through a carabiner higher up on the anchor and attach it to your belay loop with a carabiner.

5. Untie the catastrophe knot.

6. Using the sling like a pulley, lean back to release the autoblock function of the belay device, simultaneously holding the autoblock knot down in its non-gripping position while maintaining a brake hand on the rope, and proceed to lower the climber.

2. Clip another locking carabiner to the master point, and clip in the autoblocking locking carabiner on the device (carabiner to carabiner; check that both are locked). Unclip and remove the original belay device master point locking carabiner.

1. Redirect the brake strand, then tie an autoblock knot on the brake strand and attach it to your belay loop with a locking carabiner. If it's a very steep lower, or if you're lowering a heavier climber, additional friction can be obtained by tying a Munter hitch at the redirect carabiner.

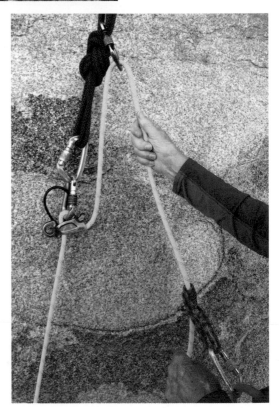

3. Now you're ready for a smooth lower in the manual braking mode, brake strand redirected and backed up with an autoblock knot.

If you are using a direct belay with an auto-blocking device and the plan is for your second to be lowered once he or she reaches your stance, you can manually convert the autoblocking device to the manual braking device mode for a smoother lower once the climber reaches the ledge or stance and is ready to be lowered.

Lowering with the Load Strand Direct Technique

The load strand direct (LSD) technique is a relatively new but simple method devised by professional guides to allow for easy lowering from an *unweighted* autoblocking device (like the Petzl Reverso or ATC Guide) when belaying the follower with a direct belay in autoblocking mode.

Instead of redirecting the brake strand, this technique simply redirects the *load* strand (the strand going to the climber), affording a quick and safe transition from belaying the follower to lowering them back down. Even if the climber is hanging from the rope, they only need to momentarily unweight the rope to allow the belayer to quickly redirect the load strand.

Load Strand Direct Lower

1. Tie an overhand knot backup on the brake strand.

2. Rig an autoblock backup on the brake strand between the belay device and the overhand backup and clip it into your belay loop with a locking carabiner.

3. Have the climber unweight the rope.

4. Redirect the load strand to a separate locking carabiner at the same master point the belay device carabiner is clipped in to.

5. Untie the overhand backup, and proceed to lower the climber.

For the LSD technique to work properly, *the redirect carabiner must be the same size or smaller than the belay device carabiner and clipped to the same master point.*

Sport Climbing Safety

The basic difference between trad and sport climbing is that trad climbing involves mostly removable gear, whereas sport climbing uses permanent gear (usually bolts preinstalled in the rock). A frequent mischaracterization is that by removing the variable of hand-placing gear, sport climbing has eliminated risk. With closely spaced bolts (thus, no lengthy runouts) and fixed belay anchors, what can go wrong on a sport climb? Plenty—and it happens with alarming frequency. Yet most sport climbing mishaps are avoidable if safety checks are carried out and a handful of routines are done preemptively.

Outdoors Is *Not* Indoors

Another misconception is that outdoor sport climbing is simply gym climbing on real rock. In many ways this is true. But since sport climbs exist in the outdoors, nature itself is not merely a character in the adventure of ascent, but the boundless stage where it all transpires. Most passionate sport climbers are outdoors people as well. Maybe not originally, or even by taste or temperament, but rather by necessity. They've shouldered big packs and logged countless miles hiking, scrambling, and bushwhacking during approaches (many sport climbing venues are in wilderness areas); have dealt with skunks and mosquitoes, heat waves and thunderstorms; have scraped an elbow and wrenched an ankle; have slept and cooked and lived outdoors, sometimes in rugged conditions; and have seen a few sunsets they'll take to the grave. To varying degrees, they've made the outdoors their own because the sport climbs we dream on are all outside. The climber transitioning from gym to crag can usually find their place in the sun, but it takes a little time to adjust. Like moving to another country. Even the most domesticated dandy can find his footing outdoors with some mentoring along the way. But it is a process.

Many sources have cataloged the technical ways we can all go south while sport climbing. Helpful, yes, but building the list is a little like counting stars: There's always more to add. A practical approach establishes a safety checklist and a handful of basic routines that we perform religiously.

Leading Sport Climbs: Basic Safety Checks

First, strap on a helmet. You can deck, slam the wall, flip upside down, and knock your head. Loose rock and dropped gear are also hazards. Again, modern climbing helmets are so light, stylish, and form-fitting that 2 feet off the ground, you'll forget you have one on. So wear a helmet.

Savannah Cummins, Red Rock, Nevada
PHOTO BY JOHN EVANS

Rita Young Shin on Platinum Blond (5.10a),
American Fork Canyon, Utah

PHOTO BY JOHN EVANS

Stopper Knot

The stopper knot is used as a safety knot in the end of a rope. It is essentially half a double fisherman's knot tied on one strand of rope. A stopper knot prevents the end of a belay rope from rolling through the belay device, and prevents rappelling off the end of the rope if rappelling with a plate, tube, or assisted braking (e.g., Grigri) device. When using two ropes, tie a separate knot at the end of each rope, as tying both ropes together can cause the lines to "barber pole," twisting around each other.

Tying a Stopper Knot

The best way to avoid a lowering accident or rappelling off the end of your rope is to tie a stopper knot in the rope's end. The stopper knot can, however, pass through a figure eight descending ring, so you'll need to use a bulkier knot if you're rappelling on an "8."

Close the System

For single-pitch routes, the belayer starts by *closing the system*. Tie a stopper knot in the end of the rope, tie the rope to the rope bag, or, best of all, tie straight into the lead rope. However you do it (stopper knots are the standard method), do it every time. Make closing the system a habit that, like all safety checks, you never, ever break.

The most common sport climbing accidents are leader falls, followed by belayer injuries while catching a fall. While sometimes serious, most leader/belayer mishaps result in scrapes and sprains. Not so lowering accidents (the third most frequent mishaps), which are usually severe.

Closing the system *simply and safely* eliminates the chance of the belayer running out of rope during the lower-off and the rope buzzing though their belay device and the climber decking out. Few climbers walk away from that.

Safety Check: ABC

"ABC" is an acronym for anchor, belayer, climber.

First check "A," the ground anchor (if it exists), usually connected to the belayer via the rope and a clove hitch. Is the anchor solid? And how's that clove?

The belayer, "B," comes next. Check your harness. Is the waist strap cinched? Are the buckles squared away? Is the rope properly threaded through your belay device, and the device securely clipped to the belay loop with the carabiner gate locked?

Now the climber, "C." Is the harness cinched up? Are the buckles good? Check. Now s*top talking and focus while you tie in*. Many climbers have started tying in, gotten distracted, and failed to finish their knot. The moment they fall or go to lower, the rope pulls through their harness and they hit the ground. People needlessly die that way. *Completion before distraction*. A well-dressed knot, snugged tight with sufficient tail. That's what you want.

Then, most important, the partners double-check each other: harness, tie-in, belay rig. To check the belay device, grab the carabiner and push on the gate with your thumb. One out of 100 or 500 times, most everyone leaves the gate unlocked. That's what you're checking for.

In a Line

If using a Grigri to belay, Petzl recommends a function test—a quick stout pull on the non-brake strand to make sure the device is preloaded and properly locks off. The anchor, belayer, and first bolt the leader will clip should describe a straight line. Now you're ready to run through the signals and climb.

Spot Her

Always spot a leader pulling hard moves off the ground. When starting off boulders or fractured ground, enlist others to help spot till that first bolt is clipped. This is standard practice, and no stand-up person refuses. Place any bouldering pads at the bottom as well. If the start still feels dodgy, consider stick-clipping the first bolt (explained shortly) and remove the chance of a ground fall.

Efficient Clipping

Every leader must have a simple, ordered method for rigging quickdraws on their harness, and to efficiently clip them into protection. Most sport climbers rack quickdraws on their right side for right-handed clips (quickdraws with gates facing left), and vice versa for their left side (left-handed clips). Experience gained in the climbing gym will pay dividends outdoors.

Many falls result from bungled clips. Sport climbing clips are normally done one-handed, with the other hand clasping a hold so you can momentarily pause and clip. A common mistake is to try to always clip when the bolt is just above your head.

Alyse Dietel, Frying Pan, Colorado
PHOTO BY JOHN EVANS

Katherine Butler making the clip,
Wild Iris, Wyoming
PHOTO BY JOHN EVANS

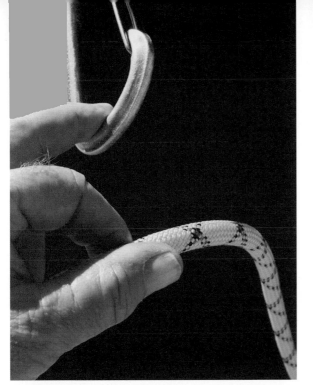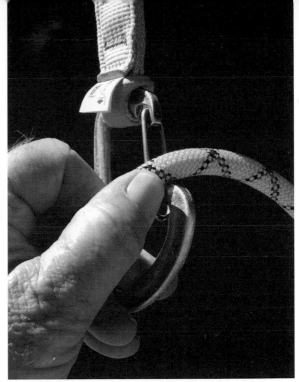

If the gate is facing right, it's easiest to clip with your left hand by capturing the carabiner with your middle finger and holding the rope with your thumb and forefinger.

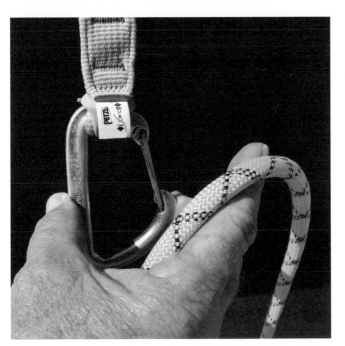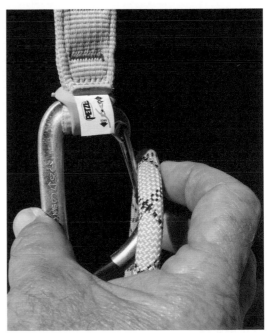

If the gate is facing right and you have to clip it with your right hand, grab the base of the carabiner with your thumb and middle finger, and clip the rope using the forefinger.

Correct quickdraw orientation. The rope runs from the inside out. The climber is moving right, and the gate is facing left. This is something many experienced climbers often botch.

Incorrect orientation. The rope runs from the outside in.

Great when you can, but the hand- and footholds rarely oblige. You might have to reach far off lower holds, or climb higher and clip lower. The trick is to find the least taxing body position on whatever holds there are, and work the clip from there. Don't try to clip off little nothings as long as the bolt is at your face. The worst time to fall is when you're just about to clip, when you have a load of rope slack in your hand.

Most experts clip the rope into the carabiner with the hand opposite the gate's position. That is, with your right hand, reach across your chest and clip the carabiner with the gate facing left, pressing the gate with your thumb. Practice clipping a low bolt at the gym—with both hands, gates facing right and left—until you're proficient. As the saying goes: Blown clips cause as many falls as blown moves.

Dangerous quickdraw orientation. The rope runs from the outside in and the gate is facing right, the same direction the climber is moving. If the climber falls, the rope can potentially cross over the gate and unclip.

Other Clipping Concerns

When you clip the "sharp end" (your end) of the lead rope into a draw, it should always run out of the carabiner, away from the wall and straight into your harness. When the sharp end runs out of the carabiner *toward* the rock, you have "backclipped,"

basically clipped the rope in backwards, which forms a small loop of rope around the carabiner. If the loop runs over the gate, and you fall, the rope can sometimes unclip itself from the draw.

Make sure to pull up slack from *above* your last draw, not from *below* the previous clip, which is easy

Peter Croft leading My Laundry *(5.10a) at Joshua Tree. He's moving to the right of the quickdraw, so the carabiner gate faces left. The rope is on the outside of his left leg, not between his legs.*

to do when the bolts are closely spaced. This results in the hateful "Z-clip"—and impossible-to-budge rope drag. When the last bolt is only a few feet below, you'll have to gather slack (to clip the higher bolt) with several short pulls. Bite the rope between pulls till you draw out slack enough to make the higher clip, but be careful here. People have lost teeth when they've fallen with a shank of rope in their mouth.

Overhanging routes are often fixed with permadraws, like the ones we clip in the gym, owing to the difficulty of cleaning them on the lower-off. Look before you clip. Rope-end carabiners, especially on popular or older routes, are often worn with sharp-edged, rope-size grooves from countless lower-offs on gritty lines. It's unlikely these carabiners will break, but the sharp edges can core-shot (cut the sheath) your rope in an instant.

Whenever you reach belay bolts with corroded or deeply grooved hardware, it's usually better to rappel off rather than lower. If the hardware is frightening, rig a few slings directly through the bolt hangers and rappel off those. Better $10 lost than your life.

In solid rock, stainless steel bolts and hangers are almost always secure. On older routes, the hardware might be suspect and, occasionally, dangerous. Infrequent loose bolts are part of the game, and can usually be tightened—but not when you find them on the lead.

It's unlikely you will find just one manky bolt on a route with otherwise solid gear. If the hardware looks sketchy from the base, or that first bolt is questionable, expect the rest to be the same, or worse. Best to arrange an escape and go to another route with solid hardware. In true junk rock, every bolt is suspect. All routes in marine environments (sea cliffs) must have glue-in titanium bolts. Even stainless steel quickly corrodes around salt water. Testing has shown that after as little as a year in tropical seaside crags, steel bolts can fail under a measly 1,200 pound load.

Rope Position while Leading

Never let the rope run behind your legs unless you're directly above a bolt. This is a guiding principle for all lead climbing, but it's more easily imagined than described.

Few sport climbs are *direttissimas*, running straight up and down, where you climb the rock like rungs in a ladder. Most routes traverse for a few moves here, require a step-through there, or pull over roofs and bulges. Overhanging and sideways motions naturally pull the rope between our legs (overhangs) and behind a single leg (traverses). A fall in this position can flip you upside down; head injuries are possible.

When climbing directly above a bolt, position the rope between your legs. If you veer slightly right or left, pay close attention to two things: the position of the rope relative to your legs, and which way the carabiner gate on the rope-bearing end of the quickdraw is facing.

When moving to the *right* of the bolt, position the rope in front of your left leg, *not* between your legs, where the sideways drag of the line can pull it *behind* your left leg. The gate of the carabiner that your rope is clipped through should face left (opposite the direction you're climbing). If you're moving *left* from the bolt, flip the rope in on the outside of your right leg. The carabiner gate should face right. Visualize this till it all makes sense—and see how it works in a gym.

With awareness and practice, you'll develop a "spidey sense" at moving and positioning the line so it can't entangle your legs. But sometimes you can't. It just happens, usually when you are maxed. An alert belayer will say, "Step over the rope." That's the immediate concern, not climbing on, because a fall with the rope behind your leg is asking for injury.

Falling

Experienced sport climbers know how to fall because they often do. It's part of the sport. Falling technique entails a handful of do's and don'ts.

Don't push off or out from the rock when you fall—when the rope snaps tight, any outward momentum is converted to inward motion and a sudden crash into the wall. If you find yourself swinging toward the wall, brace yourself with both arms extended outward with legs slightly bent, in a rappel/lowering stance. In big airy falls, grabbing the rope with both hands just above the knot helps maintain a stable posture and keeps you from flipping sideways.

If a fall seems imminent, or whenever you're reaching deep, alert your belayer by saying, "Watch me!" When the belayer comes back with "I got you," it bolsters confidence, as the belayer is at the ready. Whenever you fall, immediately yell, "Falling!"—especially if you're out of sight of the belayer.

On low-angle slab sport routes, a fall is more like a slide. On swinging, low-angle falls, a quick running/paddling motion with your feet can keep you from getting scraped up.

These descriptions cover the common physical concerns about falling, practices that are intuitive for many climbers and easily learned by the rest of us. However, the sticking point for most climbers is not so much the fall itself but the *fear* of falling.

Every fall is potentially dangerous, but especially in sport climbing, where bombproof protection bolts are typically plentiful, an informed and alert leader, given a solid belay, usually has little to fear. Trad climbing is a whole different game in this regard. Falls are potentially much longer in most cases, and the protection is almost always less secure than bolt anchors. And the majority of trad climbs are not nearly as steep as most sport routes, so our chances of hitting features as we slide down the rock (ledges, horns, flakes, etc.) are much greater. There's also the critical issue of a nut or a cam ripping out on impact, which immediately adds significant length to the fall. For these reasons, calculation (risk appraisal) is a key part of the leading equation, referred to here and elsewhere as "the protection problem." The many nuances of this vital study outstrip the scope of this manual. A leading source of information on the protection problem are the excellent books by Arno Ilgner (*The Warrior's Way*, *Espresso Lessons*, and others).

Transitions: Lowering and Rappelling

Before every lead, briefly discuss a game plan with your belayer and decide what you'll do at the anchor. If the anchor has gated cold shuts or mussy

Mussy hooks are designed for clipping in and lowering off.

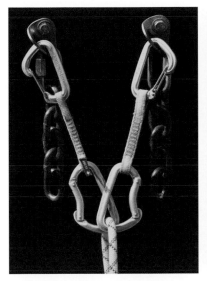

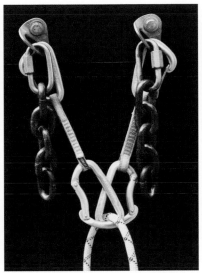

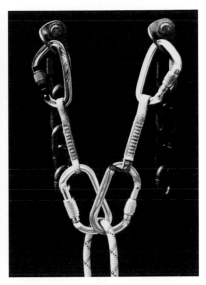

OK. Two quickdraws rigged for toproping with the gates opposed and reversed. Not ideal, since whatever chains, rings, or hardware-store doodads exist can press on the gates once the draws are weighted and potentially open one.

Better. The draws are clipped behind the chains and quick links so that when they're weighted, they won't be pressing on the hardware.

Even better. All locking carabiners on the draws for security, safeguarding against possible gate opening. The oval lockers at the master point are opposed and reversed.

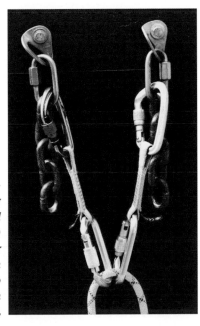

Here the bottom locking ovals (opposed and reversed) are in a better configuration for the rope to run through smoothly.

hooks (in good condition), it's as simple as clipping in and lowering off. If using quickdraws, make sure the rope-bearing carabiner gates are opposed and reversed, or, better yet, use locking carabiners with the gates opposed and reversed. With slings or a cordelette, you can easily rig a more reliable two-bolt anchor setup (see chapter 10).

After clipping in and *before* lowering, communicate with your belayer; if possible, look down and establish visual contact to make sure he or she is paying attention and is poised in the brake position.

This is a critical time, and bungled signals have resulted in numerous lowering accidents. When the climber leaned back to be lowered, the belayer had already taken the rope out of the belay device. "What we have here is a failure to communicate," said the warden in *Cool Hand Luke*. Same deal here—and the problem is largely solved by

By threading this rope through the chains then clipping it in just above with a locking carabiner (left), you're preventing wear and tear on the hardware; then the last person on the climb can lower through the rings simply by removing the locking carabiner (right). A good tactic if you're toproping with a group.

communicating before the climb, having a game plan, and carrying out that plan.

Review your climbing signals with your partner, and use the standardized commands. Devise a plan before you start climbing, and confirm every step of that plan as you go. It's worth repeating: *Experienced teams always make certain to know, announce, and mutually confirm the exact status of the belay. Those who don't will pay dearly for their negligence.*

Standard Signals Used during Lowering

Tension (or "Take")

Tension On (or "Got You")

Lower Me (or "Ready to Lower")

Lowering

Stop (or "Hold")

Tramming

If the route is severely overhanging, and no one is going to follow and clean the draws, the lower-off will leave the leader so far out from the wall, they won't be able to reach in and easily unclip the draws from the bolts.

The solution is to "tram" down by clipping one end of a quickdraw into the climber's belay loop and the other end into the rope running down through the draws. Tramming also prevents a common accident on overhanging routes that occurs when the lowered climber unclips the final bottom draw with the belayer out a ways from the wall, creating enough slack to hit the ground.

Lowering through Chains/Rings

If you're transitioning from a lead or toprope to lowering from chains/rings, you'll need to thread your rope through the chains/rings. There are two methods.

METHOD 1: THREADING A BIGHT AND LOWERING ON A LOCKING CARABINER

This method assumes the chains/rings are wide enough to thread two strands (a bight) of rope. The advantage of this method is that it's simple and you are on belay throughout the process.

Step 1: Attach yourself to the anchor with a personal tether, quickdraws, or sling.

Step 2: Thread a bight of rope through the chains/rings and tie a figure eight on a bight.

Step 3: Attach this knot to your harness belay loop with a locking carabiner.

Step 4: Untie your figure eight follow-through tie-in knot, pull the rope end through the anchor, and let it dangle at your side.

Step 5: Call for tension, get a response from your belayer, then proceed to be lowered. *Simple and safe.*

METHOD 2: TETHERING, UNTYING, AND RETYING

Step 1: Attach yourself to the anchor with a personal tether, into the anchor master point if possible. If the anchor points are separated, use two separate slings.

Step 2: Pull about 10 feet of slack from your rope tie-in and tie a figure eight loop. Clip this with a locking carabiner into your harness belay loop.

Step 3: Untie from the rope, thread it through the anchor, then retie in with a figure eight follow-through to your harness.

Step 4: Communicate with your belayer, unclip your sling/tether, and proceed to be lowered.

Transition from Toproping to Rappelling

Step 1: Attach yourself to the anchor's master point with a personal tether and a locking carabiner. Call "Off Belay" to your belayer.

Step 2: Pull up about 10 feet of rope, tie a figure eight on a bight (or overhand loop), and attach it to your harness with a carabiner.

Step 3: Untie your figure eight follow-through tie-in knot, and thread the rope end through the anchor.

Step 4: Tie a stopper knot in the end of the rope.

Step 7: Clean the toprope rigging, and you're ready to rappel.

Step 5: Unclip the rope from your carabiner and pull enough rope through the anchor to complete your rappel. If you're not able to see the end of the rope on the ground (or get verification from your partner that the end is down), go to the middle mark of the rope. If you don't have a middle mark or bi-patterned rope, measure from both ends to find the middle. And always verify that there are stopper knots in the ends of the rope.

Step 6: Rig your rappel device on your personal tether, and back it up with an autoblock attached to your harness belay loop with a locking carabiner.

Belaying Sport Climbs

Sport climbing falls can often jar the leader, especially short ones, where there is little rope out and little stretch and give in the system. Also when the rope is zigzagging through many quickdraws, as the friction in the system reduces overall rope stretch. On steeper routes, a "soft catch" can soften wrenching falls.

A soft catch requires a more dynamic belaying technique. With autolocking devices like a Grigri, where the cam locks solidly in a fall, use your stance, body position, and body movement to provide a dynamic belay. Timing is key. Anticipate the fall by bending your knees slightly. The moment the rope comes tight, simultaneously hop into the air. Every fall is different, and at higher fall factors, the impact is likely to yank you upward—be ready to brace yourself with your legs against the wall.

The dynamic belay is not appropriate for all situations. A common misconception is that a ground anchor is never required in sport climbing. Not so. Belayer accidents are frequent in sport climbing.

Method 1 *of feeding slack to the leader with a Grigri. The advantage of this method is that your brake hand stays on the rope and you never grab the device or open the cam. Keep both hands on the rope, and feed the rope into the device as you pay out the rope with the non-brake hand above it. The key is to feed slow to fast, without a sudden jerk. A good analogy is your car seatbelt: If you pull fast and hard, it will lock; if you start slow and pull smoothly (don't yank), it won't lock.*

When the leader takes an authentic "whipper" (long fall), the belayer without a ground anchor is sometimes pulled violently off their stance and slammed into the wall, or yanked up into the first quickdraw, which is hell on fingers and hands. The

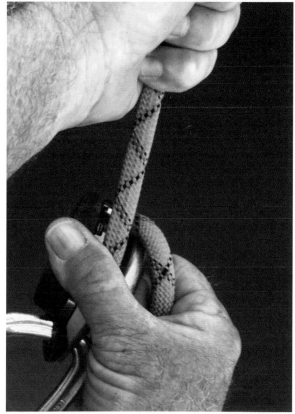

Method 2 *of feeding rope to a leader with a Grigri. The advantage of this method is that you can feed slack quickly without the device locking up, although it takes some practice to use the proper grip. The disadvantage is that if you're holding the Grigri and pressing down on the handle during a fall, the Grigri's locking mechanism won't engage. So it's important to keep a grip on the rope with three fingers of your brake hand and only press down on the Grigri's handle with your thumb. Don't grab the entire Grigri itself with your hand.*

brake hand can get knocked off the rope anytime the belayer gets launched, so plan accordingly.

A ground anchor is required on uneven terrain, where the belayer can get pulled off their perch, when the leader outweighs the belayer by 50 pounds or more, where there is a high fall factor, and when there is a real danger of a falling leader hitting a ledge or hitting the ground.

Tie off the ground anchor with the rope, which adds some stretch to the system, compared to anchoring straight in with a nylon sling, which has little stretch, or a Dyneema sling, with no stretch at all. Tie into the rope as you normally would, then clove hitch to a locking carabiner attached to the ground anchor, which can range from a sling or cord around a tree or block to a single cam set for an upward force. Most every belay is somewhat unique.

Lowering with a Grigri. If using a rope bag, make sure the system is closed with a stopper knot in the end of the rope.

When a leader can potentially hit the ground or a ledge, tie in tight to your ground anchor. When (and only when) the leader has room to fall and the fall is clean (nothing to hit), allow a few feet of slack to the ground anchor. Here, the belayer acts as a dynamic counterweight to the climber. Any fall force will launch you in the direction of pull. Take a solid stance, and be on guard to avoid getting pancaked onto the cliff.

A relatively new device, the Edelrid Olm, solves the issue of a lighter climber belaying a much heavier leader without a ground anchor. According to Edelrid: "The Ohm is an assisted braking resister that you install at the first bolt in the safety chain. In the event of a fall, the Ohm increases rope friction so that a lighter belayer can hold a heavier partner without being suddenly pulled off the ground and thrown against the wall."

The Ohm can be pre-rigged on a quickdraw, ready to be clipped by the leader to the first bolt. The device allows the rope to run freely, but the braking action kicks in during a fall. This device

Stick Clip

The riskiest part of many sport climbs is clipping the first bolt, especially when the bolt is high and the landing is dicey. Any fall is a groundfall, and those can end badly. A common solution is a stick clip—typically a 6- to 10-foot extendable pole with a quickdraw holder on the end. These allow you to clip the lead rope through the first bolt before you leave the ground. A few routes are engineered to require a stick clip. Most are not, but the device is welcome in many situations. Trango and Superclip sell premade stick clips or attachments. There is really no good reason not to stick-clip the first bolt on *all* sport climbs, which are all about movement, not risk. If there is any doubt or nervousness about the climbing to that first bolt, stick-clip it and remove the hazard. In time, this will become standard practice.

If the climber far outweighs you, a ground anchor is useful, even on flat ground. If you're belaying a leader with a ground anchor, allow about 3 feet of slack to your connection. You'll be able to provide a softer catch if you're pulled that short distance if the leader falls, providing a more dynamic belay but not losing control. When you're lowering, come tight against the anchor to help brace yourself and bolster your stance.

is particularly useful for adults who want to be belayed by their kids.

Final Thoughts on Belaying

An experienced sport climbing belayer knows more than how to best use their equipment, utilize a ground anchor, give a soft catch, and clearly communicate. They play a crucial role in supporting the "send" (the successful ascent), especially on routes that push the leader's limits, when one false move or bungled clip can spell defeat.

Practiced sport belayers develop two crucial skills: alertness and anticipation. By keeping the leader in their crosshairs, they know when she is flowing and when she is cruxing. They know the dramatic increase in forces generated by only 4 feet of slack in the rope, so they give the leader "a smile, not a mile," whereby the rope between the belayer and the leader describes a slight smiley face— enough slack in the line for the leader to move freely, but no more. They closely monitor that smile, feeding or narrowing it as required.

They anticipate the moment before a clip and feather out just enough rope so the leader can clip the bolt in one fluid move, rather than having to jerk up slack in fits and starts. They keep the cord organized as it feeds off the rope bag so the leader doesn't have to stop on 5.12 holds while the belayer battles a twisted line.

They encourage when appropriate and reassure that the leader's every move is closely monitored. They might keep some tiny tautness in the line when the leader traverses so that a loop doesn't form beneath their feet that can work behind a leg. They don't lower a leader herky-jerky, or an inch at a time, or at 20 miles an hour; instead they lower smooth and steady, placing little extra stress on the leader and the system.

They remain a voice of reason when problems arise, offering solutions, not complaints. They keep an eye out for things the leader might not see, focused as they are on the moves—like loose-looking flakes, the rope snagging on a horn, the middle of the rope coming up. The list is long, and when that list is checked by two climbers instead of one, you have a team, and "teamwork" is the word with sport climbing.

CHAPTER 13

Rappelling and Rope Ascending

Rappelling is a mandatory skill for all outdoor climbing. Even on short sport climbs, the route often ends partway up a wall, at an anchor without lowering hardware, where the only way off (without forfeiting your rope or costly gear) is to rappel. In the Alps you might take a *téléphérique* (mountain cable car) to the *top* of a peak and rappel to the *start* of the climbing. The "walk off" on some big routes involves such loose rock, thorny vegetation, stream crossings, and grueling marches that most parties rap the route. And nobody enjoys a 100 percent success rate. Crowds on the route, heat, nerves, and *fill in the blank* have driven us all off multipitch climbs; safely getting down sometimes calls for a whole lot more than clipping fixed anchors and snaking down a rope using a friction device.

The physical act of rappelling is so easy and intuitive that most newcomers catch on in minutes. For most gym climbers accustomed to getting lowered, fluid rappelling means acquiring trust and a feel for using a braking device. The body position, backpedaling down the wall at a comfortable pace while sometimes passing obstacles (roofs, different surface planes, etc.), is largely the same as lowering off a gym climb.

Rappelling mishaps count for only 5 percent of all climbing accidents, but as guides often say: Many climbing accidents can leave us injured, but almost all rappelling accidents leave us dead. Climbers fail to tie stopper knots in the rope (closing the system) then rappel off the end of the rope—the most common cause of rappelling fatalities. Rockfall and falling debris can also injure rappellers. So can losing control of your rappel and basically free-falling down the rope and the cliff. The last two scenarios are rare when rappelling on solid rock, but there are safety checks and techniques to mitigate these hazards, uncommon as they are, and we use them as default tactics. We make them habits.

That understood, we might wonder: *If rappelling is basically simple, and if one quick safety check (stopper knots) eliminates the primary risk (rappelling off the end of the rope), why is rappelling such a study?*

Rappelling itself is rarely the challenge. It's when ropes get stuck, gear gets dropped, rocks fall, anchors are bad, and the weather comes hard and fast. There usually are many ways to solve a problem of ascent. When sorting out a rappelling snafu on a big multipitch route, our options are rarely simple or totally safe. Our best insurance is knowing what might go wrong—and some methods to make things right. In the history of rock climbing, most anything that can happen during a descent *has*

The Process of Descent

Descending a route is sometimes harder and more complex than climbing up. Multipitch climbers must know how to navigate the entire process of descent—from the long list of possible hazards to the established methods to meet them.

Courtney Love rappels off Lizard Rock, Fisher Towers, Utah.
PHOTO BY JOHN EVANS

happened, and climbers have escaped unthinkable jams. There's always something to do; though for a moment we might feel stuck.

For instance, you pull the ropes through the last anchor, 120 feet above. The wind gusts just as the ends whip free, blowing the line sideways where one end hangs up on a flake, 50 feet up and right. No amount of pulling can free it. Or an unseen edge core-shots your only rope. These and other dilemmas can make descending a cliff or mountainside a task that's much more involved than merely rappelling down a rope. Nevertheless, that's where we start: How do we safely rappel down a rope using a friction device?

Rappelling Technique

Seek direct coaching by a qualified instructor for your first few rappels, which are normally done while belayed. Rappelling (rapping) is one of

Wayne Merry rappelling on El Capitan (c.1958)

Fireman's Belay

If, for whatever reason, a top belay cannot be used for a first-time or beginning rappeller (using a tube-style device), or when someone feels uncomfortable during a rappel, use a fireman's belay. Someone on the ground attentively holds the rappel rope. Pulling down on the rope creates such tension in the system that the rappeller stops on a dime—they cannot move down a rope under tension.

Fireman's belay

the few techniques where the climber is entirely dependent on equipment: the anchor, the rope, and your rappelling device. It is critical that your

Good rappelling posture: feet wide for stability, looking over the shoulder, both hands on the braking side of the device

system is properly arranged, and all of us must first be shown how. Most climbers quickly learn the basics.

A rappeller takes the same posture used when lowering off a climb: feet wide, knees slightly bent while sitting back in the harness. Keep your feet relatively high, eyes looking over your shoulder to watch where you're going. Proceed smoothly and slowly down the rappel, feeling how the friction is regulated based on the position of your brake hand and how you let the rope flow through the device. It's a little like letting out string on a kite. Too much string too fast, and the kite dives. Again, basic rappelling is so simple and intuitive, most people catch on immediately. The rappel device and your brake hand do all the work.

Joining Two Rappel Ropes

For rappels longer than half a standard (60 m) rope length, climbers often tie two ropes together to still have a retrievable system, threading one rope through the rappel anchor and tying the two ends together (noting which rope to pull down based on which side of the anchor the joining knot is positioned), then rappelling on both strands. Once at the bottom of the rappel, the rope is retrieved by pulling down the strand on the knot side of the anchor.

Knots for Tying Two Ropes Together

Standard knots for joining two ropes include the double fisherman's knot and the figure eight bend. Once weighted, the double fisherman's is more difficult to untie than the figure eight bend; but the figure eight bend, while relatively easy to untie, is bulky. Tie these knots with 5 inches of tail, and carefully tighten the knots before using them. A stiff rope makes it harder to cinch the knots tight, so be especially careful with stiffer line.

Double fisherman's knot

Figure Eight Bend

Which knot you use depends on several variables. If the diameter of the ropes is notably different, or the lines are very stiff, the most foolproof knot is the figure eight bend, backed up with half a double fisherman's on each side. This is a bulky knot, but it provides absolute security.

Figure eight bend with fisherman's backups

Flat Overhand (aka Euro Death Knot)

When American climbers visited the Dolomites and first saw Europeans using the flat overhand, they were unfamiliar with its use and thought it unsafe, dubbing it the "Euro Death Knot." We Americans were wrong about that. There is only one documented case of a flat overhand failing (in the Grand Tetons, September 1997), when it was sloppily tied with too short a tail. Be sure to leave plenty of tail and to set it snugly.

From 1999 to 2009 various tests revealed that for tying two ropes together, the flat overhand was roughly 30 percent weaker than the double fisherman's, but still plenty strong for rappelling setups. Testing also revealed that it was almost impossible to get the knot to fail, as long as it was tied with a suitable-length tail and properly tightened.

Petzl, a leading manufacturer of rappelling devices, recommends the flat overhand as the knot of choice for joining two rappel ropes together, as long as the ropes are of similar diameter and the tail is a minimum of 20 centimeters (8 inches).

The flat overhand is easy to tie and easy to untie after weighting. It presents a clean profile when pulled down the cliff during rope retrieval, reducing the odds of the rope getting jammed in a crack. For added security, back up by tying another flat overhand on top of the first one—although this adds bulk.

Remember the few cautions: The flat overhand is not recommended for tying together two ropes of drastically differing diameters (e.g., 7 mm to 11 mm), or for use on very stiff ropes. The knot should be used with discretion, well tightened (pull as hard as you can on all four strands), and tied with a long tail (minimum of 8 inches). Many experienced climbers use the flat overhand (with a second overhand backup) when they're concerned about the knot jamming in a crack when pulling down the ropes from an anchor. Otherwise they use a figure eight bend or double fisherman's.

The flat overhand is a poor choice for use with nylon webbing, and it has caused numerous rappel anchor failures when tied with a short tail. An even worse knot for rope and webbing (also the cause of numerous accidents) is the flat figure eight, which inverts at shockingly low loads as the knot rolls inward and capsizes. *Avoid using the flat figure eight on webbing.*

Flat overhand knot

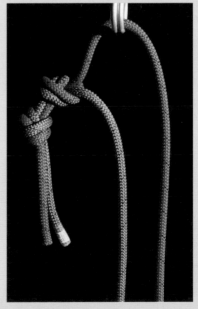

Flat overhand with overhand backup

Twisted Lines

As you progress onto steeper, more featured terrain, you'll encounter all the common rappelling challenges, starting with knots or tangles in your rope. When rope twist happens while rappelling (and it will), stop immediately. If you're not using an autoblock backup, wrap several loops of rope around your leg on the brake-hand side, pull up the rope below, and untangle it. This can take a while. If you're heading for the ground and there are partners below, they can walk out the ends (if there's enough rope), shaking out twists as they go. Either way, sort out the twists *before* you resume rappelling or the twists will jam in your rappel device.

Saddlebags

When it seems likely that your rope will hang up when you pitch the ends off the anchor (owing to bushes, broken terrain, or other climbers below), consider tying overhand knots in the ends of the rope, clipping them to a gear loop, and rappelling off with "saddlebags." This decreases the likelihood of ropes hanging up and also closes the system.

The leg wrap is useful if you need to stop temporarily to deal with rope tangles.

Rappelling with butterfly coils reduces the chance that the rope will snag in windy conditions.

Overhangs

If the overhang forms a big roof or ceiling, getting past the lip and into a free-hanging position is awkward and scary at first. Keep your feet at the very lip of the overhang and lean way back in your harness, until your feet are above your waist. Then gently push off and drop into space. This is a very counterintuitive move, since as you push off, you need to let enough rope slide through your brake hand so your upper body doesn't slam into the wall as your feet go below the roof.

Once you kick off the lip, you will quickly swing in and flip from inverted (waist lower than feet) to upright. When you keep your feet at the lip and lower your waist below your feet, you still swing in—but not nearly as far or as suddenly as if you'd simply bounded off the lip with your feet roughly at waist level, as we normally do while rappelling and lowering. By keeping your feet high at the lip and lowering your rump, you're basically sucking up the distance of the swing-in.

If the roof is poised above lower-angled rock, the moment you clear the roof you'll drop onto the face, so your feet and legs must be ready to absorb some impact (usually no more than stepping down off a chair). Learning to clear roofs on rappel takes practice, and it is tricky and unnerving for most beginners.

Rappel Devices

With a single rope (fixed line), you can rappel with an ABD (assisted braking device) or a tube device. But the most common rappel is on a doubled rope, threaded through the anchor's master point to the halfway mark, so you'll need a tube device with two slots, one for each rope strand. The rope is retrieved by grabbing one strand and pulling it through the anchors. If the rappel is longer than half the length of your rope (e.g., 35 meters on a 70-meter rope), you'll need two ropes tied together.

Rappelling with a Tube Device

When rappelling a double rope on a tube device, grab a bight of rope from both strands, stuff the bights through the device, then clip the bights into a locking carabiner attached to your belay loop. Always keep the keeper cable on the device clipped into the locking carabiner. This ensures that you don't drop the device while rigging, and keeps the device from migrating away from your belay loop while rappelling. As you thread the ropes through

Rappelling with a Black Diamond ATC XP

the device, position the brake strands down toward your feet. This lets the rope feed smoothly through the device with minimal twists—provided the line isn't twisted to begin with.

The two standard tube-style devices are the Black Diamond ATC XP and the Petzl Reverso. The ATC XP has two different friction options. One side has two V-shaped grooves (the "teeth" side for high-friction mode); the other side does not (regular friction mode). Placing the device teeth-side down on the braking side gives you maximum friction; placing the brake strands on the non-teeth side, less friction.

The degree of friction the device affords depends on the diameter of the rope, whether you're rappelling on a single or doubled rope, the

slickness and density of the rope, your body weight, and the angle of the wall you're descending.

For a steep rappel with a tube-style device, hold the ropes with both hands below the device, in the braking position, with the ropes running down between your legs. For lower-angled rappels, hold

The Black Diamond ATC XP in high friction mode

Petzl Reverso

the ropes off your right side (if you're right-handed; left side for southpaws), positioned at your hip with your brake hand. For added friction, slide your brake hand back and bend the line around your hip.

Rappel Backups and Extensions

The modern rappel backup uses an autoblock knot rigged *below* the rappel device. For the knot to grab, it only needs to hold a fraction of the rappeller's weight. Since it is on the braking side of the device, the device itself provides most of the friction and holds most of the weight. Here, the knot is like your brake hand squeezing and gripping the rope. Some instructors refer to the autoblock as the "third hand," like an angel grabbing your rope and averting catastrophe in the unlikely event that you lose control of the brake.

A prusik will also work as a backup for rappelling but often provides too much friction, especially for climbers under 150 pounds. Unlike the prusik, the autoblock can release under tension; i.e., when it's weighted and grabbing the rope.

As you rappel down, form a circle with your thumb and forefinger (like the "OK" sign) and push the autoblock down as you go, allowing the rope to freely slide through the knot. When you let go, the autoblock knot rides up and grabs onto the line, like your brake hand squeezing the rope. Releasing the autoblock, even when weighted, is as simple as sliding it back down and holding it in the "open" position with your fingers. It's a beautiful thing, and easy to rig.

The Autoblock

Tie an autoblock with a loop of 5 mm or 6 mm diameter nylon cord. A 3-foot, 9-inch length, tied with a double fisherman's knot, works well. You don't want too big of a loop, which will ride up against the rappel device and not grab. Select the softest, most pliable cord you can find, as softer cord grips better than a stiffer line. For a doubled rappel

Three-wrap autoblock with 6 mm nylon cord on a doubled rope

Four-wrap autoblock with 6 mm nylon cord on a single rope

Black Diamond ATC XP rigged for rappelling with a three-wrap autoblock backup clipped to the leg loop with a locking carabiner

Another way to rig an autoblock backup is to girth hitch the cord around your leg loop, wrap it a few times around the rappel rope, then clip it back to your leg loop with a locking carabiner. This way the cord is always ready when needed and can't be dropped. When not in use, the cord can be wrapped a few times around the leg loop and kept out of the way.

To prevent loosening the buckle on an adjustable leg loop, clip the autoblock carabiner on the inside.

rope, three wraps usually works best; on a single 10 mm diameter rope, use four wraps.

The distance between the rappel device and the autoblock backup is critical. Too long, and the autoblock will hit the rappel device, keeping it open and preventing it from grabbing. If for some reason you become unconscious and flip upside down, the autoblock will ride up and contact your rappel device, preventing it from grabbing, much like keeping it "open" with your fingers. It's not a foolproof backup.

Some harness leg loop buckles can loosen when a carabiner is clipped into the leg loop and pulled outward. When using an autoblock with an adjustable buckle at the leg loop, clip the locking carabiner on the *inside* part of your leg loop (toward your crotch) to avoid loading the buckle.

Extend It

An alternative backup, favored by many, involves extending the rappel device with a sling and rigging the autoblock clipped to the belay loop. A simple extension can be rigged with a double-length (48-inch) sewn nylon sling threaded through both points at the front of your harness (where your rope tie-in goes through), tied off with an overhand knot (redundancy at the sling). Avoid having the rappel rope run over the sling, which can singe and weaken the webbing. Go with a fat nylon sling (18 mm or $^{11}/_{16}$-inch width) over a thin (10 mm) Dyneema sling. Nylon has a higher melting point.

Here the extension is a long quickdraw with two locking carabiners.

Other advantages of extending the belay device are that partners can rig their rappels simultaneously, hastening the descent, and you can check each other's system before rappelling.

An extended rappel device with an autoblock backup. A double-length nylon sling is threaded through both harness tie-in points and tied with an overhand knot (redundancy). The rappel device is the Black Diamond ATC XP. The autoblock knot is clipped to a locking carabiner attached to the belay loop. Note the distance between the autoblock cord and the ATC rappel device. Even if this climber flips upside down, the autoblock will remain clear of the rappel device.

Rappelling and Rope Ascending **237**

PAS

A PAS (personal anchor system) allows us to extend the device—by clipping the device into a loop near the middle of the PAS—and for the end of the PAS to be clipped to an anchor.

Regarding double rope rappels, for anyone under about 125 pounds, an autoblock may create too much friction, regardless of the device. Better to use an old-school prusik above the device. Rig the prusik so that if it tightens, you can still reach up and grab the knot. Also, carry a second prusik and sling, and know basic self-rescue rope ascension (see "Prusiking") in case the prusik grabs, locks, and you need to escape.

Conclusion

An autoblock is rarely called on to safeguard the physical act of rappelling, should we get knocked

Here the PAS (a Sterling Chain Reactor) was clipped to the anchor for a tether while the rappel rope was threaded through the rings. The rappel device was extended and clipped into a loop of the PAS with a locking carabiner. An autoblock backup was clipped to the harness belay loop with a locking carabiner. Before unclipping the PAS, go through the ABCDE (see sidebar, page 240) checklist and weight the system. If everything is A-OK, unclip the PAS from the anchor and you're good to go.

unconscious from falling objects or accidentally lose control and release our brake hand during the rappel. Such mishaps are extremely rare. Two exceptions are (1) when starting a rappel from an awkward or difficult position, like swinging off a ledge into a free-hanging rappel; and (2) when rappelling with a heavy pack. Here, the autoblock lets you stop, rest, and regroup. Moreover, an autoblock makes stopping *simple, safe,* and immediate if the rappeller needs to deal with twisted lines, a snagged end, and any of the other rappelling problems that arise for every climber some of the time. Rather than wrapping your leg with the rope in order to stop on rappel, a much simpler and effective method is the autoblock.

Common Rappelling Accidents

Guide Jason Martin wrote that it's not rappelling once or twice that's dangerous; it's rappelling all the time that leads to complacency and real danger. Because a standard rappel is so physically simple to do, safety procedures are sometimes rushed or skipped. What's more, rappelling is often the last task of the day—when you're tired, daylight is fading, and the adrenaline's gone. This is the scenario for most rappelling accidents, when the same mistakes happen time and time again, so it's crucial to review what goes wrong and the proactive methods to keep things secure.

Scenario 1: Rappelling Off One or Both Ends of the Rope

Every year someone dies by rappelling off the end of a rope, usually when the rope ends are uneven during a doubled-rope rappel, the ropes are different lengths, or one rope stretches more than the other. The technical specs vary, but the fatal factor remains the same: One of the two (occasionally *both*) rope ends doesn't reach the ground. When the short end passes through the rappelling device, only one strand of the doubled rope remains

Stopper Knot

The stopper knot

A stopper knot (aka barrel knot) is essentially half a double fisherman's knot tied on one strand of rope. A stopper knot prevents rappelling off the end of the rope while rappelling with a tube or assisted braking (e.g., Grigri) device. When using two ropes, tie separate knots at the end of each rope, as tying both ropes together can cause the ropes to twist around each other.

The stopper knot can pass through a figure eight descending ring, so if you're rappelling with that device, tie a bulkier knot.

locked off. The climber's body weight rapidly pulls the free strand through the rappel anchor, and the climber hits the ground. The solution is simple and fail-safe: Tie stopper knots separately in both ends of the rope. *Stopper knots are a default strategy. Make tying them a habit, whether you need them or not.*

Scenario 2: Not Clipping Both Strands of the Rope into the Carabiner on a Double-Rope Rappel

An easy mistake to make if you're not focused, get distracted, and fail to double-check your system. A quick glance at a tube-style device can make it appear as though both strands are properly threaded because *the bights of rope are held inside the device*, even if a bight hasn't been clipped into the carabiner behind it. If only one strand is looped through your locking carabiner, the moment you lean back and weight the rope, you'll plunge to earth. No one walks away from that kind of fall.

> ## Thread Both Bights
>
> Before starting every rappel, double-check that you have threaded *both* bights of rope through your rappel device and clipped them into your locking carabiner. If you have not, your chances of survival approach zero.

Many are the stories of experts and even instructors who failed to thread both bights through their device, leaned back, and weighted the rope, only to have one of the strands pop out of the device—the climber saved by a tether or autoblock backup (yet another reason for an autoblock).

To avoid this, first tether in with a sling to the rappel anchor, rig your rappel device, rig an autoblock backup, then weight the rappel system and double-check everything *before* unclipping the tether.

Scenario 3: Not Tethering to the Anchor

This usually happens (infrequently) on alpine climbs, when rock or snow gives way underfoot. Prevent this by using a personal tether (sling, PAS, or lanyard) clipped to the anchor with a locking carabiner. Stay clipped to the anchor as you rig your rappel device and backup, then weight your rappel device and double-check your system *before* you unclip your tether.

Scenario 4: Anchor Failure

Rappelling tests your anchor; it must be stout enough to hold the rappeller's weight plus the loading spikes that occur as you naturally slow and accelerate during your rappel. Complete anchor

> ## Rappelling Safety Checks
>
> Always go through a mental checklist before rappelling: **ABCDE.**
>
> **"A"** is the rappel *anchor* and *attachment.* Closely inspect the anchor, slings, chains, etc., confirming that the rappel rope is threaded properly through the anchor. Never rely on a single piece of gear in your anchor system—a single cord, sling, or rappel ring. Stay *attached* to the anchor (with a sling, PAS, etc.) until you've rigged your rappel device and backup, double-checked everything, and weighted your rappel device.
>
> **"B"** is for *buckles* on your harness. Double-check to make sure they are buckled properly and doubled back if necessary.
>
> **"C"** is for *carabiner* and *connections.* Make sure the locking carabiner that attaches your rappel device to your harness is loading on the long axis—and check to make sure it is locked! Press the gate with your thumb to be sure. Check all the connecting knots and links in your anchor and rope system.
>
> **"D"** is for *device.* Make sure both strands of the rappel rope are properly threaded through the device and are also threaded through the locking carabiner.
>
> **"E"** is for the rope *ends.* Do the ends reach the destination point? Do they have stopper knots? Make certain they do.

failure is usually due to chossy rock breaking away rather than the anchor components blowing out. When suddenly weighted, a detached block or loose flake simply pulls off the cliff. In another recent scenario at Tahquitz Rock, three small cams were placed in a grainy horizontal crack and rigged with a cordelette. When loaded obliquely, the entire array ripped out.

Other system failures involve improperly tied nylon webbing and lack of redundancy in the rigging. Always rig your anchor system so that you never rely on a single component, be it one sling, one hardware store quick link, or one chain link, ring, bolt, or piton. There are countless possible accidents out there involving bunk gear attached to sketchy fixed anchors. Only because most climbers are vigilant most of the time are these accidents avoided.

Multipitch Rappelling

Long multipitch routes are descended using either a single rope that is doubled (30 or 35 meters on a 60- or 70-meter rope) or two ropes tied together when you rappel the length of a standard rope (60 or 70 meters) on each rappel.

The first check on a multipitch rappel is: How good (condition and soundness) is the anchor? For popular routes, the rigging is often fixed, left by a previous team. Common anchors include two bolts, a single tree, or a solid rock bollard. The only anchor you can fully trust is the bomber one you just built. Everything else is suspect till you prove to yourself (fully examine and vet) that it is solid.

Whenever descending a long route via multiple rappels, always bring extra nylon webbing, rap rings, and a knife. You may need to cut away a nest of old slings and rerig an anchor. On obscure climbs, particularly in the mountains, you might find old nylon webbing bleached white by the sun; flip it over and the same bit of webbing is bright red. Sunlight is hell on nylon and Dyneema webbing,

SMC rap rings are light (11 g) and strong (14 kN/3,147 lbs.), a good choice for carrying on long multipitch climbs where weight is a factor and the descent will involve multiple rappels. They are a poor choice for high-use fixed anchors, as aluminum wears quickly.

so carefully inspect fixed slings before deciding to use them. If the sling is stiff and sun bleached, most of its strength is gone. If the sling is burned (blackened) where a rope was pulled across it, replace the sling. It's no good. Whenever you're not tied into the climbing rope, always secure yourself by tethering to the anchor with a nylon sling or PAS.

This natural anchor was found several hundred feet up a route on Tahquitz Rock, near Idyllwild, California. Someone had obviously rappelled from it, probably to escape a thunderstorm. Although the anchor has two basic components, each "trunk" is less than 3 inches in diameter, and the master point is a nonredundant, single aluminum rappel ring (albeit rated at 3,000 lbs.). The real problem is the size of the "tree" itself—merely a sapling.

Typical rigging found at many climbing areas: two separate 1-inch nylon webbing slings, each tied with a water knot, and two rappel rings. Although the trunk is more than 12 inches in diameter and the tree is alive and healthy, note the crack it grows out of—barely 2 inches wide! Always back up suspect anchors with a separate anchor until the last climber is down.

The first person down a multipitch rappel should expect rope tangles, especially on ledgy and bushy cliffs. Rigging an autoblock backup allows two free hands to deal with rope tangles and for clipping in when you reach the next rappel stance. An additional backup is simply to tie an overhand knot on the rope below the autoblock.

This sturdy rock bollard is attached to the main structure of the cliff, and the rigging is redundant, with two separate 1-inch tubular nylon slings and two rappel rings. Bomber.

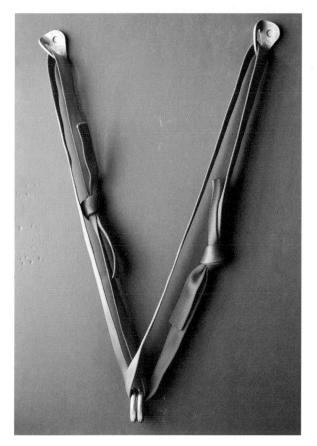

For multipitch rappelling—let us say it again—it's paramount that the rope ends are tied with stopper knots. When the first person down arrives at the next anchor, she should clip in with a sling or PAS, then unclip from the rappel device and yell "Off rappel" as a signal to let the next person know to start down. At hanging stances, the first person down should prepare the anchor with a redundant master point for all members of the team to clip into when they gain the stance. The quad system works great here.

The most common fixed anchor you'll encounter is a two-bolt anchor. An easy and bomber rappel rig is a simple V configuration. Thread two separate 5-foot lengths of nylon webbing through each bolt hanger and two rap rings, then tie each sling with a water knot.

The quad rigging allows for two separate, redundant master point clip-ins for multipitch rappelling, convenient for two-bolt anchor stations. The red sling is her rappel extension, which also serves as her personal tether. Her rappel device is at the ready for the next rappel.

Two-bolt anchor rigged with cord. Thread a length of cord (7 mm nylon here) through both bolt hangers, then tie into a loop using a figure eight bend. Pull the cord down between the bolts, tie with a figure eight loop, then add two quick links.

For multipitch rappels, many climbers don't tie the rope ends with stopper knots fearing the knots may jam in a crack, especially in windy conditions where the ropes get blown across the face. Here, tie stopper knots in the two rope ends, then butterfly coil each rope separately, draped over a sling, and clip in at both hips, holster style, letting the coils out as you rappel down.

A second method is to lower the first person on one strand while taking the other strand down as they go, until reaching the next stance. Then the second person rappels down on a doubled rope. While time-consuming, such rope management saves you time in the long run and prevents potential catastrophes.

Multipitch rappelling efficiency with a party of three on a two-rope rappel. Bob arrives first at this anchor, rigs a quad, and clips in and tethers off. Mike and Lori each rappel down and do the same. Then Bob pulls the ropes down, at the same time threading one of the ropes through the anchors for the next rappel. All three climbers clip in their rappel devices. Then Bob cleans the quad, leaving Mike and Lori pre-rigged with rappel extensions. Bob is now rappelling down to the next anchor station, where he'll set up a quad rig, clip in, then have Mike and Lori rappel, one at a time, to the station. Repeat.

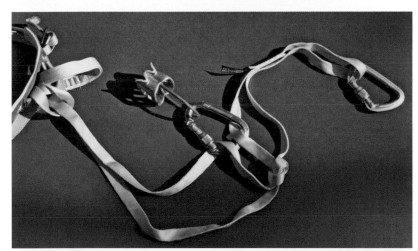

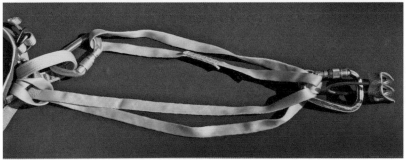

Another method for rigging a tether/rappel extension with a sling. Start with a double-length (48-inch) sling, and girth-hitch it through both tie-in points on the harness. Tie an overhand knot about halfway down the length of the sling, adjusting the knot so that when you clip it back into the harness belay loop with a locking carabiner, the length to the overhand knot is equalized. Clipping the locking carabiner of your rappel device into both loops you've created in the sling makes the sling itself redundant when it's clipped back into the harness belay loop.

Another extension method. Girth hitch a double-length nylon sling through both harness tie-in points, then tie an overhand knot halfway down the sling (on four strands of sling) for your rappel device locking carabiner clip-in point, leaving the end of the sling for an anchor clip-in point with another locking carabiner.

As the second rappels down, the first person (at the lower anchor) can pre-rig the next rappel by threading the strand (to be pulled down) through the anchor and tying a new stopper knot in the end. If the rope might snag on blocks, bushes, etc., after you pull the rope through the upper anchor, rig the two ropes so that you pull down on the thinner of the two lines. This way you'll have most of the thin rope already down before you release

Drastically Different Diameters

Beware when rapping on ropes of drastically different diameters (for example, 10.5 mm with 7 mm), and on ropes with varying degrees of stretch, such as a dynamic line paired with a static line. Otherwise the ropes can shift at the rappel anchor and change the lengths at the end points—another good reason for stopper knots. Use metal rap rings instead of rope over slings, as the friction of a shifting rope creates heat that can melt the webbing.

the other end, and the thicker rope will be last to fall. Again, a thicker rope is less likely to tangle or snag than a thinner rope.

As the second rappeler descends, she ensures that the rope is not twisting above her, which can complicate (even make impossible) the pull-down. A simple but effective trick: Take a sling attached to your harness and clip into one strand with a carabiner above your rappel device. This helps keep the strands separate and divided as you go.

When the second rappeler arrives at the stance, she clips in with her tether before unclipping from the rappel device, still holding on to the ropes. The stopper knot is untied, and the rope is pulled through the anchor. Once the rope comes down, a new stopper knot is tied in the end, and the drill is repeated.

Tandem Rappel

This technique allows two people to rappel at the same time, from the same rappel device, with one person controlling the brake hand. Primarily used in rescue scenarios, the tandem rappel also works for taking a novice on their first rappel—as with a tandem skydive, an expert controls the action. You're right there with the other person to calm his fears or, during a rescue, to offer aid. For multipitch rappelling on long alpine routes, the tandem rappel is quick and avoids rockfall caused by your partner rappelling above you.

Rigging a Tandem Rappel

To rig a tandem rappel, connect two separate slings (or a cordelette) to each rappeler's harness and clip them to the same locking carabiner at the rappel device. An MBD (like an ATC) works best. Rig an autoblock backup and attach it to your belay loop with a locking carabiner for hands-free control if you need to stop to manage rope tangles, rig an anchor, etc.

Tandem rappel setup rigged with slings. Note the autoblock backup.

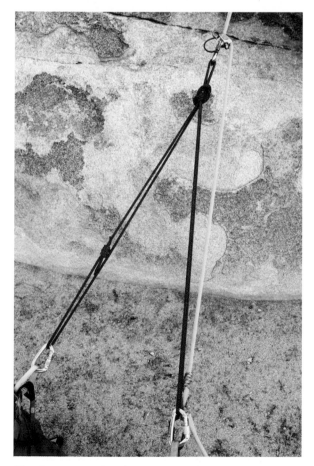

Tandem rappel setup rigged with cordelette and autoblock backup

Simul Rappel

Used by experienced climbers and military special forces when top speed is critical—and rarely if ever used when it's not. Simul (simultaneous) rappelling lets two people rappel at the same time, each on a separate strand of rope, using the other person's body and the friction at the anchor as a counterweight. The rope is typically threaded through—*not* tied off—to the anchor's master point. Rig the rope through metal rappel rings, quick links, or carabiners and not over webbing or cord—the rope may saw back and forth (due to differences in rope stretch and body weight) and burn through the webbing or cord. *The two rappelers must stay close together*, within sight of each other, watching carefully for the other person to complete the rappel

My First Simul Rap

My (BG) first simul rappel was not by choice but necessity. John Long and I had just completed the first ascent of an obscure arch formation in the Utah desert. I hand-drilled a bolt anchor for the rappel off the top, which John plucked out with his bare hands. The soft sandstone was more dirt clod than rock, so to descend with no fixed anchor—as none were possible—we were left to simul rappel off opposite sides of the slender arch. We each clipped our rappel devices into the same rope. Facing each other, eye to eye, we leaned back, the rope taut between us. We used each other's body weight as an anchor, intently mimicking each other's steps as we snailed backward, away from each other, John's eyes out on stilts as we both eased over the edge. Once the rope was firmly seated on the broad back of the arch, I breathed a sigh of relief. After descending to the open window of the arch, we enjoyed a free-hanging rappel, gently spinning in the air about 30 feet apart. A thrilling experience, but not something I would choose to repeat.

before unclipping. Unweighting one side of the rope leaves the other side unanchored. Additionally, take a long sling or cordelette and attach it to both rappelers with locking carabiners. Take utmost care with the rope ends, which absolutely must have stopper knots.

Many accidents and several deaths have occurred during simul rappels, usually resulting in a single or double fatality—accidents involving not just novices but also exceptional and renowned climbers. The general rule: ***Only experienced climbers, fully aware of all the risks and necessary precautions, should ever consider simul rappels.***

Rappelling with a Heavy Pack or Haul Bag

Rappelling with a heavy pack or a "pig" (haul bag) can be dangerous. It's also compulsory when big walls or multipitch routes require a technical descent. The weight of the pack can make a long rappel strenuous and difficult to control or, worse, flip you upside down. Once you weight the rope, the pack or bag is continuously pulling you over backward. An easy solution is to hitch a sling to the pack or haul bag, then clip it with a locking carabiner to the locking carabiner on your rappel device (carabiner to carabiner). This takes the weight off your body and puts it on the rope, which is much easier to manage.

Make certain the sling is hitched to a reinforced loop (or, better yet, two loops) on the pack. More than one climbing team has dropped all their gear when the loops on their pack blew out. Slot the pack between your legs and straddle it as you rappel, or use a long sling to rig the bag just below your feet, keeping it out of your way. The chances are high of knocking off debris when a loaded pig is dragging down the wall. So the climber with the pig raps first. And always use an autoblock backup.

Rope Management

Tossing the Rope

There is an art to tossing a rope. The key is preparation—taking a few minutes for rope management might save you hours you don't have. Several methods work well. One is to flake about half the rope (coming from the anchor) right at your feet, then butterfly coil the bottom half. Before you toss the line, check that no climbers are directly below so that you don't toss the cord onto someone's

"Rope!" *is the universal signal to be* **yelled loudly** *before tossing down a rappel rope. To prevent tangles, first butterfly coil the rope. At crowded climbing sites, when people are down below, simply lower the rope from the ends until the entire line is down.*

head. Check for loose rocks where you've flaked your rope, as the rope will launch any loose stones. If there are people directly below, yell "Rope!" and give them time to clear out before you huck the rope. At crowded crags, with people milling below, slowly lower the rope rather than hucking it. If there are trees at the base, be careful not to throw the rope too far outward and get it snagged in a tree.

Retrieving the Rope

Many people's best days of climbing have been ruined by a careless retrieval of a rappel rope. You rap to the deck after a magnificent lead and start pulling your rope to retrieve it. Just as the end of the rope passes through the rappel anchor rings, you shout "Rope!" But you didn't give fair warning, and others standing and belaying nearby can only duck as the business end bullwhips down and dashes a leg, a face, even an eye (this *does* happen).

Always be vigilant whenever pulling down a rope. If it's windy, evaluate where the rope is likely to go. If anyone is within striking distance, loudly announce that you'll soon be pulling a rappel rope. Wait for people—especially leaders on adjacent routes—to acknowledge your call, get prepared, and get out of the way *before the pull*. Calling out "Rope!" as the line comes whipping down is bad form and antagonistic. A rookie mistake—and a bad one.

1. Before pulling down the rope, look up and check for twists.

2. For long rappels, the last person—after unclipping from their rappel device—must sort out any twists and separate the two strands so that each runs straight to the anchor. You might have to walk both ends of the line out from the wall (slack allowing) to start shaking out the twists.

3. If two ropes are tied together, make certain everyone in the party is clear on which rope to pull before you head down (e.g., "pull red"). By pulling the wrong end, you are attempting to pull the connecting knot through the link or

ring at the anchor. You can't, but you might jam the rope in the process.

4. If there is any chance of rope drag chocking the pull, do a test pull after the first person rappels down. If the cord jams or can't be pulled, the top climber(s) makes necessary adjustments (e.g., a longer sling extended over an edge). Then pull-test again. The last person never raps off till you've proven via a pull test that you can retrieve the rope. A rope jam at a rappel anchor is a headache on one-pitch climbs; it's a nightmare on multipitch routes.

There is a subtle technique to pulling down a rappel rope, which takes a little practice to master—plus a few simple tricks. First double-check that there are no knots, kinks, or twists in the strand you'll be pulling up toward the anchor. Knots, in particular, will jam in the rigging. Then the only way to retrieve the rope is to re-lead the pitch or try to get to the anchor from above. Both options are hateful at the end of the day. They're generally avoidable if you stay alert.

When pulling down the line, as the free end approaches the anchor, slow your pull till you feel the weight of the descending strand (that you're pulling) start to pull the free end up toward the anchor, without your assistance. As the end passes through the anchor, make a sharp, outward tug, which jerks the end away from the wall.

A pulled rope can knock off rocks, so stay alert. If all goes well, the rope will fall without a hitch, landing on the ground in a pile. But again, the free end of the cord can generate some speed after falling 50 feet and lash like a whip—so heads up.

Dealing with Stuck Ropes

When descending big multipitch routes, stuck ropes are every climber's nightmare because they can strand you in no-man's-land. Prevention is the crucial skill, since once the ropes are stuck, your options are usually few, and most of those are *not simple* and *not safe*.

Visualizing and anticipating what might happen when you pull your rope will prevent most mishaps. Be especially vigilant not to pull your rope into a crack. With two ropes tied together, the joining knot is often the issue for the pull-down. As mentioned, a flat overhand presents a cleaner profile (with the tails pointed away from the rock) if you're worried that the knot might hang up. Twists in your rope, right at the anchor, can cause binding and make the pull-down difficult, sometimes impossible, especially if the rappel rope runs over an edge or passes over long stretches of rough rock.

When using a light "tag" line on a double-rope rappel (e.g., an 8 mm rope tied to a 10 mm rope), always retrieve the ropes by pulling the thinner line. Again, thinner-diameter ropes are much more likely to snag than fat ropes. If your rope is stuck at the anchor and you have both strands available (both strands are still through the rappel anchor), the solution is tedious but fairly straightforward: Prusik up both strands of the rope, fix the problem, and rappel back down (see "Prusiking").

The worst-case scenario is when you are left with a single strand and the rope is jammed somewhere above or to the side. Your few options are as dangerous as they are unavoidable. You can use what rope you have, if any, to lead up (placing protection as you go) and hopefully reach the jam. If you're on the ground with little cord available, you can either hike to the top, rappel in from above (if possible), or leave the cord and return with another rope and re-lead up to the jammed one. If the rope end jams at

Scenario from Hell

You're 800 feet down a 1,600 foot descent, and one end of the rope jams fast in the anchor above. The rappel route does not follow the climbing route, instead descending holdless rock you can climb only by bolting, you're out of bolts, and rescue is impossible. After exhausting all other options, you and your partner both tie in to the stuck line and, using your full weight, violently bounce on the stuck line—but it holds fast. What can you do?

The following is what Noah Müller and Mateo Bollinger did when they found themselves in this hellish scenario after climbing a 3,000-foot new route on Baffin Island in the Canadian Arctic and chose to descend a shorter, 1,600-foot wall on the flanks. After rappelling 800 feet, they went to pull the rope through the last anchor, but it jammed fast and couldn't be retrieved. They had already lost two ropes (rockfall) during the nine-day ascent and needed the stuck line—their only remaining rope—to get off. They had to get creative, or perish.

Mateo anchored the rope to the lower belay anchor with 25 feet of slack in the line, and started prusiking up the jammed line, tying an overhand knot in the rope and clipping it into his harness with a locking carabiner. Every 25 feet, the rope came tight beneath him, and he swapped out the knot with a new one tied higher on the 25-foot loop he was trailing. He kept repeating this process for 100 desperate feet, managing to set a few cams in meager cracks and clipping in the stuck line below the prusik. If the rope pulled through the anchor and the prusik held, Mateo would fall twice the distance to his last pro, and 30 percent more for rope stretch. Luckily, the rope stayed jammed for what had to be the longest prusik every done. At the high anchor at last, Mateo clipped it off with a tether—then dedicated his life to helping widows and orphans because he had just cheated death. The likelihood of this ever happening is one in a million, but that's what Mateo did when he had to.

Again, be aware that many rockfall accidents occur when a rappel rope is pulled down a cliff. Sometimes the rope jams behind blocks or loose rocks, and the vigorous pulling to free the rope launches a barrage.

The Reepschnur Method

The Reepschnur method is an uncommon rigging technique used to block a rappel rope when two ropes are tied together, allowing you to rappel on a single strand yet still retrieve your rope. It is a useful technique to know in case one of your ropes gets seriously damaged (exposed core, aka core-shot) so that you can rappel the full length of the non-damaged rope and still retrieve everything. If you're using just one rope and your rope is core-shot, rig the Reepschnur to isolate the bad half of the rope, and rappel down a single line on the good half.

The Reepschnur also allows you to rappel with your Grigri on a single strand. The larger rope is threaded through the anchor and tied to the thinner line with a flat overhand—or a bulkier knot if needed. Remember, the knot must be bulky enough to jam into the rappel rings, chain links, or quick links. Below the jamming knot, a figure eight loop is tied on the thinner line and clipped to the rappel strand with a locking carabiner. **This critical backup is absolutely necessary and is the key to securely rappelling with the Reepschnur method.**

The Reepschnur knot block. This technique allows you to rappel on a single line using a Grigri (in this example, on the right strand), retrieving your rope by pulling on the left strand.

The Reepschnur method. The blue rope is the rappel line and the green line is the tag line for retrieval. Always tie a safety backup—shown here with a figure eight loop clipped into the rappel strand with a locking carabiner. If the overhand knot pulls through the rings, your rappel line will still be attached.

Rappelling a single fixed line with a Grigri. If you take your brake hand off the rope, tie an overhand loop as a backup knot, as shown here. If the Grigri slips (as it will when unweighted), the knot will jam.

up the rope and clipping it into liberal protection placed *below* the prusiks. So long as you keep the prusiks ahead of you, keeping the jammed rope taut above you, if the rope does pull through, you fall twice the distance to your last piece of pro and—Sky Chief willing—the prusiks, and the pro, will hold. Then you double up a couple of good pieces—or build an anchor if you can—and lower to the lower anchor, thanking your lucky stars that you survived.

If the rappel does not follow the climbing route and instead descends holdless rock climbable only by bolting, you don't have a bolt kit, and rescue is impossible, you're left with an unthinkable option: prusiking up the single strand with rope jammed on who knows what. In real-world climbing, there is almost no chance of this ever happening. But it has, and climbers have still escaped. If you're curious how, read the sidebar "Scenario from Hell" and weep.

Improvised Rope Ascending

Prusiking

"Prusiking" is a generic term for ascending a rope using friction hitches, weighted by your body. Since the prusik knot was the first friction hitch used for ascending fixed ropes, the practice is still called prusiking, even when other friction hitches are used.

Improvised rope ascending skills are indispensable after taking a leader fall on an overhanging route that leaves you hanging in midair, or when you fall off a traversing climb and can't clamber back onto the route. In either case, the way out is to prusik back up the line to your last piece of protection, hoping it holds.

Your rope tie-in is your backup if the friction hitches slip; as an additional backup, tie an overhand loop below the prusiks and clip it into your belay loop with a locking carabiner.

the anchor during a big multipitch descent, a rescue might be indicated. Otherwise, you must work with what you have.

You have a rope fixed, however poorly, to the last anchor point. If the descent (rappel route) follows the climbing route, you still have a chance at self-rescue. By anchoring the free end to the lower anchor, prusik knots can be attached to the jammed rope and you can ascend the rope by prusiking

Prusik and Klemheist

A *prusik knot* is used for rope ascending and as a component in many rescue systems. It can be loaded in either direction. To tie a prusik, first make a *prusik cord* out of a 4-foot length of 5 mm or 6 mm diameter nylon cord tied into a loop with a double fisherman's knot. Buy the softest, most pliable nylon cord you can find; softer cord grips best. To tie the prusik, make a girth-hitch around the rope with your cord, then pass the loop of cord back through the original girth-hitch two or three more times. Dress the knot so that all strands are even and untwisted—a sloppy friction hitch will not grip as well. Test the knot before using it. A thinner cord will grip better, but below 5 mm in diameter, the cord will be too weak for many applications. To slide the prusik after it has been weighted, loosen the "tongue," the one strand opposite all the wraps.

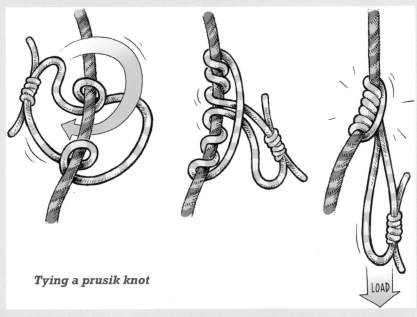

Tying a prusik knot

Tests on various friction hitches reveal that the prusik consistently has the most holding power in a wide array of cord and rope combinations.

The *klemheist knot* is quick and easy to tie, and is a good choice as a rope-ascending friction hitch if all you have available is a sling rather than an appropriate piece of cord. With cord, a 5 mm or 6 mm diameter soft nylon cord will work best. A 4-foot length tied with a double fisherman's knot gives you about a 16-inch loop. When using a sling, go with nylon (18 mm, or ¹¹/₁₆-inch width) over a Dyneema sling; again, nylon grips better and has a higher melting point. With either a sling or cord, four wraps tied on a single 10 mm diameter rope usually work well (three wraps for a doubled rope). After the hitch has been weighted, loosen the tongue (the one strand opposite all the wraps) to slide it more easily. The klemheist is configured to be loaded only in one direction.

A three-wrap prusik

Prusiking is an invaluable technique to sort out rappelling snafus, like when a shirt tail or hank of hair jams in your rappel device. You cannot move till you fix the problem, and you have to unweight your rappel device to do so. If the rappel is low angle, it may be as simple as standing on the rock to unweight your rappel device then teasing out the jam. On steep or overhanging rappels, you'll need to perform a basic self-rescue.

First back up your brake hand; you'll need two free hands to perform this maneuver. If you are using an autoblock backup, slide the autoblock up until it engages. If you don't have an autoblock backup

rigged, a simple and fast backup is the leg wrap (see photo on page 232). Better yet, tie an overhand loop on the rope *below you* and clip it to your belay loop with a locking carabiner. Tie a friction hitch (e.g., prusik or klemheist) on the rope about 1 foot above your device, then take a double-length (48-inch) sling, or two 24-inch slings girth-hitched together, and clip it to the friction hitch. Stand in the sling so you can unweight your device. Don't grab the friction hitch itself, which might slide down the rope. Don't wait for a rappelling epic to learn this simple technique. Take a half hour and practice—time well spent should things ever go south on a rappel.

Tying the Klemheist Knot with Cord

Other scenarios: You've completed a double-rope rappel, start to pull one strand down (to retrieve your rope), but the cord won't budge. There are rope twists just below the anchor, or one strand (typically an end) has wedged tight in a crack. Or you're on a multipitch rappel and cannot find the next anchor because you've rappelled *past* it. Or your rope is too short to reach the next ledge or anchor. In all these cases, and many more, you're dealing with a doubled rope (two stands), which you'll need to prusik back up to sort out the problem.

The best method is simply to tie friction hitches around *both strands of rope*. A prusik or klemheist knot are the knots of choice for rope ascending. If you don't have any prusik cord (a 5 mm or 6 mm soft nylon cord works best) and only have slings, go with the klemheist. Rig your friction hitch with a nylon sling; nylon grips better and has a higher melting point than Dyneema.

There are several prusiking methods, but the fastest, simplest rig requires the least amount of gear: two prusik cords, three regular length (24-inch) slings, and three locking carabiners.

The Basic Setup

Tie two separate friction hitches—the top one attached directly to your harness with a 24-inch sling, the other used with a foot sling (also attached to your harness with a sling). You ascend via a simple, inchworm-like technique. Stand on the bottom sling and slide the top friction hitch as high as you can reach, then immediately sit back in your harness, with your weight on the top friction hitch. Now move the bottom friction hitch up until your leg (in the foot sling) is bent at a 90-degree angle at the knee. Stand up in the sling, using your hands for balance by grabbing the rope with both hands below the top friction hitch. Then slide the top friction hitch up again as high as you can reach. Don't grab the body of the friction hitch itself—this can loosen the hitch and cause it to slide down the rope.

This sounds complicated, and is awkward to perform, but the technique is mastered quickly with a bit of practice. And it absolutely works. During the early years of Yosemite big wall climbing, before the advent of mechanical ascenders (c. 1960), most every lead was followed by prusiking.

To back up the friction hitches, take both rope strands together and tie an overhand loop below the friction hitches, then clip the loop into your harness belay loop with a locking carabiner. This is known as "clipping in short" and should be done at regular intervals (every 15 feet or so) when ascending a long way. Should your friction hitch fail (very rare), you fall to the last knot you tied in and clipped off on the very rope you're ascending.

Prusik rig with cord. The top cord was rigged by taking a 5-foot length of 6 mm nylon cord and tying a loop in both ends, with the top loop large enough to tie a prusik knot. The bottom length of cord is 11 feet long, tied with loops on both ends and a larger loop in the middle to accommodate the prusik knot.

Demonstration of basic prusiking technique to ascend a double rope, as in a stuck rappel rope scenario. With the top friction hitch slid as high up the rope as possible, hang in your harness and put your foot in the sling attached to the lower friction hitch. Stand up in the foot sling and slide the top friction hitch as high up the rope as you can (left), then hang in your harness and repeat the process (right). As a backup, tie an overhand loop on both strands and clip it to your harness belay loop with a locking carabiner.

Ascending a Single Fixed Rope

The method just described applies to prusiking a doubled rope. The thinner diameter of a single fixed rope requires additional friction, so add an extra wrap to your friction hitch. When ascending a doubled 10 mm diameter rope, two wraps of your prusik cord (i.e., four strands) is often enough. On a single cord, three wraps (six strands) are usually best. When ascending a single 10 mm diameter rope with a klemheist knot (with either cord or sling), four wraps are usually the call.

A very simple system will work to ascend a single-strand fixed rope using an ABD (like a Petzl Grigri) or an autoblocking belay/rappel device like the Petzl Reverso or Black Diamond ATC Guide.

1. Clip the Grigri or ABD device into your harness belay loop. If you're using an autoblocking belay device, clip it into your harness belay loop in the autoblocking mode.

2. Tie a friction hitch (prusik or klemheist) on the rope above your device, and attach a 48-inch foot sling to the friction hitch.

3. Slide the friction hitch up until your leg is bent 90 degrees at the knee.

4. Grab the rope above you with your non-brake hand and stand up in the sling, simultaneously pulling the rope through the device at your waist by pulling straight up on the brake strand with your brake hand.

5. Sit back and rest in your harness on the locked-off device.

6. When you're hanging in your harness, slide the friction hitch up again until your knee is bent at a 90-degree angle. Repeat the process.

Tying a slip hitch for your sling foot helps your foot stay put. As a backup, clip in short every 15 feet or so by tying a figure eight loop and clipping it into your harness belay loop with a locking carabiner.

This is an easy and quick method for a short rope ascent, but if you plan on extensive fixed-line ascending, mechanical ascenders are the way to go. In real-world climbing, nobody prusiks for anything but short distances; even then, mechanical ascenders are always favored. Prusiking is an emergency method, where the use of ascenders was not anticipated and they are unavailable.

Having the right tools in your self-rescue "toolbox" will allow you to perform improvised rope ascension no matter the scenario.

Lisa Rands demonstrates ascending a fixed line with a friction hitch and a Grigri. As she straightens out her left leg and stands up, she'll pull up on the brake-strand side of the rope above the Grigri then sit in her harness, tight to the Grigri, as she slides the klemheist back up.

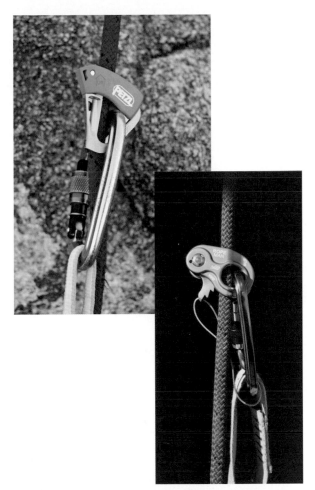

Mini ascenders like the Petzl Tibloc (left) and the Wild Country Ropeman (right) are much faster and more efficient than friction hitches for rope ascending.

Conclusion

The science and performance art of descending a big multipitch route are a little like building a bombproof belay anchor. Precautions are built into the system for dangers we'll likely never face; the safety checks and protocols are in place in case we do. Since we've schooled ourselves on the crucial techniques, self-rescue is likely. Other climbers have escaped most every imaginable jam, and so will we.

Yet for all the refinement of equipment and techniques, our *simplest and safest* defense against mishaps is educated vigilance: We know, and stay alert, for the danger signs, and take proactive measures to stay this side of trouble.

Rocks still fall. Lines still hang up. The sky would fall if it could. But the vast majority of mishaps are avoidable if we know what we are doing, stay alert, communicate, and continually double-check each other's systems.

CHAPTER 14

Multipitch Climbing

A layman, glancing at this text, might imagine climbing as a curious fusion of engineering and gymnastics. Multipitch climbing includes much more. Sport climbing is all about control—the protection, the temperature, the rock surface, our performance. If one of these factors is not ideal, our chances of success decrease. In this sense, completing a hard (for you) sport climb is a command performance made possible by controlled conditions. A big multipitch climb is more like a voyage into unknown waters, where much is out of our immediate control. Even with a detailed topo map (see sidebar), the process and the outcome are unpredictable. We might *have* to climb wet rock, battle cold and wind, traverse loose terrain, route-find, lead off sketchy protection, and tackle cruxes when dog-tired —conditions that put a hold on most sport climbing till the conditions improve. They call it "adventure climbing" for a reason, and the practice addresses a unique human need that stretches across time and was first met, perhaps in France, many centuries ago.

Spread throughout the European Alps, villages big and small are nestled between spectacular mountains. These mountains were always more than lyrical backdrops to the generations of villagers who lived and died in their shadows. They were cultural landmarks in the river of time that bore all forms away, and the shrouded summits were reminders.

Few peaks caught the eye like 6,841-foot-high Mont Aiguille, a flat-topped limestone mesa soaring off the Vercors Massif in the French Prealps. Its first ascent in 1492 marks the birth of mountaineering. But the practice didn't catch fire till 1786, when Jacques Balmat and Dr. Michel-Gabriel Paccard first climbed Mont Blanc, the highest mountain in the Alps. Ever after, the rush was on, and major peaks were climbed in succession. The summit was the ultimate goal of the alpine pioneers, and their feats, like the mountains themselves, remained touchstones for human imagination—for climbers and laymen alike.

Take El Capitan, the gray granite monolith in Yosemite Valley, California. The early paintings of Albert Bierstadt and Thomas Hill, the photos of Carlton Watkins and, later, Ansel Adams, to mention a few, burned El Cap into human consciousness, where it has lived as the ne plus ultra of natural magnitude. Every spring, summer, and fall, much as pilgrims venture to Mecca, tourists pour into Yosemite from the four corners, wander out into El Cap meadow, gape up at the Big Stone, and, with a rush of affirmation, encounter that universal sense of a shared past and present, staking their claim in a collective ethos greater than themselves. El Capitan is not an attraction but a convergence point for the great unknown.

Many climbers, like many tourists, are pleased to regard the big peaks from afar. For those like Jacques Balmat and Dr. Michel-Gabriel Paccard, who need a huge experience and a summit to remember, the means to both is multipitch trad climbing. The "why" is not so terribly mysterious.

Caroline Gleich on Sasquatch (5.9+), Little Cottonwood Canyon, Utah
PHOTO BY JOHN EVANS

An ordinary citizen might watch a climber scale an impossibly difficult sport route and applaud the leader's physical virtuosity, though the reason and significance of such a climb would likely be lost on them. But when the same citizen sees great stone monoliths like the north face of Cima Grande in the Italian Dolomites, Patagonia's 5,000-foot-high Fitz Roy, or Yosemite's northwest face of Half

Jim Bridwell scoping out new route possibilities on El Capitan, Yosemite Valley, 1970s
PHOTO BY MIKE GRAHAM

El Capitan

Dome veiled in ancient shade, some part of them knows why people should climb them, that they represent the no-man's-land that has fascinated and challenged human beings for all time. This is the promised land of big multipitch climbing, there for those who hear the calling.

Once you learn the multipitch ropes and can climb at a 5.10 standard (which most active climbers can achieve), 90 percent of the world's classic rock climbs are open to you. It's fair game from Yosemite Valley to Patagonia (aka The End of the World). A big classic, one we can dream on, pulls us from the future like a polestar, with a gravity all its own. For the inveterate trad climber, no matter the chaos of our dog days, an iconic summit always glimmers in the distance.

A Typical Topo Map

A classic trad route is more easily imagined than explained. Little of that experience is conveyed in topo maps (a schematic line drawing depicting the physical details of a climb), stories, or the methods described in this manual. The closest we can get is the ubiquitous trip report, a first-person account of a specific team scaling a particular route. Trip reports describe the personal adventure, the challenges encountered, and the solutions the team used to meet them. They're also a vivid, practical medium to demonstrate the roped safety system we've explored through the last thirteen chapters.

To that end, the following conjured trip report—a fictional team climbing a fantasy route, ostensibly in Sequoia National Park (Southern Sierras, California)—will serve as our viewfinder to see multipitch trad climbing in action. Here, pitch by pitch, through the eyes of an experienced team of two, all the information, the countless devices and techniques we have covered so far, will finally come together like pieces of a jigsaw puzzle.

Trip Report

High Times on Fuego: The Watchtower, Sequoia National Park, California (Grade IV, 5.10c)
By Troy Chalmers

Fuego (Spanish for "fire") was first climbed in 1968 by High Sierra icons Vic de Saussure and José "Pepe" Delmonico in a legendary four-day epic. The route remained a seldom-done, sixteen-pitch wilderness big wall till 1984, when Jim Martini and Dave Goldfarb free-climbed it in one long day. Ever since, Fuego has served as a rite of passage for West Coast trad climbers.

Twice I'd planned to climb the route, and the plans fell through both times. Then, over Christmas break, I ran into Rose O'Shaughnessy out at Echo Cliffs, and Rose suggested we team up for Fuego sometime that spring. Rose is a converted gym climber and promised to handle the notoriously runout face climbing, as long as I led the wide cracks. I've climbed on and off with Rose for years, and it has always been good, even when it's bad. She had a deal.

Right after New Year's I went to Rose's place, where we studied the Fuego topo and considered logistics. If we hiked in and bivouacked at the base and the route went well, we figured to on-sight Fuego in around 8 hours. The hike out from the summit follows a twisting trail along the southern rim, which most parties managed in 4 to 5 hours, which put us at 13 hours for the day, barring any hitches— and there are always hitches. We'd want the longest days possible before the blast-furnace months of June through August. We got a calendar and picked a date: May 14. We had four months to pull it all together.

Over the rest of the winter I spent part of each outing climbing the kind of pitches found on Fuego, from slabs to those wide cracks. This kept a little attention on the project. We'd also made two lists—one for rope and gear, the other for personal stuff. I had to buy a few things but found them on sale. I blinked, and it was May. We were ready.

We decided to drive up (4 hours from Los Angeles) and hike to the base on Thursday, then go for the send on Friday. That gave us the best shot of avoiding other parties, which (we heard) are swarming over Fuego most spring weekends. A couple of nights before pulling the trigger, we organized the rack and our personal gear, so when Rose swung by on Thursday morning, I just chucked my rucksack into her van and we motored up the 405. The trail at the top of Fuego winds back to the trailhead, not the base of the wall, so I'd recruited my cousin Barny to join us on the approach. When Rose and I went for the send, Barny would schlep out our bivy gear to the roadhead so we didn't have to slog back to the base to fetch it. Rose favors house music, as does Barny, so they kept it cranked all the way to Sequoia. When we finally arrived, I was so jacked I could have hiked to the Bugaboos. Would have made it too.

We parked in Buckeye Campground and hit the trail around noon. I carried a big bag of food, and we ate and guzzled water like crazy. After a mile we rounded a bend and the north face of The Watchtower came into view—a moody gray 1,700-foot arête, rearing like a citadel off the southern escarpment. For a moment we stood and stared, and life got very real. The cracks and dihedrals of Fuego were clear and striking. The rest of the way hiking in, we kept sussing out the line, checking that roof and that corner against the topo we'd saved on our phones. The closer we got, the more badass Fuego looked.

We camped at the traditional bivy spot, by a small creek 0.25 mile from the base. Luckily, we had it to ourselves and wouldn't have to contend with other parties on the wall. The weather report said partially cloudy skies next afternoon, but the night was clear. I kept drinking and eating till I passed out around midnight. Hard to knock off in the shadow of a big one, plus Barny snored like a leaf blower. Rose was asleep by 8 o'clock because she's like that.

We stoked the stove at 4:30 a.m. and started pounding coffee, water, and food—enough to take us into afternoon if it had to. We'd carry 3 quarts of water and a can of fruit juice, two sandwiches, and a bunch of energy gel packets stuffed into our pockets. We were climbing on a single 70-meter (230-ft.) rope. Most of the pitches were 100 feet or less, so we could probably get off on the one long line if we had to. The second would carry a small crag pack.

The hike from the bivy site to the base took 10 minutes under headlamps, and by the time we got rigged up, cinched on our helmets, and tied in, Rose had enough light to start up the first pitch—20 feet of difficult friction to a rusty ¼-inch bolt. For all the traffic on Fuego, you'd think someone would have replaced the damn bolt, but never count on it. Rose floated the slab, clipped the bolt with a single locking carabiner, then more dicey friction to a thin crack with an old baby angle welded to the eye. Rose didn't trust the pin and backed it up with several wires she rigged with a sliding X. A hundred feet of finger locking brought her to a small ledge. I started up.

When I reached the small belay ledge, the rope was neatly pancake-stacked by Rose's feet, and the gear I'd need for the next pitch was clipped to a sling on the anchor. Belay hygiene, I call it, and Rose was great at it—keeping the belays simple, efficient, and organized. It's easy to burn a couple of minutes at a belay, futzing with tangles and jumbled gear. We do that here, on a sixteen-pitch route, and we're a half an hour down when we reach the summit.

I clipped off the pack, snapped the gear onto my harness, and started traversing right, Rose keeping a semi-taut line so that the rope didn't slip behind my legs as I climbed into a left-facing corner and the start of a chimney that shot up for 300 feet.

I'd normally try for some multidirectional pro before wrestling that chimney, but the rope drag would get fierce after a dead-right traverse, and I didn't want to take the time and drop back down to back-clean. The topo called the chimney 5.9, which I can comfortably solo, so I crawled inside and started up. The only pro was my body squeezed into the crack, and I had to run the line 50 feet

Peter Croft leading Sidewinder (5.10c) at Joshua Tree. Note the use of long runners to reduce rope drag, and how the rope runs outside his right leg, not between his legs. To better protect his follower, he's decided to climb a bit higher before he places his next piece.

before I could sling a chockstone. Then more of the same to a monster chockstone and a belay on top from three fixed pins. I considered a direct belay, but this was alpine rock, so I played it safe and went indirect.

Above the first chockstone, the chimney narrowed and gave Rose grief with that pack on her back. I thought about Pepe Delmonico leading this pitch like a hundred years ago in lug-soled boots and was glad I was born when I was. Rose mantled onto the big chockstone and I got

Roy McClennehan on (or in) 1096, a 5.10d in Yosemite Valley, 1980s

But this is the only place we'd need a big cam, and they're awkward as hell to carry. Plus "the wide" (off-width climbing) was my thing, and I'd cranked a stack of them all winter long out at Josh. But now I wanted that cam and didn't have it.

The bigger issue was the fixed pin, jammed with so much tat (old slings), I couldn't clip the eye. Hanging from an arm bar, knee jacked in the crack, I fished a thin folding knife out of my front pocket, cut away the tat, clipped the pin with a quickdraw, and pressed on. The crack was unrelenting, but it narrowed a few times where I could place a cam and rest off a fist jam. All told, it was a classic pumper

Desert off-width
PHOTO BY JOHN EVANS

the rack together, both of us peering up at what seemed like a towering buttress of carbon steep, narrowing as it went, 1,500 feet to go. These early moments on big routes always grip and spin me, since I can never get my head around climbing the whole megillah all at once. But I could probably manage the next pitch, and that's how it went all the way up—sparked and spooked at every belay. I imagine most diehard trad climbers thrive on that experience. I know I do, and so does Rose. We were *en Fuego*.

Just above, the chimney narrowed to an off-width crack and stayed that way to the top of the dihedral, 120 feet overhead. Many thought this was the physical crux of the route, less so the climbing than the 20 unprotected feet getting to a fixed pin on the outside of the corner. This was my lead as well. Rose put me on, and I plugged into the off-width crack and started chugging upward.

I could have protected this crack with a mega cam, even toggled it up as I went, essentially enjoying a toprope.

pitch that ended on a tabletop ledge above the corner, one of the few real ledges on the route.

Rose loathes wide cracks, but the lip was sharp and the angle off-vertical, so I yelled down to forget the jamming—just lieback the thing. That's what Rose did, and

with her strength and balance, she was up the crack in no time, pausing only to clean the cams. I'd never try liebacking on the lead, but anything goes on the TR. Still, a long pitch of having her feet pasted up by her hands fairly withered Rose; when she held out her arms, they were bloated like a largemouth bass, taut to the touch. We took 5, drank a little water, and checked the topo; then Rose racked up and cast off.

The next pitch was disjoined and funky, starting with a hand traverse across a shelf with a crack in the back. There were several old fixed pins, but when clipped with

Four-piece multipitch anchor rigged with a cordelette. The bottom two cams, rigged in opposition with clove hitches, make this anchor multidirectional—good for downward, upward, and outward pulls.

Three-piece multipitch, multidirectional anchor rigged with a cordelette. The bottom cam is set for an upward pull.

Not bomber, but cinching down a bolt stud with a stopper cable works in a pinch to provide a modicum of protection.

quickdraws, the rope-end carabiner was set on the edge of the shelf; Rose clipped them off with longer alpine draws and pressed on.

A mantle put her on top of the shelf and a bolt, but some knucklehead had fleeced the hanger. Rose pushed the cable out the top of a big stopper, cinching it down on the stud, then attached a quickdraw—not ideal, but the rope didn't dislodge the stopper as she ran the rope over letterbox jugs to an old bolt ladder from the first ascent, which Rose pulled past perfunctorily at mid-5.10, careful not to Z-clip six closely spaced bolts. Then came a vertical face spangled with big knobs that she girth-hitched with double runners till she reached another stance and belayed off a fixed angle and two cams, butterfly-coiling the line as I followed, glad it was Rose's lead not mine. Damn, what a pitch! Pretty much vert the whole way with jugs in the middle, like swinging on a sky-high jungle gym.

Pitches 5 and 6 followed straight-in twin cracks that gobbled nuts but wandered so much I had to extend half the pieces with slings—and still had to downclimb and back-clean three of them, the rope drag got so bad. Pitch 6 ended at the start of a parallel-sided 1-inch crack. I couldn't skunk Rose and use all the same-size gear to build the

anchor, leaving her nothing for the 1-inch crack above. So I set a bomber #4 Camalot and used a stopper and bigger cam, well retracted, to flesh out the anchor. The pitch had wandered, so to compensate for the changing direction of pull, I rigged the belay with a quad. *Simple and safe.*

Then the infamous Fissure de Saussure, a laser-cut 5-inch gash splitting an otherwise featureless wall. A butt shot of Vic de Saussure, maybe 30 unprotected feet off the belay, half his body stuffed into the fissure, was featured on an old cover of *Summit Magazine* and gave decades of climbers the willies just looking at it. Vic, in a generational lead, only managed a couple of lousy bongs hammered into the back of the narrowing crack, which even now is rated a solid 5.10. We're lucky to have cams, which fit nicely in the bowels of that classic incision. I got by with four cams in the burly 60-foot thrasher and belayed from the only tree on the route—and big ups to Victor.

No way to lieback this one—or to climb it with a pack on—so I lowered a loop of lead rope down to Rose, hand-hauled up the pack, and Rose set to work. It took her a while, and she struggled cleaning one of the cams, which had walked back into the crack. But she was hell-bent on climbing the thing clean, and she did, though it cost her a big weeping raspberry on the back of her right shoulder and a hole in the hip of her tights, exposing a small black rose artfully tattooed onto her hip.

Rose was gasping, but she threw back her head and, in a heartfelt shout-out to the old pioneer, yelled, "Vic de Saussure can kiss my ass!"

"Or that black rose," I said. She slapped a hand over the hole and the rose and said, "Creep . . ."

"Give any dude half a chance . . ."

"Are you still here?" she laughed, jutting her chin at the rock just above.

"It's your lead, Rosemary."

"I need a minute," she said, and we took our first proper break, finishing the first quart of water and splitting one of the sandwiches and a tab of energy gel.

We'd only climbed seven of the sixteen pitches, but the topo indicated we were halfway up the wall—in a little less than 4 hours. And having a blast. Cool thing about Fuego is how it follows the only crack system up a smooth, vertical

Two-bolt anchor on a multipitch climb rigged with a quad. Here the leader will shortly embark on a short traverse to the right before any pro can be had. He's clipped his rope directly to the master point, so if he falls, the belayer should brace for a pull straight in to the wall.

fin of rock that pushes you out into space. Not every big route has the feel of a genuine big wall, but Fuego did, and I could feel it in every cell of my body.

Rose racked up and started stemming up pitch 8, a steep right-facing open book on swirled orange granite. I'd led the last three pitches, all wide stuff, so the next three belonged to Rose. At the end of pitch 8, the route disappeared around a corner. Rose traversed out of sight, took a look, came back, and yelled down that the belay was 20 feet above. Three stout tugs on the rope meant she was off belay—in case I couldn't hear her around the corner. I'd be on belay when the rope came fully tight. Luckily, I could hear her "Off belay!" but either way we had a plan to confirm the status of the belay. Without that, you got nothing.

Pitch 9 followed a shallow corner arching right, which the topo called the "leading crux" and which Rose styled with fingertip liebacking and arachnid face moves, deftly working smears and edges on both sides of the arch. Getting solid pro looked fiddly and strenuous. The shallow crack flared and leaned so much, Rose could rarely look straight into it to set gear, making most of her placements blind. We'd brought a couple of offset cams and TCUs (three-cam units), and Rose was glad to have these

because four-lobe cams didn't fit. There were several fixed pins, old and rusty. No way to ever make that lead perfectly secure, so Rose did the next best thing and sewed it up. It took her 40 minutes to lead the 80-foot pitch, and when I finally clawed onto her small stance, I told her I probably couldn't have led it free. I'd have sketched out and grabbed the pins—or something. Rose scoffed, and I said to let it be true, because it was.

The wind started gusting, and as Rose racked up for the next lead, some stones rattled down the face a ways out left. Then a second barrage, much closer, whizzed past like meteors. Nothing freezes my blood like rockfall. The heinous sound triggers some primitive fear and the impulse to run for it. Except you can't. You're lashed to the wall and powerless. Lucky for us, the next lead passed through a big roof you tunnel through at 5.8, so the roof sheltered us from the rocks—but we'd be right in the line of fire up above. Scared as we were, we didn't want to bail. Rose thought maybe we should wait a bit and see if the wind died down. Shortly it did. Probably not the safest decision, but we pressed on.

Rose slithered into the tunnel, maybe 20 feet off the belay, first doubling up on pro in case there was none above. She popped back out up higher and stormed up a hand crack, pausing on knobs and big footholds to slot a cam or wired nut. Pitch 10 ended on a tapering ledge that cut into the final corner, 60 feet straight left. Rose built an anchor off the crack behind the ledge and brought me up. The wind was gone. No more rocks hissing past, but I could still hear their echo and was jumpy as a rattler.

We were 6 hours in with six pitches to go, none harder than 5.9. That put us about an hour ahead of schedule, so we kicked back on the ledge and ate and drank, dangling our legs off the brink of the big drop, peering down at 1,000 feet of Fuego plunging into void.

The earth, as seen from up high, pulls at your guts and can scatter your mind. We'd battled up for hours, but the summit remained a vanishing point, never getting closer as solid ground fell further away, till it seemed we were adrift in a sea of rock. This uncanny feeling—that we were flying away from land and from all that's safe and known, yet somehow were making no progress at all—was maybe the reason so many climbers had bailed off Fuego, evidenced by all the tat in the fixed anchors.

We checked the topo, spotting our location way up the wall and feeling good about ourselves—till Rose spotted the black cloud bearing in from the west. Lightning came first, then one big rumbling blast of thunder. Then it was pissing down like a showerhead. We fished out our rain jackets and hunkered down—and all I could think about were more rocks washing onto our heads.

It only rained for 15 minutes—just a freak spring thundershower, common in the Sierras. The wind died but the cloud hung around, so I sloshed across the traverse, moving the belay to the base of the final corner, slick as glass from eons of runoff. Though only a 5.7, so much water still streamed down the corner that we were an hour *behind* schedule by the time I took the lead, but Rose wouldn't feed out any slack. I growled. She snickered and said, "Wipe your feet off, Tarzan."

The soles of my shoes were wet and muddy, and I hadn't even noticed. I took a couple deep breaths to slow myself down, glanced over at Rose, and said, "Watch me here . . . if you wanna learn something."

"You're very welcome," she said. I cleaned off my feet and started up.

Several sections were wet, and I had to bridge way on the outside of the chimney, barely staying on, to move past—my only pro far below and set deep in the soaking maw. After 90 feet I slithered onto a shattered terrace and a horizontal crack fixed with three solid angle pitons welded into diamond-hard rock. I set up a direct belay with an autoblocking device, and Rose grappled up the chimney with the pack (much lighter now), once more hanging off a sling from her belay loop. Rose was pretty worked, and we had to hustle to make up time, so I took the next lead as well—another burly flare, mostly dry. There were several loose flakes that I had to climb around rather than risk yanking them off on Rose.

After 100 feet I gained a small stance, and the best anchor I could manage—the only one possible in the grainy groove—was off three manky cams. I rigged them up with a quad and went with an indirect belay so that my stance and my body could absorb any fall force if

Rose came off. While Rose thrutched up the flare, I stayed braced so that no force would go onto the anchor, even though I was clove-hitched tight to the master point for stability.

We double-checked the topo, but the way was obvious: 5.8 face climbing up and right across big loose boilerplates to a hand crack maybe 20 feet away. The face was unprotected, and if the leader came off, they'd take a factor-2 fall straight onto our manky belay anchor. Running the line over 5.8 face didn't bother me much, but yanking on those creaky boilerplates just after it rained felt sketchy as hell. If we were down low, or anywhere but 1,300 feet up a 1,700-foot wall, we would have bailed. But the climb was giving us no choice. And I wasn't at all sure how to best manage the situation.

Rose did, and I watched as she rigged an indirect belay, adjusted her stance to brace with her legs for a downward force, then pulled up 25 feet of slack below her belay device and tied an overhand knot (as a catastrophe knot) just in case Lady Luck wasn't with me and I pulled off one of those plates and swan-dived past Rose in a factor 2 fall that she couldn't stop.

I'd never climbed so carefully, pulling straight down on those crumbly boilerplates and screaming out loud when I finally plugged into that hand crack and set a bomber cam. The second Rose untied the catastrophe knot, I started windmilling up the crack, like a man chased from behind.

Pitch 13 ended on a hanging stance from two cams and a bomber ³/₈-inch bolt below the most notorious run out on the climb—a continuous 5.10 slab leading to the last bolt on the route. Because you climb this slab straight off and directly above the belay, once I brought Rose up and she took over the lead, if she ripped off the slab she'd fall directly onto me—and also straight onto the belay for yet another factor 2. I eliminated both hazards by climbing the slab, clipping that last bolt, then dropping down and rigging the belay—one of the boons of climbing on a long rope. When Rose reached me in nothing flat, I handed her the rack; she floated the slab with a toprope then blazed over easy face climbing to a belay off juniper bushes in a big crumbly recess. Rose led the next pitch as well, following a hand crack and flakes 100 feet to a traverse dead right and the belay on another bushy ledge.

We'd flashed the last four pitches in less than an hour but were still running late. The sky was darkening, the wind was starting to swirl, and little cascades of sand and pebbles were sloughing onto us from above. We had to get the hell off this wall. Now, speed was safety.

I swarmed up the crack then hand-traversed right to a fixed pin maybe a dozen feet from Rose and her belay off those bushes. Rose said the crux was tricky and right past the pin—meaning that once I unclipped, if I pinged I'd take a big swing right straight onto Rose and those bushes. So I stayed clipped to the pin and started traversing right, the rope now doubled behind me. The rope drag was awful, but I made the traverse OK. Now on a good stance, I tethered off to the anchor, untied my end, and pulled the rope through the fixed pin down and left. Then I tied back in and bombed up pitch 15, the last hard bit on the route—a 60-foot lieback up a big exfoliating flake.

The flake was frighteningly thin in spots, which is where the first ascent used some aid. Four rusty old ¼-inch Rawl bolts, festooning from the grainy wall just right of the flake, were all there was for pro. Some easy friction above the flake landed me on a shattered terrace, where I rigged a belay off a huge block keyed into a hollow. I put Rose on tension for a sec, and from the lower belay at those bushes, she pendulumed left to the fixed pin, cleaned the draw I'd left before the traverse, then smoked up the flake and joined me on the block.

The wall just above kicked way back, joining a low-angled ridge above this last pitch, which the topo called "Easy 5th Class." We were mostly above the rockfall zone, but that sand kept raining down and the slab was littered with loose flakes and teetering blocks, so no telling.

We felt a couple of big raindrops. We had to move, but we had to stay focused because we both knew this is where people die, when it gets "easy" and the adrenaline starts wearing off. And it was. We were running on fumes—dehydrated, sunburned, and hungry as hell. But we focused and carefully checked each other's systems.

Rose wouldn't need much pro, but she racked plenty to be certain, and I put her on a hip belay so she could move at top speed, saying I'd start simul-climbing the moment she hit the end of the rope.

"Won't be a minute," she said and shot off, fairly running, placing several just-to-be-sure cams and wisely taking a line that avoided the rope, or her feet, knocking off one of those flakes or blocks. She quickly ran out the 70-meter rope. I cleaned the anchor and Rose charged on, the two of us simul-climbing up and over the rubbly ridge, which melded into a woody escarpment. The wind started howling as big random drops pocked the ridge. We'd cut it pretty close.

I joined Rose on a grassy slope about 50 feet into the trees. I stripped off my harness and personal gear, changed into my sandals, and started coiling the rope as Rose stuffed the gear into the crag pack. We staggered up the slope and hit the rim trail right as rain drilled the treetops like buckshot. But we were safe now, on a flat, well-traveled path including a rusty tin trail sign that read: "Buckeye Camp Roadhead—7.8 miles." Five miles later the rain had stopped and the wind was gone, but we'd run out of water and energy gel, had been going for 14 hours straight, and were starting to bonk. Needing a break, we collapsed in a heap. I told Rose that Fuego was my last climb, that she'd have to leave me for dead. I'd never make it back to the trailhead. It was my honor and pleasure to know her, and for us to—

She held out the 16-ounce can of guava-pear juice she had secreted in the pocket of her rain parka and which I'd totally forgotten about. "Rose!" I said. "By any other name—"

"Drink," she said, handing me the can, which we shared and savored, experiencing a kind of resurrection there on the muddy trail. The haze between trees was graying fast, so we strapped on our headlamps and lumbered down the trail.

Nearing the roadhead at last, Rose asked, "What do you know about Keeler Needle?"

"Funny you should mention that, Rose . . ."

Every Trip Report is a case study of a climbing team making a variety of decisions to meet the specific challenges of a given climb. The sidebars that follow offer a closer look at a few basic issues—common to all multipitch trad climbing—that were briefly touched upon in the Trip Report.

Choosing a Big Multipitch Route

Most climbers pick a multipitch route based on a five-star rating in a guidebook, rave reviews on Mountain Project, what tradition insists are must-do classics, or when word comes in from friends who have photos and stories that stoke our embers. When you find another climber who shares the same stoke, the game's afoot, and you dive headfirst into the project. Study the guidebook. Read all the trip reports. Get a feel for the route from firsthand sources. Climbing a big multipitch trad route is serious business, and research helps avoid a shit show, because some of them are. The big routes don't always play fair. Technique and equipment forever evolve, but the skills that see us through remain the same: knowledge and experience, vigilance, fitness and fortitude, and preparation.

Picking a Partner

An ideal partner is skilled, experienced, and doesn't look to bail when the pressure rises. Team up with someone you really know, not some stray you snagged off a "partner finder" forum. That's like blind dating. Many climbers have tried that, once, and were lucky to escape off a climb without bones showing. Limit partnering with strangers to gym climbing, bouldering, and short crag routes, where you can get the measure of the stranger near the deck, not five pitches up a big wall. Big routes always give surprises, so you don't need more from a strange partner. In a perfect world, every partner is your equal. Maybe better. But perhaps more important is how you mesh as a team, which hinges on lots of intangibles, though it often boils down to compatibility under pressure.

Mountainproject.com

Mountainproject.com is the best worldwide resource for detailed route info. Up-to-date comments vet out the discrepancies in articles and local guidebooks and reach a public consensus on route difficulties, protection problems, belay strategies for combining pitches, what length rope to bring, whether we need a #4 Camalot, and so forth. Most of the data you need to know is pretty much right there.

Preplanning

Climbing writer and educator Willis Kuelthau offers the following "7 things to do to plan ahead for your first multipitch climb":

- Do as much research as you can before you go onto the route. Study the route—where it begins, where it travels, and where it ends.

- Study how to get down. If you're rappelling, find out where the anchors are.

- Have a copy of the topo or guidebook with you when you do the climb.

- Ask any friends that have done the climb to give you beta.

- Look for information on how long you're going to be on the climb.

- Know exactly what gear you'll need for the approach, climb, and descent.

- Be ready for the terrain you'll encounter—that way you'll know exactly what to do when you get there.

Let People Know Where You're Going

If nobody knows where we are going, they won't know where to look if we turn up missing. So always leave an itinerary with someone, preferably someone near and dear. Whoever gets the itinerary must be able to understand it. A friend left a guidebook with her dad with her route highlighted; her dad had to find someone else who could decipher the guide. Provide an estimated time of return, and always check back in once done, allowing a big enough time window for weather delays or changing a flat tire—*before* sending in the troops.

Multipitch Checklist

- Pick a route appropriate to your experience, skill, and fitness.

- Plan ahead. Know the route; check the weather forecast.

- Pack sufficient food, water, and appropriate clothing.

- Go light as possible.

- Don't rush; take breaks.

- Watch your time.

- Use sunscreen.

- Stop and enjoy the views.

Ultralight

"Ultralight" concerns both the weight and the amount of gear we pack (and have to carry) for a climb. Modern gear is lightweight by design, and we need little beyond our rack for short routes. The ultralight MO comes into its own for all-day adventures. Four factors to consider:

1. **Where You Fit on the Performance—Comfort Spectrum.** For the person trying to climb the Mountaineer's Route on Mount Whitney (at 14,505 feet, the highest peak in the Lower 48 and a 22-mile round-trip), say, car-to-car in a day (a fit team can do so in roughly 12 hours), the focus is on performance, and every extra pound matters. A casual team in "tour mode" might take two or even three days for the same venture (a day to hike in, a day for the route, and a day to hike out). This team favors comfort over exhaustion and will pack their bag accordingly, taking stuff that would slow the performer. The only "better" in any of this is what best suits your personal style and preference.

2. **Skill Level.** The more you know (skill), the less you need. As you gain experience, you naturally grow more efficient—and stop carrying gear you won't use. Ounces mean pounds, and pounds mean pain.

3. **Fitness.** The fit person goes faster and needs less stuff to sustain her over the short term. Or she goes with a pedestrian pace and lugs a few luxuries because she likes them. Fitness gives us options.

4. **Grunt Factor.** The expert often takes almost nothing extra, or is often willing to schlep a few treats for the pleasure they give—like an actual camera instead of a cell phone, a summit beer, and so forth. Wishing to pay off all that effort, some grunt out a few more pounds. Lighter is not always "more better."

Trad Learning Curve

Injuries from "acts of God," like lightning and rockfall are statistically rare, and even these are often avoidable if you know the conditions under which they commonly occur. Accept that there's a learning curve requiring training and education, mentors, and serious immersion so the dangers are known and understood. Then add some years working up the ladder. Accident reports are full of people who tried to "hack" the process. "Acceptable risk" assumes that the person knows what those risks actually are, and this is always an inexact science owing to so many variables, especially weather. Experienced hands factor in a certain margin of error for what we expect and plan for.

The High Price of Climbing Gear

Modern climbing gear is a blessing to use and a curse to buy. A top-end GORE-TEX rain parka, weighing less than 8 ounces, costs more than a top-shelf Italian suit. A common refrain within the outdoor world is: Never pay retail for anything. If you can't scam that rope or those cams, look for sales. Manufacturers continually update their line, so last year's model is still plenty good. Popular items can be had for a price because they are often overstocked. A hundred other reasons make it possible to find nearly everything on sale. Most any professional climber will readily admit that if they don't get stuff for free, or with a pro deal, they buy it out of bargain bins.

Crag Pack

Don't buy a cheap book bag for trad climbing. They're poorly made and fall apart. Get a good one, with minimal pockets and doodads. Small technical day packs are great deals because they are basically just nylon, reinforced straps/gear loops, and zippers. Good ones can be found on sale for $50 and will usually last a few years unless you haul them a lot. Ambitious trad climbers will likely need two crag packs: one big one ($100–$250) for humping gear and ropes to the cliffside; a smaller one for taking on big multipitch routes, as needed. Myriad sizes and designs are widely available.

Have a System

The experienced hand has developed a personal system, a basic way of operating and organizing her personal gear and going about her business. This makes her more efficient and helps eliminate chance. Over time, she has standardized her gear into her personal system, keeping things the same till she finds something better, or a more efficient MO. This way her stuff reliably performs as expected and she can concentrate on safety and performance.

In climbing, most gear is clipped to gear loops on your harness, and no two people "rack" their gear the same way. Some prefer the bigger devices up front; others like it toward the back (rare). Some like slings, belay devices, and free carabiners on the left; others like them on the right—or on both sides. The point is to arrive at a consistent system so that in a pinch, you can instinctively grab stuff you know is there. If you go clipping stuff on any which way, you'll fumble to find what you want; at some time, that will cost you.

Making adjustments on the fly is part of the adventure, but without a basic system, we have nothing to adjust. The person who has a personal system knows, in general terms, what she is doing. Otherwise we're just winging it, which results in a junk show more often than not.

Someone without a personal system—no matter their skill level—is disorganized and incompetent, is always scrabbling with unfamiliar gear and needlessly wasting time. Get your stuff squared away. Develop a personal system.

Cell Phones

Most smartphones feature GPS navigation, RDS radio receivers, video calling capability, and more—but none of these work when the battery dies. External batteries and portable solar rechargers are helpful, but not if you drop your phone in the stream. That happens. It's unlikely that your and your partner's phone will both go down, unless you lose the signal, which usually cuts out in the wilds, especially in canyons and valleys. *Phones break and often go down, so always bring a hard copy of the topo when climbing a big multipitch route.*

Weather

The long days of summer are typically the hottest as well, so it's vital to know when a climb gets sun or shade. Professional free climbers never tackle their project when it's baking in the sun. Tommy Caldwell and Kevin Jorgeson climbed El Cap's Dawn Wall in January (often at night, with headlamps), and Alex Honnold free soloed Freerider in morning shade.

Layer Up and Down

A layering system allows us to adapt to wild swings in temperature, especially in the mountains, where afternoon thunderstorms can quickly drop the temperature 30 degrees or more. Even in blazing midsummer Yosemite, veterans carry a lightweight rain jacket and a knit ski hat, just in case. Big Yosemite routes start from the Valley floor (4,000-foot elevation) and top out in another climate zone, 4,000 feet higher. Same goes for Long Peak (The Diamond) in Colorado and countless other mountain walls. Modern outdoor garments let us layer up and layer down as needed.

Climbing behind People

Climbing behind people is not a good idea. You can't control the team above you, who can drop gear and trigger rockfall. Usually the rope is the culprit, when it's pulled over debris-strewn ledges. Passing another team can be problematic. Who can rightfully demand that a team allow you to pass simply because you're faster? That puts them in the rockfall zone, and they got up early to avoid that. On marble-hard climbs, a pass by an expert team might be fitting. But it's never a right; rather it's gifted by the upper team. Expect crowds to swarm over popular routes. To avoid conflicts, get up early, bivy at the base, or pick a nonpeak time (weekday, off-season, etc.) when heading for a trade route.

Carry or Haul the Pack?

Nothing can tank a great multipitch climb faster than hauling a bunch of tackle you don't need—or not having what you *do* need. The right balance is different for every team, but most experienced climbers go minimal. That often means the second carries a light crag pack, and the team climbs on a single long rope to avoid trailing another line,

Alex Honnold passes Rita Young Shin during a speed ascent of The Nose route, El Cap.
PHOTO BY JOHN EVANS

even a skinny 8 mm. The leader, as needed, can lower down slack on the long rope and hand-over-hand up the pack. It's sometimes tricky, but usually doable.

For high-standard climbing, however, the second can't follow hard pitches with a heavy pack (containing approach shoes, water, lunch, jackets, first-aid kit, headlamps, etc.), so a thin trail/haul line (like an 8 mm half rope) is the ticket. Plus it facilitates quick descent if the route involves long rappels to escape. Often a 70-meter rope is long enough to rap most routes; a 60-meter usually isn't (a doubled 60-meter line is only 98 feet long).

Personal Gear and Accessories

A fair-weather climbing outfit might include stretch tights or sweat bottoms (sturdy nylon blends), polyester tech T-shirt, and a superthin fleece top you wrap around your waist (or jam in the crag pack). Both partners often carry cell phones and a small battery (in the pack) to recharge one if they have to. Worm-drive into a body crack with a cell phone in your pocket, and kiss that phone goodbye. Of course there's no reception in most wilderness areas, so you carry your phones to store topos and take photos and video.

The crag pack has the food and water plus two superthin rain jackets and two beanies—just in case—and two headlamps, which don't weigh anything. Most big routes require approach shoes as well. The crag pack might weigh 25 pounds at the base, but it quickly gets lighter as you drink the water—by far the heaviest cargo. Speed climbers might take little to nothing more than the rope and their climbing gear. If all goes well, they're off the wall before getting blindsided by thirst and hunger. If things go wrong, they suffer.

Off the Deck

Open face climbing straight off the ground is exciting, especially at dawn. You're cautious gaining that first bolt or placement, so you don't deck. If you have to run the rope again, you need some pro soon enough, or you're quickly high enough to deck once more. Always factor in rope stretch and belayer flex/movement when running the rope off the deck.

Rope Management

US Navy SEALs have a saying: "Slow is smooth and smooth is fast." On a big multipitch route, taking time to manage the ropes always saves time higher up. A few rope snafus can be the difference between descending in daylight and strapping on the headlamps. Jammed ropes are also a leading cause of teams getting benighted on the cliffside.

Whenever you're on a ledge, if one climber has led a pitch and is leading the next pitch as well, "pancake stack" the rope (tightly flaked in about a 2-foot-diameter pile, patting it down occasionally with your foot), then carefully "flip the pancake" for the next lead. At hanging stances, as you belay the follower, butterfly-loop the rope on top of your (normally semi-taut) tie-in strand, short to long, starting with a loop that hangs down about a foot; then make ensuing loops about 2 inches longer. Then butterfly-flip the rope (transferring it on top of the new belayer's tie-in).

If you're swapping leads from a stance, butterfly the rope long to short, starting with the loops hanging down to foot level; then make each loop progressively shorter.

Never let your rope hang below your feet. Once the leader begins the next pitch, if a dangling loop snags on a flake or a bush, it's a big problem and a time suck to fix. The leader must either downclimb to the belay or anchor off to a protection point as the belayer raps down to free the snag then ascends back to the belay stance. Better to manage the rope like a boss.

Multipitch Belay Strategy

On popular multipitch routes, 90 percent of the time it's this easy: After leading the pitch, place three bomber pieces and rig them with a cordelette. Anchor yourself to the master point with a pear-shaped locking carabiner, then rig a direct belay (using an autoblocking device or assisted braking device) by clipping the locking carabiner of the device straight into the master point. **Remember, a direct belay with a MBD is not recommended,** since it puts your hand in an awkward, dangerous, and untenable brake position. For belaying the leader, switch back to an indirect belay, with your belay device clipped through your belay loop.

The quad is the biggest recent innovation for multipitch anchor. By splitting the four strands (two and two), you'll have two distinct master points to clip into.

If your anchor is marginal (with less than bomber pieces, sketchy rock, etc.), common on obscure routes and alpine climbs, use the indirect belay for the second (i.e., with your belay device clipped to your harness belay

Multipitch belay at Tahquitz Rock, California. The leader is ready to go, and the belayer has put him on belay. When the leader unclips his clove hitch, he'll clip his rope to the top piece, which already has a quickdraw waiting. The leader's rope is butterfly-looped and ready to pay out without any tangles. Once up on the pitch, if the leader falls, the upward force on the belayer would soften the impact, and the right-hand piece in the anchor, placed for an upward pull, would keep the belayer from getting yanked too far upward.

Gear changeover. Each climber is clipped to a quad master point.

Three-point quad anchor. The belayer is belaying the follower with a direct belay using the Petzl Reverso in autoblocking mode.

This four-piece cordellete rig affords two masterpoints, each with four loops: one master point at the bottom carabiner; another at "the shelf," where the top carabiner is clipped into all four upper loops.

loop). Clove-hitch yourself taut to the anchor's master point, then take the best possible stance and brace yourself in the direction of pull. Use your stance and body position, along with the friction of the belay device, to absorb the force of any fall, with little or no loading on the anchor.

Back-Cleaning

The route wanders and zigzags. Or, more typically, the only available protection, which you very much need, is to the side of the climbing route—or deep in a chimney. Or maybe the rope runs hard around a corner or over a roof. Point is, whenever the lead rope describes hard angles, even if extended with runners, rope drag can stop us cold. It's often just a single placement that causes dire drag. The common solution is to battle the rope drag and climb higher till you can place a higher piece, then downclimb and "back-clean" the piece that's causing the drag. Remember that after you clean the lower piece, if you fall and the top piece blows, you are looking at a much longer plunge. Prevent this by *making certain the highest protection is bomber before back-cleaning anything below*. Double it up if you have to. Even create a distributed anchor if the placements are sketchy. Either way, that top piece must be solid.

"ROCK!"

Like "Fore!" in golf, "Rock!" is the universal shout-out to warn those below of a falling rock or dropped piece of gear. The narrowest shave experienced by many climbers is a close encounter with falling rocks. When our brains are flooded with adrenaline, memories are set all the deeper. Most anyone who's had a rockfall incident can replay the scare like it happened that morning. You can usually judge the size of a falling rock by how loud your partner yells "ROCK!" A blood-curdling scream—take cover. A mini-fridge might be coming your way. Frightening as it is, try to calculate the trajectory of the rock, and take whatever evasive action you can, however small. Small shifts at a hanging belay have saved more than a few climbers from rocks that would have otherwise taken them out. A split

second and a slight shift in body position can make all the difference. In multipitch areas known for rockfall, never intentionally climb below other parties. On ledges on multipitch routes, be especially vigilant when pulling your rope around near the edge of the cliff. It's usually a rope dragging over loose terrain that triggers rockfall.

Protect Yourself

On big multipitch routes, when you're climbing on-sight (first time on the climb), it's reckless to pass obvious protection points. Pause and slot a cam or drop in a nut, then carry on. It only takes a second. Many seasoned climbers have sustained permanent injuries—even perished—from falling off what they considered "easy" terrain.

Clean Shoes

In more than thirty-five years of guiding, I (BG) can remember only two instances when I took a leader fall while guiding a client. One was when a hold broke; the other was due to dirty shoes. I'd been standing on a dirty, wooded ledge, and halfway up the pitch, my foot slipped on a smear I was confident would stick. After I fell I checked my shoes; the soles were caked with dirt.

On multipitch climbs, watch out for ledges that have dirt, grit, lichen, or seepage. Before each lead, check each shoe, and brush off the sole with your hand. For hard slab climbing, take extra time—rub the sole with your palm until it squeaks.

Outside Your Comfort Zone

A short refrain from the untold story about mega trad routes. Imagine this: You read the topo, see the rating, and think you're golden; but somewhere during your ten-pitch gauntlet, the route makes you do something far outside your comfort zone, which no one can control or quantify. As conditions changed, each of the previous eight pitches had sprung a fast one on countless other teams, which accounted for all those bail-off slings on anchor after anchor.

The Big Picture

We can argue endlessly about the best way to distribute the load on a three- or four-piece anchor and how to rig the array to withstand a factor-2 fall—and miss the real-world fact that factor-2 falls are rare, that 99 percent of any falling scenario involves the top piece of protection (the last piece the leader has placed) absorbing virtually all the loading. Yes, we always need bomber belays. But our main focus is to always strive for solid primary placements, especially on the lead, which is where the majority of accidents occur. Don't miss the big picture and myopically focus on the belay anchors when the real issue is lead pro, since 99 percent of the time, that's what holds the fall force.

The Fall Factor

The fall factor is derived from a simple calculation: the total distance of the fall divided by the length of the rope out from the belay device. Anything approaching a fall factor of 1 or higher is a serious jolt on the belayer and a tough catch.

On a multipitch climb, if you're leading with no pro 30 feet above the belay, and fall, you'll sail past the belay and fall at least 60 feet before rope stretch kicks in—and you'll log the dreaded fall factor 2.

For multipitch climbs, debate continues about how best to rig and anchor for a potential fall factor 2. Should you clip the lead rope into the anchor's master point or the topmost piece in the anchor? There is no simple answer due to the variables, the most obvious being the strength of the anchor.

One solution is to always avoid the possibility of a factor-2 fall. If you're forewarned that the route has fall factor 2 potential, as long as have enough rope (and assuming the anchor is reliable), the leader can clip the anchor's master point, continue into the next pitch and up to the first good gear placement, then lower back down to the belay, thus eliminating the possibility of a fall factor 2. The drawback here is that if climbing off the belay is delicate and tenuous, rope drag (built up at the end of the pitch) may be significant.

$$\text{FALL FACTOR} = \frac{\text{length of fall}}{\substack{\text{length of rope} \\ \text{between} \\ \text{belayer and climber}}}$$

Calculating the fall factor

Another solution, provided the anchor is reliable, is for the leader to lower some distance (say, 20 feet) *below* the anchor, tie off to a robust placement, and belay from there. The next leader can then clip into the anchor's master point, no longer looking at a fall factor 2, since more rope is in the system from the belay device. If enough force is generated in the leader's fall to yank the belayer upward, that movement will soften the impact force—a good thing, as long as the belayer doesn't lose control and there's no ledge for the falling leader to hit.

If all the placements in the anchor are bomber, the leader can clip the topmost piece of the anchor, creating a gap of a few feet between that clip and the belayer's device. In this scenario, the fall factor is less than 2, but considerably more force is generated at the clipped piece, since the force is multiplied due to the pulley factor (a force of x 2 minus the friction factor = 1.6 x. Ergo, the clipped piece must be bomber and the belayer should be well braced, or they'll get pulled violently toward the piece and into the wall.

Another solution, with a solid anchor, is a direct belay, which is normally not recommended for lead belaying. A direct belay eliminates the multiplied force and the slamming of the belayer, but it is not recommended with an assisted braking device (e.g., Grigri) due to the device's solid lock-off, which transfers more impact force onto the anchor. A direct belay with a Munter hitch solves this problem, since it slips a little bit when engaging, thus softening the force on the anchor. Since the maximum friction is generated when the two rope strands are parallel to each other, the Munter provides a more ergonomic brake position for the belayer—but in the scenario just described, the catch will be a hard one (gloves recommended).

When using a direct belay with a Munter hitch, create a backup system by conservatively estimating the distance to the leader's next stance and protection point; clip a manual braking device (MBD) like an ATC into the rope at the estimated spot, and tie a catastrophe knot on the brake strand just below it. Then you'll be ready to switch from the Munter to the MBD after the leader has clipped their first piece of protection.

Hanging belay at Red Rocks, Nevada. Here Mike Moretti pays out the leader's rope, clipped to the right bolt of a two-bolt anchor with a locking carabiner, thus eliminating a factor-2 fall potential. He's attached himself to the master point with a clove hitch and braced himself for an upward pull if the leader were to fall on this traverse up and right from the anchor. He's adjusted his stance so that he's created some distance between his belay device and the first point the leader's rope is clipped into. His rope is well managed—butterfly-looped across his tie-in strand.

If the anchor is sketchy, you're treading on thin ice, and both climbers are finished if the anchor fails (usually because all the pieces were placed in a weak rock feature). Here, belay directly off your harness (to limit the

A Munter hitch direct belay rigged for a fall factor 2 situation. This is a tough catch, so it's advisable to rig a backup, just in case. Make a conservative estimate of the length of the leader's runout to the first piece, clip in an MBD (like an ATC) that distance down the rope, and then back it up with a catastrophe knot on the brake-strand side. In a worst-case scenario, if the leader falls and the belayer loses control, the backups will come into play.

The maximum friction you can generate with a Munter hitch belay is when the two rope strands are parallel. For a tough catch like this, gloves are recommended.

impact force on the belay anchor) with an MBD, and back it up with a catastrophe knot on the brake-hand side. Brace yourself in the best stance you can muster, and do your best to absorb the impact force with your legs and torso. Note that with an MBD, the brake-hand position is up, not down. If you completely lose control, the catastrophe knot will jam into the belay device—averting disaster as long as the anchor holds. In all these scenarios, a catastrophe knot (one that will jam in your belay device) serves as your last line of defense should you lose control of the belay.

The first line of defense is not to fall in the first place. Fifteen pitches up a seventeen-pitch route is a heartbreaking place to bail and face a series of long, tedious rappels. But know that many accidents occur when a leader won't give up and casts off onto unknown moves with marginal control—the proverbial "going for it." Practice downclimbing on moderate highball boulder problems, and develop a foundation for mental control when you need it most. Using sound judgment—knowing when to back off—is a hallmark of a solid leader. Hubris makes us dead.

Doug Robinson sums it up nicely in his article "The Whole Natural Art of Protection": "Learning to climb down is valuable for retreating from a clean and bold place that gets too airy. And having the humility to back off rather than continue . . . a thing well begun is not lost. The experience cannot be taken away."

Belaying the Leader

It's especially important for the belayer to carefully watch the slack in the rope when the leader is climbing straight off a ledge, or any feature the leader might clip should they fall. A piece placed for an upward pull, as part of the anchor array or clipped in separately, will help the belayer hold a solid stance and not get yanked up the wall.

During any leader fall, the rope will stretch about 30 percent of the length of the rope that's out between the belayer's belay device and the leader's tie-in knot. Thirty feet of rope out means a 39-foot fall—less rope stretch if the lead line is clipped through various protection points and carabiners; more stretch if the rope is only clipped through a piece or two.

If you're leading out of sight of your belayer and encounter some dicey moves, a good signal to your belayer is "Watch me!" so they can monitor the slack and get into a "heads-up" mode.

Sasha Digiulian and Jon Cardwell on Misty Wall, Yosemite Valley, California

PHOTO BY JOHN EVANS

Caroline Gleich leading Sasquatch (5.9+), Little Cottonwood Canyon, Utah

PHOTO BY JOHN EVANS

The Jesus Nut

"Jesus Nut" is a term made infamous by helicopter mechanics during the Vietnam War. The then ubiquitous Bell UH-1 "Huey" helicopter had one and only one giant stainless steel nut (the Jesus Nut) that screwed onto the top of the main rotor mast, keeping the main rotor blades attached to the chopper. As the saying went, "If the nut fails, the next person you will see is Jesus."

In multipitch rock climbing, the Jesus Nut is the first, most vital piece the leader clips into directly off the belay, eliminating the potential for the dreaded fall factor 2. If the top piece in the anchor is solid, that piece can serve as the Jesus Nut, eliminating the chance of falling directly onto the belayer's device.

Direction of Pull

Whenever you traverse to Point A, arrange a piece of protection, then ascend to Point B and place protection there, you've created an angle in the lead rope. A fall at any point above *the second piece of pro* (Point B), and the direction of pull will bisect any angle you've created in the rope system. Because this angle is invariably oblique, it puts a sideways pull on the pro at Point A. If that pro is not multidirectional (like a nut placed only to withstand a downward force), it could easily get levered from the crack.

The leader's goal is for the rope to run in a relatively straight line by judicious use of slings, eliminating a conflagration of varying directions of pull on all the pieces of the system. At any angle created by a zigzagging rope through various pieces, if the leader falls, the resulting direction of pull will bisect every angle created.

Rita Young Shin on
Cosmic Girl, Yosemite
PHOTO BY JOHN EVANS

Setting Nuts

Setting nuts is standard practice. A firm tug sets them in place and ensures that nominal rope drag won't lever them from the crack. Setting nuts with extreme force is not only needless but hateful. Violent yanks take only seconds, while the poor follower, hanging off glossy carbuncles, might spend minutes trying to wiggle lose a stopper literally welded into the crack. If something more than a firm but moderate yank is needed to set a nut, you chose the wrong size or the wrong placement. If that's all you've got, and you desperately need it, you might have to welt it, and you might have to hold the follower on tension while they bust out the nut tool and go to work. Most parties take the protection they need and no more, so forfeiting a nut here might imperil the team higher up. Leaving gear on routes is a badge of shame, but sometimes it cannot be avoided.

Check Ahead

Always eyeball the next pitch close enough to decipher what gear will likely be needed. Always carry what you need—and a little more. What leaders often misjudge on big trad routes is not hardware but the number of runners and alpine draws they'll need to avoid dire rope drag.

Carrying Double-Length Runners

When carrying a double-length (120 cm) sling, rather than carrying it bandolier style (i.e., doubled, over one shoulder and under the opposite armpit), drape it over one shoulder, across your chest, and around your back, then clip it loop end to loop end with a carabiner. This makes it much easier to deploy on the lead; you simply unclip one loop end from the carabiner.

Single-length slings can be easily carried over the shoulder. For double-length slings, clipping the ends to a carabiner as shown allows for quick deployment.

Nonverbal Climbing Signals

On big routes, communication can be difficult when the pitches are long and the wind is strong. Make a game plan in advance. A guide will often tell a client: "When I get to the next belay, you probably won't be able to hear me. When I pull up all the rope and it comes tight to your anchor, I'll have you on belay." Another method is to use three stout tugs. When the leader reaches the belay, builds the anchor, and ties in, they give three stout quick tugs on the rope (meaning "Off belay"). The belayer tugs back three times ("Belay off"). The leader pulls up the slack until it comes tight to the anchor, and the follower gives three tugs ("That's me"). The belayer tugs back three times (meaning "Belay on").

Stay Hydrated!

Hydration is a safety issue, since our physical and mental wherewithal declines, sometimes alarmingly so, once we get dehydrated. Staying hydrated is a three-step dance.

1. Keep drinking throughout the day. Heat, humidity, exertion, and clothing all affect our hydration, often in ways we're unaware of because our minds are dulled from lack of water. Many accidents (the majority the result of human error, and thus avoidable) occur when people are tired and dehydrated.

2. The amount of water we need to stay hydrated depends on many factors. Play it safe, and always stay ahead of thirst. Few conditions require constant guzzling. Casual sipping at frequent intervals is a no-lose strategy. Thirst is *not* our best indicator of how much we need to drink. High-stress, high-effort work like trad climbing requires our full attention. When so engaged, we often forget to drink till we're dying of thirst. If you wait till you're thirsty, you've waited too long. Keep drinking at regular intervals to stay ahead of thirst, if only by a sip or two.

3. Hundreds of hydration aids are available (powders, liquids, and gels). Electrolyte replacements are especially helpful. It is important to keep the body's carbohydrate content up while exercising. Mixing in protein is helpful in this regard, as the body can metabolize these mixtures faster than food. Remember the cardinal rule: *Always stay ahead of thirst.*

Stay Fueled Up

Big work requires calories—loads of them. How you get your calories is your business, but get them you must or

On the Nose Route, El Capitan

your body will cannibalize itself for the fuel you didn't take on beforehand. Sports medicine tells us that you want a significant glycogen cache going into game day (or the start of a big climb), which can't be gotten with a big carbo load the night before. Rather, start eating a larger-than-usual percentage of carbohydrates, increasing the ratio as you go, for *the last three days* before the big route. It's unrealistic to eat much food during a climb, but you need something to avoid bonking. Energy bars and gels are handy here. Most climbers try various options and find out what works best for them.

Wilderness First Aid

Injuries frequently occur in the wild places, and people are left to deal with the skill and knowledge they have—or wait till others arrive who can assist. Adventure sport athletes (trad climbers included) are the likeliest to suffer serious injuries in the wilds, and they also are the most likely to know nothing about wilderness first aid. Play it smart and take a "wilderness first responder" first aid class. They are widely available, inexpensive, and usually can be completed in a few weekends.

Headlamps

Always keep a headlamp in your pack, removing it only to recharge or swap out batteries. Backup batteries (even for rechargeable units) are likewise standard kit items. Leading manufacturers all have a basic model that's also a great deal and works well in most situations. Lithium batteries are the first choice for cold weather. They're far pricier than alkaline batteries but last much longer in cold conditions. Rechargeable nickel metal hydride (NiMH) batteries also perform well in the cold but lose power between charges, so carry a few alkalines (excellent at holding their charge) as backups.

Bivouac ("Bivy")

In the vocabulary of multipitch climbing, a bivy refers to spending the night on the wall. Planned bivys are an integral and unforgettable part of the trad climber's experience. There's no better way to get to know a cliff than to spend the night on it. Most big multipitch routes feature ledges along the way that serve as traditional bivouac spots; teams aim for these and plan accordingly. A minority of routes—usually super-steep aid climbs—lack suitable bivy ledges, necessitating hanging bivys, an experience like none other, and one not to be missed.

Up until the late 1980s, hanging bivys involved sleeping in uncomfortable mesh or nylon hammocks that mashed a climber like a sardine in a tin and afforded fitful

El Cap bivy
PHOTO BY JOHN EVANS

sleep at best. The modern "portaledge"—consisting of a taut nylon floor or bed stretched over a suspendable (and adjustable) aluminum tube structure, complete with a water- and windproof, zip-up nylon fly has brought the very comforts of home to the steepest cliffside, allowing onboard cooking on small stoves and the ability to wait out stormy weather and saw some serious logs in what amounts to the master bedroom of a tiny house. It's not uncommon for a team snug in such lodgings to while away the evening dining on fine viands, sipping craft beers or a splash of vino, listening to house music on one partner's smartphone while the other partner is videoconferencing with kith and kin staring up from the deck, or even conferencing from another country. We climbers have never had it so good.

Benighted: Pulling a Forced Bivy

Climb enough big multipitch routes and eventually a storm, a jammed rope, or (fill in the blank) will stall you out and you'll get benighted—forced to spend the night either on the route or on the descent. Planned bivys include food, water, and shelter (at least a pad and sleeping bag), the very things you'll do without during a forced bivy. On big, time-consuming routes, many parties bring wool hats, pile coats, and superlight rain jackets (or some such combination) just in case. Any more and you might as well *plan* for a bivy and haul a bag.

It used to be that many forced bivys happened on descents, when the way felt too hazardous to negotiate in the dark. Modern headlamps are so bright, you can climb with them, so it's less likely you'll get stuck on the wall because of darkness. The issue is almost always the cold. If an unplanned bivy seems likely, look for a sheltered alcove (out of the wind) if there's one to find, as opposed to just gunning for the top and having to spend the night in slings or on a crappy stance.

No matter how close you hunker to your partner, as darkness falls and your teeth start to chatter, it's just going to be you and your thoughts, feelings, and sensations. These are teachable moments, for sure, at once both hateful and enlightening.

Projecting

An adventure project is a big deal because it's often the next step, possibly an achievement that crowns our career up to that point. Projects mean upping our game in terms of effort, skill, and commitment. For weekend warriors, it often means learning new skills or refining the ones we have. For both the pro and the weekend warrior, the sci-ence of projecting is basically the same, and increases our odds at succeeding. Here are a few steps:

- **Objectify the venture.** This is basic information gathering. What is involved, start to finish, and what are the specific demands? Why do people fail or succeed? Talk to whoever knows. Read magazine and web articles, especially trip reports. Get a general feel for the project and decide if it's right for you.

- **Commit to the project.** If a project hooks you in, commit to exploring the possibility of doing it. Develop an action plan so that day trips/adventures work toward your project, at the exclusion of what does not. Practice what you hope to play.

- **Evaluate and work on weaknesses.** What do you need to develop to bag the project? Often it's a matter of more of the same, meaning endurance. Incrementally work toward your goal, bringing weaknesses up to speed on smaller ventures that simulate the project. There often are tutorials for the big classic climbs: "Road to Astroman," and so forth.

- **Create a timetable.** Once you commit and start working toward a project, your progress will determine a future date to aim for. Give yourself a window, but set a target date, basically a deadline, without which your focus might flag.

- **Timing.** Weather-dependent projects might entail short holding patterns if it's snowing, say, or even if you're not "feeling it," but avoid lengthy delays. Enthusiasm and urgency get the fire burning, but both can quickly go cold if the wood gives out through delays.

- **Pull the trigger.** The hardest part of most projects is the first step.

That said, projects are a strange animal, predictably unpredictable. Short-term projects are the ones we usually get done. Focus and enthusiasm are most easily kept over the short term, lest we find something else to do. And doing, not planning, is our prerogative. As celebrated climber and BASE jumper, Steph Davis, once said, "Things don't stay the same long enough to make long-term plans."

Kevin Jorgeson on Blue Collar (5.13d), a project on the north face of Yosemite's Higher Cathedral Spire that he sent after fifty days of effort

PHOTO BY JOHN EVANS

Well-Rounded

Most accomplished trad climbers are competent with all techniques—and that never comes naturally for anyone. You get well-rounded by working your weaknesses as hard as (or harder than) your strengths. That's stressful and annoying, and we feel like bumblers. So we practice what we're good at, climbing only those routes on which we can shine. If not addressed, weakness leads to fear, and to avoiding any adventure that exposes our weakness. This puts many trad climbs out of reach because classic multi-pitch routes are typically long and multifaceted, requiring general competence—including the skill set we lack.

For instance, most people initially hate wide cracks. No part of your body fits into them. You flog, grunt, thrutch up an inch and slide down two, grinding the skin off knees and elbows. But most big classics feature some wide, often a lot of it. When your frustration from avoiding feels worse than "the wide," you'll return to the flared chimneys and off-width cracks till fear and bumbling morph into skill. Then your options are practically unlimited.

Standard Rack

The following *standard rack* will allow you to climb most routes in trad climbing areas. Buying more large nuts (like hexes) will save you money if you're on a budget, but camming devices will provide more versatility. Few experienced climbers carry a full range of hexes, or any hexes, these days.

- 2 sets of wired nuts from 0.2 inch to 2 inches (e.g., Black Diamond Stoppers, sizes 2–12)

- 1 set of micronuts (e.g., Black Diamond Micro Stoppers, sizes 2–6)

- 1 set of hexes or tricams from 1 to 2.5 inches (e.g., Black Diamond Hexes, sizes 5–8; Camp (Lowe) Tricams, sizes 2–4)

- 1 nut tool

- 1 set of small camming devices 0.3 to 0.75 inch (e.g., Metolius Master Cams sizes 00, 0, 1, 2, 3)

Racking up

- 2 sets of camming devices from 0.4 inch to 3 inches (e.g., Black Diamond Camalot C4s sizes 0.3, 0.4, 0.5, 0.75, 1, 2, 3)

- One 4-inch camming device (e.g., Black Diamond #4 Camalot)

- 6 quickdraws with carabiners

- 6 single-length (24-inch) slings

- 2 double-length (48-inch) slings

- 2 cordelettes (18–20 feet of 7 mm nylon cord or 5 mm to 6 mm tech cord)

- 30 carabiners

- 4 to 6 locking carabiners

CHAPTER 15

Risk Management

The previous fourteen chapters sought to explain and illustrate the roped safety system, standardized into methods so basic that anyone with working knowledge can walk into a climbing gym, pass a 60-second safety check, and climb all day without incident. If the system were less reliable, climbing gyms could never exist. Lawsuits would close their doors in a week.

Gym accidents do happen, but rarely, and occur from what aviation calls "pilot error." Scarlet let the rope run under her leg, fell, tripped on the rope, and smacked her shoulder. Belayer Jack bungled the lower-off, and Jill hit the mat. John Long forgot to finish his tie-end knot, climbed a route, went to lower off, and decked (it happened). Given proper training, we can easily prevent these mishaps through vigilance and safety checks.

Note that indoors we use the same shoes, chalk bag, harness, and belay device we use outside. We use the same knots. We use the same belaying and lowering techniques. Our safety checks and signals are the same. We use many of the same climbing techniques. If the game is so similar, why do accidents continue to happen outdoors, when indoors they are the exception?

Outdoors, we have to rappel, route-find, and tackle climbs larger than a 40-foot wall of multiplex board. There's loose rock outside, sharp edges, sudden and violent storms, and "acts of God" never encountered indoors. *Yet analysis overwhelmingly shows that objective dangers are rarely the cause of outdoor climbing accidents.* This introduces a subtle but profound

Joshua Tree Search and Rescue Team in action at Joshua Tree National Park, California

shift in the way we approach climbing safety. The main focus is not on the ways the mountain or the environment can harm us (while this remains a

Ander Rockstad at Wild Iris, Wyoming
PHOTO BY JOHN EVANS

vital concern), but rather on the many ways we can lose focus, bungle techniques and safety checks, and essentially invite injury. Put differently, *the vast majority of climbing mishaps are self-inflicted*. The principal dangers are not "out there" but within.

Longtime YOSAR (Yosemite Search and Rescue) officer John Dill studied the most serious climbing accidents that occurred in Yosemite Valley over a two-decade period (during which fifty-one climbers died). Dill estimates that 80 percent of those accidents were "easily preventable." Many survivors told Dill that they lost their good judgment just long enough to get hurt. It's a complex subject.

Nevertheless, Dill found at least three states of mind that frequently contribute to the majority of outdoor climbing accidents: ignorance, casualness, and distraction.

Ignorance is being unaware of potential danger. *Casualness* is not taking things seriously enough—complacency reinforced by repeatedly getting away with poor safety habits. *Distraction* is when our mind wanders away from a critical task *while we're doing it*.

Not all acts of God are avoidable through attentiveness. Objective dangers dramatically increase in

Molly Mitchell on Stranded at Sea (5.12a R), Vedauwoo, Wyoming
PHOTO BY JOHN EVANS

mega-scale areas like the Karakorum in Pakistan, notorious for savage storms. Even in pacific venues like Yosemite, freak late-summer storms have killed more than a few teams that were caught unprepared ("ignorant"). A little research, widely available, might have spared the victims. And if we go to the Karakorum, we go by choice, knowing the hazards. For the trained and vigilant climber who stays on decent rock in moderate climates, statistics clearly show that acts of God rarely get us. Then what is left to go wrong?

Anchor failure.

In the gym, lower-off and protection anchors are I-bolts fastened to the steel superstructure of the wall. There is a one in a million chance these bolts will ever fail. When trad climbing outdoors, we mostly hand-place removable anchors in an endless variety of cracks and on natural features, placements ranging from bombproof to marginal—and sometimes they fail.

Great emphasis and endless debate on anchor rigging techniques lead some to believe that belay anchors are the principal safety issue. Catastrophic belay anchor failure is extremely rare, and is usually

Remember the Motto

"Gravity never sleeps." Neither can we. Accident reports overwhelmingly show that the danger is largely within, and that eternal vigilance is the one quality most likely to bring us safely home.

- Pay attention and allow no distractions while performing crucial tasks.

- Don't engage in conversation when tying in, clipping into anchors, rigging, making transitions, and performing technical protocols.

- Make it a habit to double-check your systems—then check your partner's as well *before* engaging.

Jay Smith on Hall of Mirrors, Glacier Point Apron, Yosemite

due to committing to a weak rock structure, like a loose block or flake. The most common rock climbing accident is simply this: The leader places a single point of protection, falls, the protection fails, and the leader gets hurt. We call this challenge the "protection problem."

Belay anchors demand extreme vigilance. But if solid belay anchors were not widely available on popular routes, and recreational climbers could not learn how to rig them, belay anchor failure would happen more frequently, and it does not. Factor 2 falls—when a leader falls directly onto the belay anchor—are also extremely rare. The issue here, one that every word, sentence, and paragraph in this book has led to, is the protection problem.

It is simplistic to say that this is the only threat facing trad climbers, but even world-class pros know that as long as they follow the safety checks and hold their focus, the protection problem is their basic concern. What then is the best strategy to manage the protection problem?

Never fall. If we never fall we never tax the protection, however good or bad. This is impractical, because even experts fall on easy terrain, and experienced climbers get bored on simple routes. Better to become an expert on protection devices and how to judge them. Millions of climbers have done so; but the protection problem still looms large when the *only* protection is middling or worse, a challenge all trad climbers face at least some of the time. Whenever you do, follow the Trad Climber's Credo: The harder the climbing (for you), the safer it should be. If the belay is sound, the protection is solid, and there's nothing to hit should you log a short to moderate fall, many feel justified in giving it a try. If the climbing is simple (for you) but potentially dangerous, the risk might be worth taking, especially if it eliminates an even greater risk, like climbing quickly over easy but loose rock during a storm to avoid both rockfall and getting stranded in a danger zone. But to push your limits on chossy rock when the protection is poor and there are ledges to hit—that's not asking for trouble;

that's making it. In rare situations when the stars align, pro climbers (who know their limits) might take a calculated risk. Even a big one. *For the rest of us, the safest play is to push our limits only when the penalty for falling is small.*

But this is a nuanced subject that requires deeper study. The Trad Climber's Credo is designed to manage risks. It also casts the *protection problem* in strictly physical terms, when physical climbing ability is rarely the limiting factor.

Picture Sam, a 5.12 climber high on a long trad route, who's facing a 20-foot runout off so-so wired stoppers. The topo says the runout is 5.9—in theory, a trivial grade for a 5.12 climber. Why are Sam's

Evan Wisheropp running it out on a first ascent, Moab, Utah
PHOTO BY JOHN EVANS

knees knocking? Because he's scared. He's facing a risk scarcely found in sport climbing, a moment of truth that he best answer truthfully: *Can I climb 5.9 under this pressure, with real stakes in the game? Can I keep my head together for the next 20 feet, on terrain I could easily climb on a toprope. But here, I have to lead, and if my nerve fails me and my game comes apart, I'm taking the ride for sure.*

This is the challenge igniting the core of all trad climbing, where the moment of truth awaits us all whenever we push our limits. *The key is knowing that grace under pressure is a skill that can and should be slowly developed.*

Provided he is an adventurer at heart, Sam, a proven 5.12 climber, can learn to flash a 20-foot runout on 5.9, as long as he works up to it. He practices doing runouts on ridiculously easy terrain, building confidence as he goes, toggling up the difficulty as his mind gets solid with managing the risks—always a slippery task. And if at the moment of truth his answer is *No*, he doesn't question his own judgment and go anyway. Everyone has a limit. Respect it.

That, in a nutshell, is the Trad Climber's Credo. It remains a strategy to manage risk—according to our overall skill—not ignore it.

That said, ambitious trad climbers are certain to encounter situations where fear has the upper hand but we have to attempt that runout anyhow.

We get off-route and must climb our way back to safety, which sometimes calls for distressing risks. Or for many reasons, we can't retreat and have no choice but to tackle a runout and go with lousy protection. The critical factor is not the rating but our comfort level when tackling the risk at hand. If we've successfully managed lesser risks, we are in a stronger position to succeed. As legendary American climber Jim Bridwell used to say, "My mind is my protection."

Acceptable risks are based on our judgments. In trad climbing we must correctly judge the soundness of the rock and our protection. We must have a solid grasp about how hard we can climb without falling when the protection problem is real. Success often depends more on a strong mind than on strong fingers. Topo maps rate each pitch, valuable data for sure. But we still have to decide: Do we go or not, which is the moment of truth that keeps many climbers on short, bolt-protected sport routes. For others, those who seek a giant step into the unknown with no guarantees, the freedom to choose electrifies their lives, knowing that the hazards are always there. Mastery in this regard is less about huge numbers than about staying within ourselves. Managing the protection problem was best summarized by Socrates, 2,500 years before technical climbing was ever invented: *Know thyself.*

We still talk about Icarus, but he died.

CHAPTER 16

Leave No Trace

Experiencing the natural world carries with it a sense of timelessness that's prized by many people. For the places we go and the routes we climb, we're grateful to find what the pioneers discovered decades, even centuries ago—exactly as they found it back in the day. We preserve this gift by making good on the promise to *Leave No Trace*.

We practice Leave No Trace principles from the moment we arrive at the crags. The following steps help keep the climbing sites we all share as clean as possible, with minimal damage to the climbing area and the surrounding terrain:

- At popular climbing areas, use the outhouses located at most parking areas *before* you embark on your approach to your chosen cliff.

- Always use marked climber's access trails where available. If there is no marked trail to the cliff, minimize your impact by walking on permanent surfaces (e.g., a sandy wash, rock slab, or barren ground).

- At popular, easy-access crags, avoid making a beeline from the parking lot straight to the crag without first looking for an established path or trail. Walking off-trail can ravage vegetation and cause soil erosion if enough people do it over time.

- If traveling in a group in remote, pristine areas where no trails exist, fan out instead of walking single file, and try to walk on the most durable surfaces, avoiding fragile flora. Don't leave rock cairns to mark the path—this removes the route-finding challenge for those who prefer to experience it on their own.

- If nature calls and you're far from any outhouse, deposit solid human waste well away from the base of any climbing site. Dig a cathole 4 to 6 inches deep. Cover and disguise the cathole when you're done. Pack out all toilet paper and tampons in a ziplock bag. Urinate on bare ground or rock, not plants. Urine contains salt, and animals will dig into plants to get at it.

"Leave No Trace" means just that: Pack out everything you bring in, including all trash and food waste (apple cores, orange and banana peels too). Set an example for your group by collecting any trash you find. Be a steward, plan ahead, and always carry a trash bag when you venture to the crag.

Additional Leave No Trace principles worth following:

- Don't monopolize popular routes by setting up a toprope and then leaving your rope hanging on the climb, unattended.

- If your climb begins from a campsite and the site is occupied, ask permission to climb from the campers there.

- Minimize chalk use. After working a route, clean off any tic marks with a soft brush the moment your work is done.

John Cardwell on Misty Wall, Yosemite Valley
PHOTO BY JOHN EVANS

- Protect everyone's access to climbing areas by being courteous, beginning with parking in designated areas and carpooling whenever possible.

- Noise pollution is an intrusion few appreciate—from blasting tunes to screaming while attempting hard climbs. Be considerate and aware of those around you, and limit your noise.

- Pick up all food crumbs, and don't feed any wild critters; this habituates them to human food and encourages them to beg and scavenge, sometimes chewing holes in backpacks to get at food.

- On multipitch routes, if leaving your pack at the base, remove your food and place it in a squirrel-proof container, such as Tupperware.

- Consider leaving your dog at home—dogs dig and root up vegetation and stress native wildlife in rural areas. If you do bring your dog, remove any dog poop from the base of the cliff and the approach trail. Not all climbers are comfortable around dogs no matter their breed or behavior. Respect that as much as you do your dog's "rights."

- Leave all natural and cultural objects so others can experience them in their natural setting. If you are climbing in a national forest or national park, obey all regulations per gathering firewood and other objects.

For more information on Leave No Trace ethics, visit lnt.org.

Rappel off the Nautilus Formation, Vedauwoo, Wyoming
PHOTO BY JOHN EVANS

Alyse Dietel on Ancient Art, Fisher Towers, Utah
PHOTO BY JOHN EVANS

The way most old climbers tell it, their fond-est memories are rarely about conquests; rather, they're about their relationship with partners and the vertical world. When we go there ourselves, a charged silence reaches back to those who worked out a way before us on the rock. Decades later, at the juncture of back then and not yet, we rope up for a route and climb it right now—riding old routes into the future. Preserving that future for the climber yet born is every era's mandate in the adventure of ascent.

Off Belay

The goal of this manual was to increase our knowledge and understanding of the roped safety system, using *safety and simplicity* as guiding principles. As we've discovered, this is far from straightforward work. Unconditional facts and figures are especially illusive. Lab tests simulate but never duplicate real-world climbing because outside the laboratory, the "playing field" continually changes. What's more, climbers use a diversity of ropes and slings, each with slightly different specs. Even with a standardized system (using all the same equipment), the exact forces at play in any roped system, on any given rock climb, are basically unknowable. In some regard we are left to devise methods and protocols without unassailable facts, which raises an interesting question: What passes for actual knowledge as it pertains to outdoor climbing?

Some rules of thumb seem objective given our present equipment and how we use it, just as our basic protocols seem evergreen. It's hard to imagine a time when it's fine to belay off crappy anchors, to take our brake hand off the rope, and to skip being vigilant about our safety checks. Basic physical phenomena like gravity, direction of pull, and load multiplication, to mention a few, will not change in 100 or 1,000 years, even as the "best" way to manage these forces continues to evolve. Nevertheless, the knowledge that keeps us alive is less like a series of proofs and more like a *conversation* occurring within a bubble that moves through time. Imagine the bubble having a porous membrane allowing new information to come in and outmoded methods to trickle out. Those steeped in the present conversation look back through the bubble and say, "Wow! I can't believe we ever did that." Just as climbers a century hence will look back at this manual and wonder the same thing about our methods.

It's curious to realize that at no time does this "conversation" resemble a jigsaw puzzle, where gaps need only to be filled by inviolate pieces as yet undiscovered. Such a model assumes that knowledge is bounded when it's probably infinite, meaning there are infinite gaps. We will never complete the entire puzzle and achieve absolute knowledge and security about rock climbing. At any point in the conversation, people will look back, sigh, and say, "If they only knew . . ."

Yet most any experienced trad climber can travel alone to a new area, meet other experienced climbers, partner up, and climb with relative security day after day, year after year without major incident. Prevailing knowledge, while far from absolute, is "good enough" for an experienced climber to make decisions sufficiently informed that trust in the system is their privilege. The risks increase when climbers push their limits, especially when exploring new terrain; but the basic system is still so reliable and relatively easy to master that climbers have a right to their confidence, provided their decisions are well informed.

That's the most any instructional manual can hope for: to increase a climber's odds of making

Peter Croft begins Figures on a Landscape (5.10), Joshua Tree, California.

informed decisions. There is a daunting amount of information for the novice to download and make their own, but once this is put into practice, it quickly becomes instinctive and second nature. Provided we stick with established routes on decent rock, most of our doubts have been answered by previous parties. Loose rock, if any, has usually (but not always) been trundled off; reliable belay anchors have been established or, at any rate, are known to exist; the route has been charted and rated by consensus, the descent or downclimb established.

With basic competence, if you climb within your abilities, stay vigilant, and use safety checks, your principal concern will almost always boil down to the *protection problem*: Can I arrange solid and reliable gear to adequately protect me on the lead in the event of a fall? When this checks out, as often it does, the game is simplified to the most basic challenge of them all: Can I climb this thing?

The electrifying experience of answering this question is the reason we started climbing in the first place. The aim of getting competent with all this gear and all these techniques is to free us up to climb. But since Old Man Gravity never sleeps, informed decisions are always required. The most benign slab climb remains an adventure because the outcome is never determined beforehand. Embracing such challenges is not for everyone; of that we may be sure. But for those of us with a restless spirit and daring dreams, the adventure of ascent is like none other, and helps make our world go round.

Safe climbing!

—John Long and Bob Gaines

Glossary

ABD (assisted braking device): A device that locks off the rope when a load is quickly applied. The most commonly used ABD is the Petzl Grigri.

aid: Means of getting up a climb using other than natural rock features such as handholds, footholds, and cracks, usually by hanging on the rope or equipment to rest and make progress up the climb.

aid climbing: Using equipment for direct assistance (like stirrups for your feet), which allows passage over rock otherwise impossible using free-climbing techniques.

aid route: A route that can only be ascended using aid climbing techniques.

alcove: A cave-like formation or depression in the rock.

AMGA (American Mountain Guides Association): A national organization that trains and certifies professional climbing guides and instructors, promotes safety in guiding, and accredits guide services.

Aliens: Brand name for one type of spring-loaded camming device (SLCD).

American Triangle: A rigging method whereby a sling or cord is threaded through two anchor points and tied in such a manner as to create a triangular configuration that unnecessarily increases the forces on the anchor points. The larger the angle at the base of the triangle, the greater the force on the two anchor points.

arête: A narrow ridge or an outside edge or corner of rock.

arm bar: A technique for climbing an off-width crack by inserting an arm into the crack and utilizing counterpressure between the palm on one side of the crack against the triceps.

ATC (Air Traffic Controller): A belay/rappel device made by Black Diamond Equipment.

backpacker coil: A method of coiling a rope, also known as the "butterfly coil," that reduces kinking in the rope during coiling and facilitates carrying the rope like a backpack.

backstep: Placing the outside edge of the foot on a hold and turning the hip into the rock.

bail: To descend or retreat without successfully completing a climb.

bartack: A high-strength stitch pattern used by climbing equipment manufacturers to sew slings and webbing into loops.

bashie: A piece of malleable metal that has been hammered into a rock seam as an anchor; used in extreme aid climbing.

belay: Procedure of protecting a climber by the use of a rope.

belay device: A piece of equipment into which the rope is threaded/attached to provide friction for belaying or rappelling.

belayer: The person managing the rope on the end opposite the climber; responsible for holding the climber in the event of a fall.

belay loop: A sewn loop on the front of the climbing harness to which a rappel or belay device is attached with a locking carabiner; used when belaying and rappelling.

beta: Prior information about a climb, including sequence, rests, gear, clips, etc. "Running beta" is when someone instructs the climber on how to do the moves as they climb.

beta flash: Leading a climb without falling or dogging, but with previous knowledge on how to do the crux moves, such as seeing someone else do the climb.

BHK: Short for "big honking knot," a double over-hand on a bight forming two redundant loops; commonly used as a master point knot on a toprope setup using an extension rope.

bight: A bend in the rope where the two strands do not cross; used for knot tying, threading into a belay device, etc.

big wall: A long climb traditionally requiring at least one bivouac, but which may take just a few hours for ace climbers; *see wall.*

bivi: *See bivouac.*

bivouac: To spend the night on a route, usually planned for on a big wall climb; also called bivi.

bolt: An artificial anchor placed in a hole drilled for that purpose.

bomber: Absolutely fail-safe (as in a very solid anchor or big, big handhold); sometimes called bombproof.

bombproof: *See bomber.*

bong: An almost extinct species of extra-wide pitons, which today have been mostly replaced by large chocks or camming devices.

bouldering: Short climbs on small boulders or cliffs performed without a belay rope, usually utiliz-ing a small "crash pad" to fall onto and a "spot-ter" for safety. Climbers do "boulder problems," where the solution is deciphering and executing a series of moves to complete the problem.

bridging: *See stemming.*

bucket: A handhold large enough to fully latch onto, like the handle of a bucket; also called a jug.

buttress: An outside edge of rock that's much broader than an arête.

cam: Short for spring-loaded camming device; also refers to the single lobe or cam or camming device; also a verb used to describe the act of counterforce wherein a downward and outward force is created against the walls of a crack.

Camalot: Brand name for one type of spring-loaded camming device (SLCD) manufactured by Black Diamond Equipment. The Camalot was the first SLCD with two axles, which affords a greater range of placement for a given size.

camming device: Common term for a spring-loaded camming device (SLCD).

campus: To climb an overhanging section of rock using the arms only; a method of training grip, contact, and upper body strength.

carabiner: A high-strength aluminum alloy ring equipped with a spring-loaded snap gate.

CE: Certified for Europe.

ceiling: A section of rock that extends out above your head; an overhang of sufficient size to loom overhead; sometimes called roof.

chalk: Carbonate of magnesium powder carried in a small "chalk bag," used to prevent fingers and hands from sweating and to provide a firmer grip in warm conditions.

chalk bag: A small bag filled with chalk and carried on a belt around a climber's waist.

chickenhead: A bulbous knob of rock.

chimney: A crack of sufficient size to accept an entire body.

chock: *See nut.*

chockstone: A rock lodged in a crack.

choss, chossy: Dirty, loose, rotten, and otherwise unappealing rock.

Class 1: Mountain travel classification for walking on relatively flat ground and trail hiking.

Class 2: Mountain travel classification for hiking over rough ground, such as scree and talus; may include the use of hands for stability.

Class 3: Mountain travel classification for scram-bling that requires the use of hands and careful foot placement.

Class 4: Mountain travel classification for scram-bling over steep and exposed terrain; a rope may be used for safety on exposed areas.

Class 5: Mountain travel classification for technical "free" climbing where terrain is steep and exposed, requiring the use of ropes, protection hardware, and related techniques; *see Yosemite Decimal System (YDS).*

Class 6: Mountain travel classification for aid climbing where climbing equipment is used for balance, rest, or progress; denoted with a capital "A" followed by numerals 0 to 5 (e.g., 5.9/A3 means the free climbing difficulties are up to 5.9 with an aid section of A3 difficulty).

clean: Routes that are mostly free of vegetation or loose rock, or where you don't need to place pitons; also the act of removing chocks and other gear from a pitch.

clean climbing: Climbing that requires only removable protection, no pitons necessary.

cleaning tool: A metal pick used to poke and pry nuts from a crack; also known as a nut tool.

cliff: A high, steep, or overhanging face of rock.

clove hitch: A secure and adjustable hitch used to attach a rope to a carabiner.

cold shuts: Metal hooks commonly found in pairs as anchors atop short sport climbs to facilitate lowering off; can be open, with gates, or welded shut.

cordelette: A short length of cord, normally 18 to 25 feet in length, often tied into a loop, used to equalize multiple anchor points. For nylon cord, 7 mm is the standard diameter. High-strength (Technora or Spectra) cord is often used in 5 mm or 6 mm diameter.

crack: A fissure in the rock varying from extremely thin and narrow to as wide as a chimney.

crag: Another name for a cliff or rock formation.

crash pad: A portable foam pad used in bouldering.

crimp: A hand grip where the first knuckle is extended and the second knuckle is flexed, allowing the fingertips to rest on a small ledge.

crimps: Small but positive sharp edges.

crux: The most difficult move or sequence of moves on a climb, typically marked on topos with the difficulty rating.

dihedral: An inside corner of the climbing surface formed by two planes of rock, like the angle formed by the pages of an open book; also called an open book.

direct belay: To belay directly off the anchor.

downclimb: A descent without rope, usually when rappelling is unsafe or impractical.

drag: The resistance of the rope running through carabiners, commonly referred to as rope drag.

dynamic rope: A climbing rope with built-in stretch to absorb the energy of a fall, typically around 9 percent stretch under body weight and up to 35 percent in a big fall.

dyno: A dynamic move or explosive leap for a hold otherwise out of reach.

edge: A small hold, or the act of standing on an edge.

edging: Using the very edge of the shoe on any clear-cut hold.

EN: European Norm.

equalette: An anchor-rigging technique using a cordelette, tied by forming a U shape with the cordelette, then tying two overhand knots at the center point, about 12 inches apart. A carabiner is clipped into each loop of cord between the knots to create a self-equalizing rig with minimal extension. The four strands, or arms, of the cordelette can be attached to various anchors.

exposure: A relative situation where a climb has particularly noticeable sheerness.

extension: The potential for an anchor system's slings or cord to lengthen if one piece in the anchor system fails, transferring the force onto the remaining anchor or anchors.

fall factor: An equation that calculates the severity of a fall: the total distance of the fall divided by the length of rope from the belay.

finger crack: A crack climbed by wedging and jamming the fingers into the crack.

finger jams: Wedging the fingers into constrictions in a crack.

fireman's belay: A technique used to belay a rappelling climber by pulling down on the rope below the rappeller, creating tension that stops the rappeller from further movement down the rope.

first free ascent: The first free climb of a route previously climbed by aid climbing.

fist jam: Placing and wedging a fist sideways in a crack with the fingers curled inward toward the palm, providing a secure enough jam to pull on.

fixed anchor: Any permanent anchor left for all climbers to utilize, typically bolts or pitons.

flag: A climbing technique using a limb as a counterbalance.

flakes: A wafer or section of rock where a crack runs parallel to the plane of the main rock structure, as opposed to a "straight-in" crack that runs perpendicular to the plane of the main rock face.

flaking a rope: Uncoiling a rope into a loose pile, with one end on the bottom and the other end on the top of the pile; also called stacking a rope.

flared crack: Any crack that increases in dimension either inward or outward.

flash: Free climbing a route from bottom to top on your first try, without falling or hanging on the rope.

footwork: The art and method of standing on holds.

Fox System: A toprope rigging technique using an extension rope to create both a tether and an extended master point.

free: *See free climb.*

free ascent: *See free climb.*

free climb: The upward progress gained by a climber's own efforts, using hands, feet, and any part of the body on available features, unaided or free of attending ropes and gear. Rope is only used to safeguard against injury, not for upward progress or resting. Opposite of aid climb; also called free or free ascent.

free solo: Free climbing a route without the use of a rope.

friction hitch: One of several hitches tied around a rope using a piece of smaller cord or a sling, which grips when weight is applied but can be loosened and slid up the rope when not under tension; commonly used to ascend a rope and in self-rescue techniques.

Friend: The name of the original spring-loaded camming device (SLCD) designed by Ray Jardine and marketed by the Wild Country Company in 1977. The word "friend" became a generic term for any SLCD.

frog step: Bringing one foot up, then the other, while keeping your torso at the same level, forming a crouched or "bullfrog" position.

gaston: To grip handholds with the hands in a thumbs-down position, then pull outward, like prying apart elevator doors. Can also be one hand in the thumbs-down position on a handhold above and to the side of the body.

girth hitch: A hitch used to connect webbing or cord around a feature to create an anchor by looping around the object then back through the sling or cord.

gobies: Hand abrasions.

Grade: A rating that tells how much time an experienced climber will take on a given climb, referring to the level of commitment required by the average climbing team; denoted by Roman numerals.

Grade I: A climb that may take only a few hours to complete.

Grade II: A climb that may take 3 to 4 hours.

Grade III: A climb that may take 4 to 6 hours, typically done in half a day.

Grade IV: A climb that may take a full day.

Grade V: A climb that normally takes two days, requiring a bivouac.

Grade VI: A climb that normally takes two or more days on the wall, requiring several bivouacs by the average party.

Grigri: A belay device with assisted braking manufactured by Petzl.

gripped: Extremely scared.

ground anchor: An anchor used to secure a belayer at the base of a climb.

hangdog, hangdogging: Hanging on the rope to rest; not a free ascent. Sport climbers will often "hangdog" up a route to practice the moves and prepare for a later "free" ascent.

headwall: A much steeper section of cliff, found toward the top.

heel hooking: Hooking the heel on a large hold on overhanging rock above your head and pulling with the leg much like a third arm.

hex, hexes: *See hexentric.*

hexentric: A six-sided chock made by Black Diamond Equipment that can be wedged into cracks; commonly called a hex.

highball: A term used to describe bouldering problem that is high off the ground.

hip belay: To belay by wrapping the rope around your waist to create friction.

horn: A generally small, knoblike projection of rock.

indirect belay: To belay from the harness, not directly off the anchor.

jam: Wedging feet, hands, fingers, or other body parts to gain purchase in a crack.

Joshua Tree System: A rigging technique for toproping using an extension rope and a V configuration to create a master point over the edge of the cliff.

jug: A handhold shaped like a jug handle.

jumar: Term commonly used to refer to a device used to ascend a climbing rope; also a verb; i.e., "jumaring" the rope means ascending the rope.

killer: Extraordinarily good.

latch: To successfully grip a hold.

layback: Climbing maneuver that entails pulling with the hands while pushing with the feet; also called lieback.

laybacking: *See layback.*

lead: To be the first on a climb, belayed from below, and placing protection to safeguard a fall.

lieback: Climbing maneuver that entails pulling with the hands while pushing with the feet; also called layback.

liebacking: *See lieback.*

line: The path of the route, usually the line of least resistance between other major features of the rock.

lock-off: Hanging by one arm on a single handhold with enough strength to allow the other hand to release its grip and move up to a new handhold.

loop strength: The minimum breaking strength of a sling or cord when tested in a single, continuous loop; like a Dyneema sling sewn into a loop with bartacked stitching, or cord tied into a loop with a knot.

lunge: An out-of-control dynamic move; a jump for a far-off hold.

magic X: *See sliding X.*

manky: Of poor quality, as in "a manky finger jam" or "manky protection placement."

mantle: A series of climbing moves enabling you to grab a feature (like a ledge) and maneuver up to where you're standing on it, usually accomplished by pulling up then pressing down with one or both palms while bringing up one foot (similar to getting out of the deep end of a swimming pool).

mantleshelf: A rock feature, typically a ledge with scant holds directly above.

mantling: The act of surmounting a mantleshelf.

master point (aka power point): The equalized point in an anchor system; the point a climber clips into.

micronut: A very small nut used mainly for aid climbing.

mountaineering: Reaching mountaintops using a combination of skills (such as rock climbing and ice climbing), usually involving varying degrees of objective hazards.

move: One of a series of motions necessary to gain climbing distance.

multipitch: A route with multiple belay stations (rope lengths).

Munter hitch: A hitch used for belaying that requires no gear other than a carabiner.

natural anchor: An anchor made from a feature occurring in nature, such as a chockstone, rock tunnel, horn, tree, boulder, etc.

nut: A wedged-shaped piece of metal designed to be used as an anchor in a crack; also called a chock.

nut tool: A metal pick used to tap and pry nuts to facilitate removal, or "cleaning."

off-width: A crack that is too wide to use as a finger, hand, or fist jam but too narrow to get inside and climb as a chimney.

on-sight: To successfully climb a route without prior knowledge or experience of the moves.

opposition: Nuts, anchors, or climbing maneuvers that are held in place by the simultaneous stress of two forces working against each other.

overhang, overhanging: A section of rock that is steeper than vertical.

peg: *See pitons.*

pinch grip: A handhold where the thumb pinches in opposition to the fingers on either side of a projection.

pinkpoint: To lead (without falling) a climb that has been pre-protected with gear and rigged with quickdraws.

pins: *See pitons.*

pin scar: A mark of damage left in a crack by repeated placement and removal of pitons.

pitch: The distance between belays.

pitons: Metal spikes of various shapes that are hammered into the rock to provide anchors in cracks; sometimes called pins or pegs. These types of anchors were common up to the 1970s but are rarely used today.

power point: *See master point.*

pre-distributed: Tying off an anchor system for an anticipated force in only one direction.

pro: *See protection.*

protection: The anchors used to safeguard the leader; sometimes called pro. Until the 1970s, protection devices were almost exclusively pitons—steel spikes that were hammered into cracks in the rock. Since then, various nuts and camming devices have almost replaced pitons as protection devices. These chocks and cams are fitted into cracks, and the rope is attached to them. In the absence of cracks, permanent bolt anchors are installed into the rock. The leader clips into the protection and proceeds to climb past it. If the leader falls, he or she will travel at least twice the distance from above the last point of protection (rope stretch adds more distance).

prusik: Both the knot and any means by which you mechanically ascend a rope.

quad: A rigging technique accomplished by doubling a cordelette and clipping it to two anchor points, quadrupling the strands. Two overhand knots are tied in the four strands, and carabiners are clipped to two or three of the four strands between the knots, creating a self-adjusting anchor system with minimal extension.

quickdraws: Short slings with carabiners at both ends that help provide drag-free rope management for the leader.

quick link: An aluminum or steel screw link often found on rappel anchors, mostly bought from hardware stores, although some manufacturers make CE certified quick links for climbing (like the Petzl Maillon Rapide).

rack: The collection of gear a climber takes up the climb.

rappel: To descend by sliding down a rope, typically utilizing a mechanical braking device.

rapping: Informal term for rappelling.

redirected belay: To belay by running the rope through a belay device attached to the harness, then back through an anchor.

redpoint: To lead a route from bottom to top in one push, clipping protection as you go, without falling or resting on protection.

RENE: Acronym for Redundancy, Equalization, and No Extension.

Rocks: Brand name for a line of passive nuts developed by Mark Valance and sold by Wild Country.

roof: A section of rock that extends out above your head; sometimes called a ceiling.

rope direct belay: To belay from an extended master point using the climbing rope.

R-rated climbs: Protection or danger rating for climbs with serious injury potential; protection may be sparse or "runout," or some placements may not hold a fall.

runner: *See sling.*

runout: The distance between two points of protection; often refers to a long stretch of climbing without protection.

sandbagging: The "shameful" practice of a first ascent team underrating the actual difficulty of a given route.

second: The second person on a rope team, usually the leader's belayer.

self-adjusting: An anchor system that adjusts to withstand a force in multiple directions.

send: To climb a route, start to finish, without falling—and any *attempt* to do so.

sharp end: The lead climber's end of the rope.

shelf: The pre-equalized point on a cordelette directly above the master point knot; all loops must be clipped for redundancy.

shred: To do really well; to dominate.

sidepull: Pulling on a vertically aligned hold to the side of the body.

signals: A set of commands used between climber and belayer.

slab: A less than vertical, or low-angle, section of a rock face.

SLCD (spring-loaded camming device): *See Friend.*

sliding X (aka magic X): A self-adjusting sling rigged between two anchor points.

sling: Webbing sewn or tied into a loop; also called a runner.

smear, smearing: Standing on a sloping foothold and utilizing friction in order to adhere to the rock.

"soft" ratings: Ratings deemed harder than the actual difficulty of a given route.

spring-loaded camming device (SLCD): *See Friend.*

sport climbing: Similar to traditional rock climbing but with protection and anchors (bolts) already in place. Instead of using nuts and cams, the climber uses quickdraws, clipping bolts for protection. Most sport climbing is face climbing and is usually only one pitch in length, but can be multipitch. With the danger element removed, the emphasis is on technique and doing hard moves.

spotter: A person designated to slow the fall of a boulderer, especially to keep the boulderer's head from hitting the ground.

stance: A standing rest spot, often the site of a belay.

static rope: A rope with almost no stretch.

stem, stemming: The process of counterpressuring with the feet between two widely spaced holds; also called bridging.

stopper knot: A safety knot tied on the end of a rope to prevent accidents.

Stoppers: Brand name for one of the original (and now one of the most commonly used) wedge-shaped tapered nut deigns; sold by Black Diamond Equipment.

sustained: Climbing adjective that indicates the continuous nature of the climb.

tail: The length of the end of a rope protruding from a knot.

TCU (three-cam unit): A type of spring-loaded camming device (SLCD) with just three cams instead of four.

tensile strength: The minimum breaking strength of a sling, cord, or rope when tested on a single strand.

thin: A climb or hold of relatively featureless character.

thread: A sling or cord looped through a tunnel in the rock structure.

topo: A detailed diagram showing a climbing route up a cliff.

toprope: A belay from an anchor point above that protects the climber from falling even a short distance.

toproping: *See toprope.*

trad: *See traditional rock climbing.*

traditional rock climbing: Climbing a route where the leader places gear (nuts and cams) for protection and anchors, to be removed later by the second or "follower"; as opposed to sport climbing, which relies solely on bolts for protection and anchors; also called trad climbing.

traverse: To move sideways, without altitude gain.

tricam: A mechanical wedge that acts both as a nut and a cam.

tweak: To injure, as in "a tweaked finger tendon."

UIAA: Union Internationale des Associations d'Alpinisme.

undercling: Grabbing a hold (usually a flake) with the palm up and fingers underneath the hold, then pulling outward with the arm while pushing against the rock with the feet, much like a lieback.

V system: The universal bouldering language, established in the early 1990s at Hueco Tanks, Texas. Ratings range from V0 to V16, with V0 being the easiest and V15 being roughly equivalent to 5.15b YDS.

vector: A measurement of force and direction in anchor systems.

wall: A long climb traditionally done over multiple days, but which may take just a few hours for ace climbers; *see big wall.*

water knot: A knot used to tie a loop of webbing.

webbing: Synthetic fiber woven flat like a strap, used to make slings. Nylon webbing was used exclusively for slings up to the 1990s; now slings are also made from Spectra and Dyneema webbing.

wired: Known well, as in "a wired route."

work, worked, or working: To practice the moves of a difficult route via toprope or hangdogging.

X-rated climbs: Protection or danger rating for climbs with groundfall and death potential.

YDS: *See Yosemite Decimal System.*

Yosemite Decimal System (YDS): The American grading scale for identifying technical difficulty of routes, where 5 denotes the class and the numerals following the decimal point indicate the difficulty rating (5.0 to 5.15), usually according to the most difficult move. Subgrades (a, b, c, and d) are used on climbs rated 5.10 and harder.

Z system: A raising system that uses a 3:1 mechanical advantage.

Acknowledgments

Special thanks to Ron Funderburke, writer and former education manager for the American Alpine Club, and now director of education for the Colorado Mountain School, and Philippe Westenberger, head of product for Edelrid, one of the most innovative gear manufacturers in the business. Ron and Philippe both reviewed the text, and their feedback was invaluable in ensuring the material is current, clear, and accurate. And a huge shout-out to climber, ultra runner, photographer, and SMC marketing director John Evans, who gave us full access to his spectacular library of climbing images (including the cover photo), which breathed life and gusto into otherwise technical material.

Thanks to Steve Grossman, curator of the North American Historical Archives, for his help with the historical photos.

Thanks to all the climbers and guides who graciously posed for photos, including: Tony Sartin, Tony Grice, Patty Kline, Mike Moretti, Erin Guinn, Michael Baines, Steve Schwartz, Terri Condon, Lisa Rands, Mike and Lori Satzberg, Roddy McCalley, David Kerner, John Lauretig, Francisco Kim, Alex Nunez, Chris Norwood, Frank Bentwood, Farai Muchenje, Melissa Popejoy, and Casey Stroud.

And last but not least, thanks to FalconGuides editorial director David Legere, senior production editor Meredith Dias, and layout artist Melissa Evarts for putting it all together.

Index

About the Authors

John Long is an acclaimed rock climber and author of more than forty books, including several in Falcon's catalog. He is one of the most prolific adventure writers out there and has authored magazine articles, screenplays, documentary films, and television and movie scripts, as well as instructional rock climbing books.

Beginning in the mid-1970s with his historic one-day ascent of The Nose route on El Capitan, Long became a mainstay in the world of extreme sports and adventure. He and his elite group of climbers, the "Stonemasters," ushered in a new era of big wall climbing with their epic climbs in Yosemite National Park and elsewhere. In the years that followed, John transitioned from rock climbing to international exploration, traveling around the world from the jungles of Southeast Asia to the North Pole. Some of his many achievements include the first coast-to-coast traverse of Borneo and the discovery and exploration of the world's largest river cave.

John has also built a successful television and film career, producing the *International Guinness Book of World Records* television show before moving to feature films. The Sylvester Stallone movie *Cliffhanger* is based on one of John's stories.

In recent years, John has continued to write books and articles and to work in television and film. He is also an Adidas Ambassador and frequently works with them at various events around the country.

Bob Gaines began rock climbing at Joshua Tree National Park in the 1970s. Since then he has pioneered more than 500 first ascents in the park.

Bob began his career as a professional rock climbing guide in 1983 and is an American Mountain Guides Association Certified Rock Instructor. He is the coauthor of *Rock Climbing: The AMGA Single Pitch Manual*, the textbook for the AMGA's single-pitch instructor program.

Bob has worked extensively in the film business as a climbing stunt coordinator. He has coordinated more than forty television commercials and was Sylvester Stallone's climbing instructor for the movie *Cliffhanger*. Bob doubled for William Shatner in *Star Trek V: The Final Frontier* as Captain Kirk free soloing on El Capitan in Yosemite.

Bob has worked extensively training US military special forces, including the elite US Navy SEAL Team 6, and is known for his technical expertise in anchoring and rescue techniques.

He is also the author of *Best Climbs Joshua Tree National Park, Best Climbs Tahquitz and Suicide Rocks, Toproping: Rock Climbing for the Outdoor Beginner, Rappelling,* and *Advanced Rock Climbing* and is coauthor of *Climbing Anchors* and the *Climbing Anchors Field Guide* (with John Long).

Bob's other passion is fly fishing. He currently holds fourteen International Game Fish Association world records.